The Barbarian Withi

D1286601

BOOKS BY WALTER J. ONG, S.J.

Frontiers in American Catholicism (1957)

Ramus, Method, and the Decay of Dialogue (1958)

Ramus and Talon Inventory (1958)

American Catholic Crossroads (1959)

Darwin's Vision and Christian Perspectives (1960)
(Editor and Contributor)

The Barbarian Within (1962)

BOOKS CONTRIBUTED TO:

Twentieth Century English (1946)

Immortal Diamond (1949)

English Institute Essays 1952 (1954)

Problems of Communication in a Pluralistic Society (1956)

The Catholic Church U.S.A. (1956)

Literature and Belief (1958)

Religion in America (1958)

The Critical Matrix (1961)

The Barbarian Within

✣ AND

OTHER FUGITIVE ESSAYS

AND STUDIES ✣

BY WALTER J. ONG, S.J.

THE MACMILLAN COMPANY : NEW YORK

"The Jinnee in the Well Wrought Urn" and "A
Dialectic of Aural and Objective Correlatives" first
appeared in *Essays in Criticism* (Oxford, England);
"System, Space, and Intellect in Renaissance Symbolism" first appeared in *Bibliothèque d'Humanisme
et Renaissance,* published by Librairie E. Droz; "Wit
and Mystery: A Revaluation of Mediaeval Latin
Hymnody" first appeared in *Speculum,* XXII, 3 (July
1947), copyright 1947 by the Mediaeval Academy of
America; "The Myth of Myth" first appeared (under
the title "Myth and the Cabalas") in *The Modern
Schoolman,* Vol. XXVII, No. 3 (March 1950); "Educationists and the Tradition of Learning" first appeared in the *Bulletin* of the Ontario Secondary School
Teachers' Federation, Vol. XXXVII, No. 6 (Decem-
ber 1957); "Wired for Sound" first appeared in *College English,* Vol. 21, No. 5 (February 1960),
copyright 1960 by the National Council of Teachers
of English.

Second Printing 1968

The Macmillan Company, New York
Collier-Macmillan Canada Ltd., Toronto, Ontario
Macmillan New York, London

PRINTED IN THE UNITED STATES OF AMERICA

Library of Congress Catalog card number: 62-12425

For

ALDEN AND ROSEMARY FISHER

Contents

Preface

WITH THE EXCEPTION of the culminating essay, after which this collection is named, these essays and studies are indeed fugitive geographically, having been published in a great many scattered places, from Oxford in England and Geneva in Switzerland to Ontario and Ohio and Wisconsin. Most of them have appeared from 1954 on, but two —"Wit and Mystery" and "The Myth of Myth"—date somewhat earlier. The lengthy final essay, "The Barbarian Within," is here published for the first time.

In subject matter, too, these essays and studies range widely. But despite this fact, or perhaps because of it, they tend to structure themselves around certain themes. In the order of material in this collection, the first of these is the relationship of literature to the human person, a relationship that persists despite the unremitting and necessary struggle of art to "create" an "object" out of the human situation or to find an "objective correlative" within this situation.

The personalist theme involves a subsidiary theme, that of voice itself, the most sensitive manifestation of personal presence and the normal mode of communication opening persons to one another and rendering fertile the grounds on which relationships with the object world are established. The human word serves divergent ends, on the one hand revealing the presence of a person, transobjective and unique, and on the other trafficking with objects and indeed helping constitute the "object" that literary art devises.

The world of voice is not at all the same as the world of space, for it is less an object-world than a temporal one. Since, as Professor Rudolph Allers once phrased it, space is the universal symbol of order, an oral-aural world holds special terrors for the emotionally or the intellectually insecure, for whom order is at best a precarious pose. Unlike constructs in space, which create an illusion of permanence, the vocal performance of man, like his acts of intellection, has no permanence but alternates with silence. What is said tells off against what is not said, reminding us that total explicitness is impossible to human beings: one always means (implicitly) more than one says (explicitly) or, in another sense, says (implicitly) more than one means (explicitly). In being to some degree necessarily occult, myth is a by-product of this limitation of human voice. It exists by virtue of what it says not explicitly but symbolically. *Mythos* complements *logos*.

The limitations of voice, and of intellection as reflected analogously in voice (far more sensitively than in vision), make themselves felt in games with language, in word play, in "wit," with which one of these essays is concerned explicitly. Of course, if one supposes that words are adventitious to a system of thought purportedly wordless at its optimum, a system of thought in turn superimposed upon an utterly thought-less and word-less world of Newtonian "objects," word play is only an elaborate and even perverse form of doing nothing at all. But if one is aware of the way in which things themselves are words, and of the way in which thoughts are words even more intensely, word play, like other play, becomes a serious thing, involving the interlocking of the verbal and the extraverbal in our cosmos. Thus word play proves thoroughly serious in many a medieval hymn, particularly those concerned with the central Christian mysteries of the Trinity, the Incarnation, and the Eucharist.

A further theme in the present essays and studies interrelated with the foregoing is that of education. Education is intimately connected with the study of the word, for it is essentially a communications process, and one most central to society—the process whereby society reviews what it knows about everything while it undertakes to pass what it knows on to its newer members. Formal education, especially in societies that use writing, begins normally with the study of the media of thought and communication. Twentieth century society is at present reorienting its educational procedures because of the way in which the media have been reconstituted, and it needs to reorient these procedures still more. Grammar has become merely a part of the much larger field of study known as linguistics, which takes as its point of departure the spoken rather than the alphabetized, visualized word. The shift to the oral-aural approach is in turn related to the shift from Latin to the vernacular in formal education over the past few generations (this change took place much later than today is commonly supposed) and to the maturing of vernacular studies, which can be measured by the rise of the now aging New Criticism.

A final theme of these essays and studies is a modification of the initial theme concerning the human person. This final theme is more directly that of the self and other, of the isolation of the self, which our literature and philosophy both reflects and reflects on today. The peculiar relationship of the person and things within the "wilderness" culture of the United States is touched on, an early instance of the literature of isolation is turned up in St. Ignatius Loyola, and finally the outsider inside society today is examined in contemporary and historical perspective. Outsiders have always been with us, and indeed we are all in a sense outsiders to one another, and yet our age has made the outsider its own in special ways, concerning itself more than any preceding age has done with the abstract notions themselves of outsidedness, or isolation, of otherness, and promising to develop an awareness that will in some measure ameliorate our situation, even though this is too deep-rooted and too necessary for any natural cure.

Since, despite a community of themes, each of these essays and studies stands on its own feet in the context in which it was first drafted, those which have been published before have not been revised here to any appreciable extent but are presented in their original published form except for the alteration of a few words here and there and the curtailing of a passage in "Latin and the Social Fabric" which repeated some observations on the epic already elaborated in "The Vernacular Matrix of the New Criticism."

The following essays and studies in this volume were first printed by the publishers here indicated, to whom grateful acknowledgement for permissions for the present reprinting is hereby made. "The Jinnee in the Well Wrought Urn" and "A Dialectic of Aural and Objective Correlatives" were published in *Essays in Criticism* (Oxford, England) in 1954 and 1958 respectively, "Metaphor and the Twinned Vision" in the *Sewanee Review*, 1955. "Voice as Summons for Belief" appeared in 1958 in *Thought* and in *Literature and Belief* ("English Institute Essays," 1957; New York: Columbia University Press, 1958), edited by M. H. Abrams. "System, Space, and Intellect in Renaissance Symbolism," of which abridged selections had earlier been printed in *Explorations* (Toronto, Canada), first appeared in complete form in *Bibliothèque d'Humanisme et Renaissance* (Geneva, Switzerland) in 1956. "Wit and Mystery: A Revaluation in Mediaeval Latin Hymnody" appeared in *Speculum* in 1947; and "The Myth of Myth" in the *Modern*

Schoolman in 1950 under the title "Myth and the Cabalas." "Educationists and the Tradition of Learning," the Fourth J. W. Ansley Memorial Lecture, appeared in 1957 in the *Bulletin* of the Ontario Secondary School Teachers' Federation and in 1958 in the *Journal of Higher Education.* "Grammar in the Twentieth Century" was published in *Problems of Communication in a Pluralistic Society* (Milwaukee, Wisconsin: Marquette University Press, 1956), ed. by Reynolds C. Seitz; and "The Vernacular Matrix of the New Criticism" in *The Critical Matrix* (Washington, D.C.: Georgetown University Press, 1960), edited by the late Paul R. Sullivan. "Latin and the Social Fabric" was published by the *Yale Review* in 1960, and "Wired for Sound" by *College English* also in 1960. "Personalism and the Wilderness" appeared in the *Kenyon Review* in 1959, and "St. Ignatius' Prison-Cage and the Existentialist Situation" in *Theological Studies* in 1954.

W. J. O.

Saint Louis University

WORDS ARE MORE THAN THINGS

ONE

The Jinnee in the Well Wrought Urn

I

THIS is the age which has repudiated books about the girlhood of Shakespeare's heroines. Criticism in the English-speaking world within the past few decades has made it its business to guarantee the autonomy of the work of art as constituted within its own limits. Every effort has been made to clear the art object of accretions, to focus attention on it as freed of irrelevancies concerning the author's life, his friends and his problems, or of errant speculation about the previous or subsequent history of characters, if any—from all that might be styled the personalist irrelevancies adventitious to the work of art in its own totality. The effort has been reasonably successful. The once undisputed popularity of biographical excursion has been severely curtailed. It maintains itself with effort even in concert program notes.

The compulsions responsible for the present emphasis are many and complex, and they operate in quite diverse quarters simultaneously. The conviction that it is neither the potter who made it nor the people, real or fictional, to whose lives it is tangent, but the well wrought urn itself which counts, has been fed indifferently out of studies of Donne or Pope or Coleridge, out of trenchant criticism working through contemporary literature, out of theory spun from clues picked up in St. Thomas Aquinas, and from innumerable other sources. Indeed, the ability it manifests to pick up nourishment almost anywhere at all is convincing testimony to the essential truth of the conviction in question: it is in accord with facts as they are.

In a sense, the current emphasis on the work of art as such simply exploits by reaction a special weakness of nineteenth-century criticism such as Hazlitt's or Lamb's. Associated with commitments of rhetorical theory through long centuries, this weakness was not even new. But the present age found it singularly ripe for attack, and the past few decades have, by a kind of inner compulsion, set themselves to forging weapons for the antipersonalist armory. This compulsion is discernible in T. S. Eliot's submersion of the individual's subjective talent in an objective tradition (of which, to be sure, the subjective talent is simultaneously the expression), and in the attack launched by F. R. Leavis and others against a criticism based on measuring fictional characters by "real life"—by their seeming adaptability to ultrafictional projection. The same compulsion is seen everywhere in the persistent emphasis of American criticism as represented by such work as that of Cleanth Brooks or Kenneth Burke.

But a change of heart, however carefully defined, is setting in, as a close reading of recent critical credos, such as those of Leslie Fiedler or of Richard Chase, shows. The compulsion to beat the personalist horse loses force as the impression gains ground that he has shown no unambiguous signs of life for a long while. Beating him becomes a bore, and we want something newer and more interesting to do.

However, it is not quite clear to me, nor perhaps to many others, that the horse is really dead. A phenomenon so universal and persistent as the personalist deviation in criticism, it would seem, still deserves rather more explicit consideration than it has received. It has been written off in places at which it might well have been looked into. Personalist deviationism is, after all, not merely the last infirmity of feeble sensibilities. Dr. Johnson, who is honestly admired by most objectivist critics and is cited by Mr. Fiedler as a practitioner commonly acknowledged as extraordinarily good, not only stands for an approach to literature that is frankly moral, in a distressingly simplified fashion, but could state bluntly to Boswell that "the biographical part of literature is what I love most." (The personalist horse does seem dead and shrunk to a heap of bones when we try to imagine a present-day critical collection with *that* for a title-page motto.)

This is not to say that the personalist approach to a work of art is to be advocated. If I may be permitted a personal deviation of my own, I myself subscribe wholeheartedly to the practice and theory of focusing primarily on the work of art itself and feel no desire to defend the personalist approach as a substitute technique. It is not defense of the personalist drift, but explanation, that is needed. The personalist deviation is here to stay, not only in program notes but in serious discussions of literature which, apparently unaffected by recent critical trends, continue to pour from the presses. For some it may be a racking experience to own that the personalist approach is still established as the dominant approach in most classrooms. But there it is, all the same.

However objectionable, the personalist approach manifests a persistency that itself clamors for explanation. If the urn really is the issue, why is it always in peril of being overlooked or tossed aside? If you so much as whisper that there is a jinnee in the urn, most onlookers will be only too willing to drop the urn without further ado. Broken, it will let the jinnee out, and they can ask him a few questions. While decrying the tendency to behave this way, we may be excused for asking what accounts for the presence of the tendency in the first place.

II

There are countless ways in which works of art fray out into personalities and thus give the personalist distraction a foothold within the art object itself. The most obvious, that of character in literature or even in the plastic arts, is both so straightforward and so complicated —with the curious susceptibility characters exhibit even for getting themselves psychoanalyzed—that it hardly need be mentioned. But there are other footholds, some closely approximating to this. There is the autobiographical strain which persistently fertilizes fiction. Or there is the obverse autobiography of a Scott Fitzgerald, where not only are the novels cut to the measure of the author's life, but this life itself is lived to the measure of the novels—type and antitype are generated not only simultaneously but reciprocally as well.

Or there is the fact that groupings of works by author have a tough and ready viability not found in groupings by classes. The body of works by Shakespeare—plays, sonnets, and other poems all together —forms a whole in a way more integrated than that formed by the body of Elizabethan sonnets or by Elizabethan drama. *Sweeney Agonistes* belongs with *Tradition and the Individual Talent* in a way it does not with Pound's *Cantos* or with a poem by Auden.

Or again, there is the fact that the final stage of interest in a poet's work creates inevitably the poet's shrine, which is consecrated to the poet's person and thus may as well be his birthplace as something more readily connected with his works. The Shakespeare Memorial Theatre is at Stratford, not on the south bank of the Thames. Or, once more, the personalist distraction intrudes itself by reason of the sense of communion which rides through the contemplation of a work of art. At the threshold of consciousness, there hovers the awareness that others, or at least another, knows this work in the intimate way that I do. What would be an intrusion on our attention, if only an object were concerned, is thus transmuted into a sharing in terms of this injection of personality, however vague it may be. One wonders if there could be any artistic experience at all if the contemplator were a human being entirely alone in the universe.

This is not all. The very genesis of works of art is often—perhaps always and necessarily—derivative from personal relations and tensions. That the muses are conceived of as persons and not as clouds or waves bears testimony to a state of mind elusive but real. Certainly the artistic impulse is at a kind of peak when the person-to-person relationship takes possession of the whole field of life in a crisis terminating ordinarily in marriage. For the great majority of persons, this is the only time anything like artistic creativity even remotely threatens in their lives. Even those whose creative activity persists testify to the earlier period of intensification of impulse and the readjustment demanded for continuation. There is Villon's verse testament executed "en l'an de mon trentiesme aage," or Mr. Eliot's pertinent remarks about those who want to continue to write poetry after their early youth. The crisis adverted to here is one which hardly exerts itself so immediately in the case of scientists.

Even where there is readjustment and the period of artistic impulse associated in one way or another with entrance upon the plenary personal relationship of marriage is past, the personal drive continues in the production of works of art. Frank accounts of artistic development, such as Stephen Spender's recent account, throughout are replete with personal relations and tensions, which, again, would have an entirely different status in the life of a mathematician or physicist or perhaps even a metaphysician.

It would be hard to disprove the statement that the impulse to produce a work of fine art simply cannot arise except within a framework of personal give-and-take, a *you-me* situation, set up within the artist's mind. The lack of artistic impulse among animals is a simple corollary of the dead quiet which Rilke found so terrifying in the animal eye. J. S. Mill's attempt to define poetry as something not heard but *over*heard is largely traceable to the impulse of the abstractionist, scientific mind to extricate poetry from the network of personality in which it is in-volved. But the attempt is successful, or at least titillating, precisely in so far as it removes the sensorily ascertainable audience and replaces it with a mysterious audience suggesting the bottomless depths of a pure personality, disengaged from the crudities of sense perception and existing only in the vibrant tension which makes a *me* separate from a *you*.

Creative activity is often—again, perhaps always—powered by the drive to accomplish, in terms of the production of an object of art, an adjustment or readjustment in certain obscure relationships with other persons. The state of protest in which artistic activity is so often framed is evidence of how matters stand here. Only persons are liable to protest. You cannot protest to a fact or to an object. Although you speak of pro-testing against it, you can only protest about it to some *one*. In a dis-cussion of Lionel Trilling's recent book, R. P. Blackmur very properly suggests the artistic sterility of a feeling for systems—impersonal things —and the fact that existing politics is good not *for* literature, but "to *aggravate* literature." These sensitively conceived remarks underscore the value of high-potential person-to-person situations in generating the artist's product.

Even critical activity is dependent on this person-to-person situation for its coming into being. Another way of putting this is to say, as it is commonly said, that criticism is a social activity in a way in which scentific activity is not. Although in science there is queston of back-ground, there seems to be no question of a personal *mise en scène* as a condition of scientific activity in the way in which there is in critical activity. Even when questions as to who says what about whom are not obvious at the surface, issues involving such questions are likely to be found in the depths, where the wells of criticism, like those of the poem, are driven deep in the personal situation in which the critic find himself. The goddess of criticism is a kind of in-law of the muses, and there is some question of an underground passage between the watering places to which she brings her devotees and the springs of Helicon.

III

The artistic situation differs from the scientific, against which it is helpful to set it here, precisely in centering about an externalized, man-made object. The persuasion that the object itself must be primary is thus both sound and promising. But the object is not free of involvement in tragedy simply because of its primacy as object. Although it stands solidly—or pretty solidly—on its own feet, it is none the less a harbinger of disappoinment and of death. For once we have granted to the work of art the kind of autonomy which the artistic situation demands, once we have decided to allow it to slough its irrelevancies, which would disssipate its own objective being in the confusion of personal issues out of which it perhaps arose, a further question presents itself: Is it not in the last analysis cruel to face a human being with merely an object as such, a being which is less than a person? As soon as contemplation enters beyond a certain stage of awareness, is not the human being going to be unsatisfied if he cannot find another, a person, a *you*, in whatever it is he is concerned with?

It seems that he is going to be unsatisfied, precisely in so far as he drives this contemplation of the object to its ultimate—in so far as he takes it in its maximum of seriousness. We consider here the case not of passing attention to a work of art but the case of plenary attention, serious and protracted and repeated. Contemplation of this sort involves love, and the question is whether it can be carried on, or how far it can be carried on, without some suggestion of reciprocity. Projected into an unpeopled voia, love becomes only the ultimate refinement of self-torture. And while it is true that contemplation of a minor object of art may not involve the full psychological mechanism of love in all its complications, still, in proportion as the object of art pretends to be serious, it at least sets in motion this tremendous mechanism, which demands for full satisfaction the reciprocity of another person.

Man's deepest orientation is personal. He cannot give himself fully in an outpouring of love unless someone else is *there*, with at least the capability of giving a self in return. Otherwise, psychological disaster threatens—the disaster which takes such heavy toll of serious writers or artists.

The morass of personality which surrounds the work of art in ways only briefly hinted at here establishes the personalist aberration as a permanent threat. As contemplation enters upon a more serious stage, the human being is driven by the whole economy of what it is to be man to find opposite himself, in that which he contemplates, a person capable of reacting in turn. This drive is primordial and will not be denied. It can be deflected from the object, as it ordinarily is, by a refusal to take the object in total seriousness, by a smile, a shrug of the shoulders, by an acknowledgment, if only subconscious, that somewhere or other the poem will break down, will ultimately reach a point at which it is incapable of eliciting further love—unlike a person, who can go on eliciting love without limit.

When the personalist aberration sets in, or in so far as it sets in, the resolution of the state of tension is otherwise effected. The movement of love goes on, but persons—the characters of the novel, the artist himself responsible for the object, the peopled parlor where the Ming vase was displayed, or the woman who ran her fingers over the cool jade—will begin to haunt the attention, not as within the work of art itself but as constituted more and more in their own right. This personalization is, of course, unsatisfactory, even to the compulsion from which it derives. It is only an evanescent appeasement, for these persons do not exist in the present situation controlled by the object, and it is an existent and responsive person that human nature demands. But the personalist drive, if still frustrated, has had a kind of say.

The nature of the frustration here can be misunderstood. It turns not on the fact that the work of art is man-made but on the fact that it is an object. Drilled at least from the time of Walter Pater to focus all aesthetic questions on the man-made art object, we are likely to overlook the fact that the fundamental impasse here presents itself at a more basic level than that of art itself, and that the impulse to focus the difficulty at the level of art is only another manifestation of the tendency to keep the potential of personality around an object at a maximum. The art object, with its immediate social context, is an easier point than the natural object at which both to study and to project the personalist aberration. That for both operations we today automatically avail ourselves of the object of art rather than of the natural object testifies perhaps to the waning power of the imagination in our present culture.

In more primitive cultures, it has been otherwise. It has been otherwise in the earlier history of the culture of the West. The nature cults react to the impasse created by the person-object situation not only on the artistic, but upon the natural level as well. Hebrew and early Christian critiques of the nature cults of antiquity attack the cults precisely on such ground. In the analysis offered by the writer of the Book of Wisdom, it is man's orientation toward personality which has betrayed him in his contemplation of natural objects, so that he pretends that the objects themselves are persons, imagining "either the fire, or the wind, or the swift air, or the circle of the stars, or the great water, or the sun and the moon, to be gods that rule the world." The pre-Hellenic nature cults are accused of pretending to close a circuit where it cannot be closed, of failing to own that the person-to-person drive must push on past the person-object situation to find a response which plays back. While the objects of nature are indeed redolent of Person, the Person must be not in, but beyond them. The error lies in the self-deception which tries to turn the object into a person instead of squarely facing the impasse.

Centuries later, this same critique is extended to the Greco-Roman world and given additional dimensions by Paul in the opening of his Letter to the Romans. Men have allowed themselves to be misled in imputing what is proper to the invisible and incorruptible God (personality as such is not visible, the human person, in so far as merely visible, being rather like an object) not only to human beings but to birds and four-footed animals and creeping things. Here the aberration of idolatry, of misplaced personalism, is presented as intimately connected with other deep psychological displacements. The deterioration of the sexual aspect of marriage in an idolatrous society is not a mere accident, for treating objects like persons and persons like objects suggests a basic imbalance sure to make itself felt in this deepest of human personal relationships.

IV

It would be difficult to assign the precise differences between the place of the artist and the art object in contemporary society and their place in the Judaeo-Hellenistic world. It is, however, certain that the shifts that have produced the modern world have radically altered the focus of the personalist crisis. Men are less and less inclined to impregnate inanimate nature with personality, at least in any crass fashion, although it is well to recall that in Mr. Eliot's later poems, as H. Marshall McLuhan has recently pointed out, the quite convincing speakers seem to be sections of the landscape. Even apart from reflections suggested by this and the many related phenomena which everyone can think of, it would be too simple to maintain that the old apotheosis of natural objects has simply been removed and the apotheosis of the objects of human art put into its place. But it is certain that a great shift has taken place from the former to the latter kind of apotheosis.

Between Greco-Roman times and the present, the crudity—indeed, the childishness—of almost all medieval and Renaissance purely rhetorical theory, which stands in such strange contrast to the sophistication of theological, philosophical, and even, within its limits, what we might today call the paraphysical or paramedical theory of the same periods, and which lags far behind rhetorical practice, betrays the fact that through the Middle Ages and the Renaissance the object of art had not aggregated to itself any large concentration of serious intellectual issues. No especially crucial questions attached to objects of art, not because earlier ages had an adequate apparatus of theory for explaining away the questions, but rather because the object of art failed, it would seem even in the case of serious artists, to become in any urgent way the psychological crux for things. It was idolatry of nature, implemented indeed by art, but only implemented, which long remained the real threat. The idolatry of art seems only during the Renaissance to have begun to appear as something more than a mist on the horizon.

Whatever the complete details of its history, the shift in emphasis from nature to art has matured today in connection with several related phenomena. There is the elaboration of rhetorical and esthetic theory which has marked the past few centuries, there is the cult, half-explicit but quite real, of the artist who is martyr to his craft and burnt up wholly in its service, and, finally, there is the present insistence on focusing the object of art itself to the careful exclusion of its personalized periphery.

The first of these phenomena, the elaboration of theory, is simply testimony to the fact that the work of art itself is now somehow capable of focusing the central issues of human existence. The second points immediately to the personalized aspect of these issues, for in figures such as those of Kafka or Proust or Joyce—at least as they exist as symbols in men's minds, for, as to their persons, we cannot presume to frame a definitive answer—we find the human being who has given himself to the work of art so completely as to blur the distinction between himself and it, presenting himself to it, as though it were a person, in an act of total abandonment, and thus endowing it, by what must be the ultimate fiction, with the marrow of his own abrogated personality. For the devotee of the martyr-artist, the blurring here is accomplished not at the periphery of the work of art by shading this periphery out into personalities, but rather at the very center of the work, where the personality of the artist has so annihilated itself as to be defined by nothing more than the work. The autobiographical bias in the work here does not stand in relationship to a life retained in its own right as real. The autobiography has consumed the life in its telling. The real life has been terminated in a foundation sacrifice: a human being has been put to death in order to serve as the ultimate substructure of the artistic edifice. To serve even the cause of the natural fertility which underlies the fertility of art, neither Moloch nor any other Baal could ask for more.

It is in association with such phenomena as these that the present insistence on the autonomy of the art object acquires its high seriousness. The concentration on the object is hardly a passing infatuation of a school of critics. It is a specialized focus of a persistent problem at the center of human life. If the object of art has become less religious today in being less often explicitly directed toward an extratemporal goal, it has also become more religious in bearing more directly the weight of religious issues. The object-person question pressing on the art object today is not a mere prop tangential to human living. It is the axis, the quiet pole that bears the weight and movement of all.

The assertion that in works of art it is the object itself which counts thus treads such crucial ground that it must be made with great honesty, which means with circumspection and humility. Not only the truth of the situation, but its awkwardness as well, must be faced. This awkwardness derives from the fact that, farfetched as it may seem when applied to less important works of art, the principle apparently holds that, in a valid but not exclusive sense, each work of art is not only an object but a kind of surrogate for a person. Anything that bids for attention in an act of contemplation is a surrogate for a person. In proportion as the work of art is capable of being taken in full seriouness, it moves further and further along an asymptote to the curve of personality.

The very insistence on the object-existence of the work of art, the insistence that it be set off from another reality, clean and self-possessed, involves an anomaly. For it is not an object, but a person who is self-possessed. It is only persons who, in their deep interiors where no other creature can enter, are cut off clean from the rest of the world, poised alone. The object situation itself is really the crux, the ultimate impossibility—a situation which by its very structure points away from itself to another world of persons, which carries in itself its own dissolution. The very way in which we envision the object-situation as clean, cut off, is derived not so much from the object as from our own personalist bias. We have forgotten the lesson of Gestalt psychology. This is humiliating for those who must deal with objects, as we all must. But it will do no good to blink the facts and pretend that they are otherwise. And it will perhaps do no harm to understand and sympathize with the recurrent impulse—shall we say, of the undergraduate?—to get away from it all and back into the vibrant world of personalities again.

The fact is that, in the last analysis, as a matter of full, serious, protracted contemplation and love, it is unbearable for a man or woman to be faced with anything less than a person—and thus, tragically, even part-way unbearable to be faced only with other human persons, where the personal relationship is inevitably enmeshed in material situations involving objects, and where even the human being, measurable, definable, partakes of the nature of object at the same time that he is person. In all our moves, our motivation, perhaps in secret and by indirection, bears toward the countermove, hopes to find itself really a countermove. Our great fear is that we are not being loved. Our gaze on the object, we peep anxiously from the corners of our eyes, alert for someone's response somewhere.

This situation keeps the jinnee in the urn and promises to keep him there for good. Try as you may, he will not be exorcized. What is worse, he will always threaten to prove more interesting than the urn itself. For he is a person, or—since it is hard to be certain about jinn, themselves folklore creatures grown out of the person-object crisis and representing an ambiguous and unsatisfactory compromise, for some Moslem writers make them angelic or demonic persons, but others mere diaphanous animals—at any rate, if he is not a person, he behaves enough like one to betray the bias of the human heart.

❧ TWO ❧

A Dialectic of Aural and Objective Correlatives

Soun ys noght but eyr ybroken.
—The eagle to Chaucer in
The House of Fame

I

THE likening of a poem to a monument or to some sort of object is as old at least as Horace's 'Exegi monumentum aere perennius.' Nevertheless, a certain fixation upon the analogy between a poem and an object is characteristic of the present English-speaking world. Here a great deal of criticism feeds on this analogy, which is featured not only in titles such as Cleanth Brooks's *The Well Wrought Urn* or William K. Wimsatt's *The Verbal Icon,* but also in the substructure of much of our most active critical thinking and writing. In his "Science and Poetry," I. A. Richards deals with a poem as the "skeleton" of a "body of experience," as a "structure" by which the "impulses" making up the experience are "adjusted" to one another. In their highly influential *Theory of Literature,* René Wellek and Austin Warren answer their own capital question regarding the mode of existence of the literary work by explaining it as a "structure" of norms or "stratified system" of norms. T. S. Eliot's great critical essay, "Tradition and the Individual Talent," underwrites the poem as a "monument," and treats of tradition with no discernible attention to vocalization as such. Poetic tradition is considered without explicit attention to the radically acoustic quality of the dialogue between man and man in which all verbal expression has its being. Accordance with tradition is for Mr. Eliot a matter not of harmony or counterpoint, but of objects which "fit" in with one another. The creative process is envisioned as outside the world of voice, in terms of chemicals (objects) "working" on one another. Despite his own

26

recent disavowal, Mr. Eliot's "objective correlative" is deservedly famous, for it provides support for a whole state of mind fixed on a world of space and surfaces. It is noteworthy that by the time of *The Confidential Clerk,* the symbol for artistic performance is even more committed to the visual and tactile. Sir Claude Mulhammer, the unsuccessful artist—poet in the larger sense—is presented as a spoiled potter.

This tactile and visualist bias is shared by poets themselves when they speak of their own achievement. Archibald MacLeish, always a sensitive register of contemporary critical and literary trends, in his *Ars Poetica* compares a poem to a whole series of nonvocal, visually and tactually apprehended "objects":

> A poem should be palpable and mute
> As globed fruit
> As old medallions to the thumb
> Dumb
> Silent as the sleeve-worn stone
> Of casement ledges where the moss has grown—
> A poem should be wordless
> As the flight of birds.

This has, of course, a certain validity. It suggests earlier Imagist preoccupations with poetry which is "hard" and "clear"—made up, that is, of images (with a bias toward visual images) rather than of words. It likewise suggests still earlier Platonic and Aristotelian theories of poetry such as the "kodachrome theory" espoused by Sir Philip Sidney (poetry makes the grass greener and the roses redder). But it is a far cry from Sidney's and others' notion of a poem as a *speaking* picture.

II

Many of the critics just cited as preoccupied with objects, structures, skeletons, and stratified systems have pressed the point that poetry belongs primarily to the world of voice and sound, but in doing so have based their explanations perhaps too innocently on spatial analogies. To consider the work of literature in its primary oral and aural existence, we must enter more profoundly into this world of sound as such, the I-thou world where, through the mysterious interior resonance which sound best of all provides, persons commune with persons, reaching one another's interiors in a way in which one can never reach the interior of an "object." Here, instead of reducing words to objects, runes, or even icons, we take them simply as what they are even more basically, as utterances, that is to say, as cries. All verbalization, including all literature, is radically a cry, a sound emitted from the interior of a person, a modification of one's exhalation of breath which retains the intimate connection with life which we find in breath itself, and which registers in the etymology of the word "spirit," that is, breath. "Whoever loses his breath loses also his speech," and, we might add, his life as well. The cry which strikes our ear, even the animal cry, is consequently a sign of an interior condition, indeed of that special interior focus or pitch of being which we call life, an invasion of all the atmosphere which surrounds a being by that being's interior state, and in the case of man, it is an invasion by his own interior self-consciousness. Not that man's interior through this invasion entirely exteriorizes itself, loses its interiority. Quite the contrary, it keeps this interiority and self-possession in the cry and advertises to all that is outside and around it that this *interior* is here, and, refusing to renounce itself, is manifesting itself. Precisely because he does not renounce his own interior self, the cry of the wounded, suffering man invades his surroundings and makes its terrible demands on those persons who hear it. For this invasion, under one aspect a raid or sally into others' interiors, is also a strangely magnetic action, which involves not so much one's going out to others as one's drawing other interiors into the ambit of one's being. The voice of the agonizing man, we say, "captivates" others' attention, their very selves, "involving" them, as we have recently learned to put it, by pulling them into his own interior and forcing them to share the state which exists there.

There is, indeed, no way for a cry completely to exteriorize itself. A mark made by our hand will remain when we are gone. But when the interior—even the physical, corporeal interior, as well as the spiritual interior of consciousness—from which a cry is emitted ceases to function as an interior, the cry itself has perished. To apprehend what a person has produced in space—a bit of writing, a picture—is not at all to be sure that he is alive. To hear his voice (provided it is not *re*produced from a frozen spatial design on a phonograph disc or tape) is to be *sure*.

'Soun ys noght but eyr ybroken,' says the loquacious and pedantic eagle who soars through Chaucer's dream in *The House of Fame*. The frightened, airborne Chaucer had not only his heart in his mouth as he heard this, but his tongue in his cheek as he reported it. He sensed that this simple reduction of sound to "broken" air and thus to spatial components was psychologically unreal, much too facile. Today we have the same awareness as Chaucer, set in a more complex context. We know that we can study sound in measurable wave lengths, on graphs and on oscillographs, calibrating it in a thousand different ways. But we also know that this spatial reduction of sound, which externalizes it completely and enables us to handle it scientifically and with impeccable accuracy, has one supreme disadvantage. Through such study we know everything—except sound itself. To find what the sound *is,* we must make it really exist: we must hear it. As soon as we hear it, all its mysterious quality—the thing which makes it really different from a measurement or a graph—asserts itself once more. And this is precisely what makes it *sound.*

In its ineluctable interiority, related to this irreducible and elusive and interior economy of the sound world, all verbal expression, and in particular all true literature, remains forever something mysterious. Like the self or person, the word refuses to submit completely to any of those norms of clarity or explicitness (which means "unfoldedness") such as we derive through considering knowledge and communication by analogy with sight. It refuses to be completely exposed (as a surface) or explicated (unfolded) or explained (laid out flat) or defined (marked with boundary lines) or to be entirely clear (separated from its ground or background) and distinct (pricked out).

What I am trying to say here is not properly conveyed by stating simply that utterance, and in particular the true literary work, has "depth." For depth is a concept which can be resolved, ultimately if circuitously, in terms of surfaces. Interiority cannot be. For I mean by interiority here precisely the opposite of surface, that which does not have surface at all, and can never have.

Language retains this interiority because it, and the concepts which are born with it, remain always the medium wherein persons discover and renew their discovery that they are persons, that is, discover and renew their own proper interiority and selves. Persons who do not (in one way or another) learn to talk remain imbeciles, unable to enter fully into themselves. The pitch of utterance which bears toward the interior of the speaker—and by the same token toward the interior of the hearer, who repeats in his own interior the words of the speaker and thereby understands them—can never be done away with, despite the fact that the same utterance must always have some reference, at least oblique, to exterior reality as well. Because of this double reference of language, to person and to object, "I do not understand *you*" can be tantamount to "I do not understand the *things* you are trying to say."

But if all language faces some toward the interior, and the interior of both speaker and hearer, of all the forms of language literature has in a sense most interiority because, more than other forms of expression, it exists within the medium of words themselves and does not seek escape from this medium. In some sense, most, if not all, other forms of expression do ambition such escape. Typically, scientific expression does. It hedges words about with definitions and restrictions of all sorts in order to keep them to a certain extent from leading their own uninhibited life in the mysterious interior world of communication between persons wherein they came into being. It drives toward complete explanation. It bends words to extrinsic ends at the expense of intrinsic in the sense that it tries to keep their reference to "objective" reality under a kind of surface control. Science relies heavily on diagrams or on diagram-type concepts. And, insofar as it is quasi-scientific, so does my present discussion here.

And yet science works its designs on language here with only partial success, for two reasons. First, the scientific policing of terminology is itself a linguistic activity, not a technique of object-manipulation, and hence itself exhibits a certain mysterious interiority. At any moment in its development, even science, not to mention philosophy, is only arrested dialogue.

Secondly, as its source for its own proper terms science can avail itself only of a stock of words or morphemes which have come into being in a curiously nonscientific way. Science must establish itself within an already going language grown into being through nonscientifically controlled etymologies. Thus scientific conceptualization and expression is tempered everywhere with nonscientific relicts, and always will be. In the last analysis, all science must in some fashion be perpetuated by explanation in nonscientific terms, for otherwise no one could be inducted from the world of ordinary human speech into the world of scientific meanings but would have to be born into this latter world. This is to say that, basically, science can invent no entirely new words, only new combinations of those words or morphemes which it has inherited from history, that is, from the interior world in which person has communed with person over the eons in the age-old dialogue which is central to the story of mankind and which is carried on in the curious interiority of the world of sound. Still, because this world in which it operates is interior and hence mysterious and unexplained, science and philosophy itself must seek in some way to exteriorize it. For this is the business of science and, in a somewhat different way, of philosophy, to explain, to "open up" or to "open out," to explicate and unfold the mysteries, that they may remain mysteries no longer—to some extent, for in part they will always so remain.

III

Although it is not to be equated with science, criticism is in some degree explanation, and has something of this same scientific bent. Unless it is to be itself a poem, criticism of a poem must involve some elucidation. Its ultimate object may be to introduce the reader more fully into the mystery which is the poem, but its technique will be to some extent to "clear up" certain things.

It should be owned that criticism, more than science, does acquiesce somewhat explicitly to the mysteriousness of language. A look at its very meaning, supported by its own complex etymology, makes this fact clear. For criticism means radically judgment, which in turn means not explaining or diagramming but *saying* yes or no. The critic, as a sayer of yes or no, is a denizen of the sound-world. The notion of judgment, the action of the saying yes or no, simply cannot be reduced in terms of spatial analogy. Thus the fact that criticism or judgment, which is a notion certainly applicable in one way or another in all sciences, attaches itself most conspicuously to operations on literature—or to works of art, which, as will be seen, are in their own way "words," too—bears stubborn witness to the fact that literature moves certainly in the realm of the word. More than that, it bears witness to the fact that literature (and art) exists in a particular relationship to the interior of man, to that "selfless self of self, most strange, most still," as Gerard Manley Hopkins describes it, which lies forever folded in its own mysterious decision expressed by the word—"fast furled, and all foredrawn to No or Yes."

Such considerations or perspectives must, I believe, temper our critical ambitions to reduce the work of literature—most typically the poem—to some sort of object. For, although, as Eliot justly maintains in his essay mentioned earlier, works of literature are "not the expression of personality but an escape from personality," and in this are unlike ordinary dialogue, they are nevertheless not quite an escape to an object, a thing adequately conceivable, even analogously, in terms of surfaces and visual or tactile perceptions. Works of literature consist in words, and, as we have suggested, words themselves retain in themselves ineluctably something of the interiority of their birth within that interior which is a person. As cries, they go "out," but they are not extensions of, or projections of interiority. In this sense Camus's and Sartre's view of man as an interior exteriorizing itself is quite inadequate to the totality of the human situation. We are more accurate if we keep our metaphors closer to the world of sound and think of speech and of works of literature as "amplifications" or, better, as intensifications of an interior. All words projected from a speaker remain, as has been seen, somehow interior to him, being an invitation to another person, another interior, to share the speaker's interior, an invitation to enter in, not to regard from the outside. The Hegelian master-slave dialectic manifests a brilliant partial insight, but it does not cover the whole of the person-to-person relationship revealed by voice considered as voice.

In so far as all works of art are in some measure utterances, expressions emanating from the human psyche, they, too, partake of this interiority. Even the works of pottery in *The Confidential Clerk,* to resume Sir Claude's musings, in this sense consist in words, resonant with human life, for Sir Claude goes on to identify his experience of pottery as a mode of communication between persons:

> But when I am alone, and look at one thing long enough,
> I sometimes have that sense of identification
> With the maker of which I spoke—an agonizing ecstasy
> Which makes life bearable . . .

IV

The piece of pottery serves to join the often otherwise unknown artist and observer—uniting those into whom the word enters, or who enter into it. But if a piece of pottery or any other object of art can be said to consist in a word or words, works of literature can be said to do so even more. They consist not only in words, they consist of words. For this reason they remain most mysterious among all works of art—more mysterious, even, than music, which, divorced from words, is pure voice, but voice with a human point of reference missing.

It is a commonplace that Aristotle once observed that music is the most "imitative" of arts. This implies that, in so far as art is imitation, music is the most consummate art—a paradoxical notion if our idea of imitation is formed chiefly by reference, even analogous reference, to the world of sight and space. For what construct existing outside itself does a work of Beethoven or Bartok "imitate"? However, Aristotle's remark need not be interpreted in terms of such constructs. It seems to contain in germ an idea which can be developed in another way, although from Aristotle's point in intellectual history this development could not yet be explicitly realized, especially since he appears to have conceived of music regularly in conjunction with voice. The idea is this: Among the arts, music enjoys a kind of primacy in so far as the sound world has a primacy over the space world in artistic creation because all art must always in some fashion be more voice than "object." Pure music, that is, melodic or harmonic sound without words, although it is defective in not being a human voice, still has a certain primacy even over the human voice because of its existence totally within sound. Music is sound exploited as pure sound, symbolizing directly no "object" at all. Music suggests what voice might do in the way of pure communication of interior to interior, of person to person, of knowledge to knowledge and love to love, if only voice did not find itself involved also in representing objects and hence involved in the tangle of explanation in which the human voice operates and which is half its excuse for being.

But by the same token, because music is not directly involved with the opacity of objects—except in so far as it is assimilable to an object itself, and this it is only at the very minimum, being pure sound, "noght but eyr ybroken"—music manages to shirk half of the twofold responsibility of the human voice, which in giving utterance to the human word looks inward and outward simultaneously. In its purer forms, music, while it is not inward in the sense of being purely subjective, nevertheless is inward in that, while it speaks, it says nothing—that is, no*thing*. Pure music shrugs off all effort at *re*presentation. It is pure presentation. But because of this calculated irresponsibility, to which it owes its bewitching beauty, music bears within itself the germ of its own disintegration. Unconcerned about symbolizing an object despite the fact that it is a denizen of the sound world, the realm of voice, and that it capitalizes on this situation, music utters a "word" which actually falls short of being a voice. For the human voice, interior though it be, achieves its inward perfection only by bearing outward too. In being a voice about nothing outside, music amplifies only a fictional interior. In being about no object, in the last analysis it also is the voice of no person. For this reason, the more music becomes pure music, the more it risks being identified with mathematics, as the history of the arts in antiquity and the Middle Ages shows, and thus being viewed not really as sound at all. By carrying the artistic process to one of its extremes, music thus reveals the impossible tensions under which all art works and which all art must strive ceaselessly to resolve with never the hope of complete success. These tensions manifest themselves most spectacularly in the realm of sound, for all art, as voice or word, exists with special reference to this realm.

V

If it is desirable that criticism go beyond its admittedly healthy interest in the art "object" or the "objective correlative" by giving more explicit attention to the oral-aural commitments of all art, and particularly of literature, one can suggest that the perspectives open to the phenomenological and existential outlooks ought at this point to be exploited to a greater extent by American and British critics. Now is the time to infuse into criticism awareness such as those of Louis Lavelle, Martin Buber, and Gabriel Marcel, which make it feasible to deal to a greater extent with language as sound, with correlatives which are not merely "objective," or, for that matter, merely "subjective" either, but which transcend this objective-subjective classification (itself derivative from an unreflective visualist notion of reality). We need the Kierkegaardian sense of dialectic, as well as an awareness of the existential implications of dialogue—that is, of all expression viewed for what it basically is, an exchange between an "I" and a "thou"—such as registers variously in the works of post-Hegelians like Jaspers or Camus. (In *The Fall*, only one person's speech is recorded, but the direct partner to the dialogue becomes the "I" who is the reader, and the person speaking, it is to be noted, is a judge—one who decides, says yes or no

—who is a penitent judge, aware that he is one himself made to be judged.) If it is not too much to expect that these typical Continental developments take root in our still basically Anglo-Saxon critical soil, certain problems of criticism, hitherto highly intractable, can be dealt with much more satisfactorily.

There is first of all the problem of the "boundaries" of a literary work. Any criticism which insists that each work be regarded as a whole, somewhat in the sense in which an object is felt to be a whole, and that the value of any items in the work depends on the interior organization of the work, will feel the work as having definite boundaries. It will be disconcerting to find, for example, in the influential textbook, *Understanding Poetry,* of Cleanth Brooks and Robert Penn Warren, where works do have definite boundaries, the admission that "it is sometimes said that a poet's work is really one long poem of which the individual poems are but parts." Messrs. Brooks and Warren do not undertake to refute this view. But it is a puzzling view if we wish with Brooks and Warren to take each poem individually as a discrete object existing in its own right, a unique "well wrought urn"—unless we are willing to recall that the well wrought urn, too, as a "word," is like the individual poem, a moment in an age-old conversation in which what goes on within the artist's psyche and registers in his work echoes the whole evolution of the cosmos. From this latter point of view the single poem is discrete somewhat in the abstract way in which a moment in a dialogue is discrete—only somewhat more than nonpoetic moments in a dialogue, at least in that it provides a unit for pause and meditation. It communicates a unique something which cannot be quite laid hold of outside the poem. But, while standing by itself more than a riposte in a conversation might do, this something does not stand entirely by itself. Each literary work marks a definite advance over what has gone before and is big with promise for the future, and this precisely because it is not a mere object, but something said, a "word," a moment in an age-old exchange of talk. Thinking and speaking of a literary work as a moment in a dialogue engenders an awareness of its "open" or unbounded historical potential, and of its unlikeness to a discrete "object." It appears as something like a Sartrean *pour-soi* as well as an *en-soi.*

A second area or problem of criticism which can be dealt with in terms of oral and aural performance is that of the literary genre. Just as a poem or other work of art as word resists complete framing as an "object" thought of as clearly and distinctly outlined in space, so it resists complete framing in terms of types and genres. For these represent an attempt to define, to delimit, to mark off, and in this way conceal a visualist approach to knowledge, feeling, and communication which is—I must repeat—a necessary and inevitable approach for purposes of explanation, but which can never be entirely satisfactory in the case of works which are, again, not objects but moments in a dialogue. Awareness of this state of affairs enables us to explain in some sort an annoying fact that we all know, namely, that, in a very real sense, among all the diverse works of a writer such as, for example, Jonathan Swift (to take one who used a great variety of genres), whether these be lyric poems or prose travel fiction or literary hoaxes of the Bickerstaff sort or satirical pamphlets or sermons—in all these diverse works, there is a certain unity greater than that found in the genres to which these various works belong. The basis for this unity is that they are all the utterances, the word, of one man.

Thirdly, explicit attention to the mysterious oral-aural nature of the work of literature enables us to account more fully for the function of the critic—and even for the fact that criticism is constantly worrying over the function of the critic. For, once we recognize explicitly the fact that all poetry and all literature is, from one point of view, a moment in a dialogue, the rôle of the critic becomes both cleared and more complicated. If the art "object" which is "made" of words were really that—an "object"—alone, one could talk about it without becoming involved in it in the way in which, despite everything, the critic is constantly becoming involved. However, since it is not simply an object, but also something that someone (a historical person, speaking in a certain place at a certain historical time and after certain historical literary events) utters after and because others have uttered something else, and since the work of the critics is also something that someone utters after and because others have uttered something else (this something else being both the work of art and its antecedents, as well as other criticism), the lines of literature and of criticism are necessarily interwoven. They are interwoven as words are interwoven, each belonging to a certain moment in the totality of activity emanating from human life in history. Seen this way, criticism is perhaps somewhat less the poor relation of literature than it is sometimes made out to be. It is part of the total dialogue in which all literature exists.

The art "object," literary or other, precisely in so far as it is an "object," invites being treated with words. For, in spite of everything, words are more intelligible, more alive, and in this sense more real than what we perceive in space, even analogously. We use words to process, understand, and assimilate spatial conceptions. We learn *from* sight, but we think *in* words, mental and vocal. We explain diagrams *in* words. The art "object," in so far as it is an object with at least an oblique spatial reference and not a word, has somehow divorced itself from the flow of conversation and understanding in which human life moves. It must be returned to this flow, related somehow to the continuum of actuality, that is to say, to what concrete, existent persons are actually saying and thinking. Undertaking to talk about the art object, the critic undertakes to effect this relationship or reintegration. But in doing so, he must somehow violate the work of art in its effort to subsist alone. For by talking about it he advertises the fact that it does not really and wholly and entirely exist alone.

Moreover, the critic is likely to violate the work of art in another and opposite way. For, in so far as he does more than merely initiate into the experience of a given work of art, help create a climate of empathy—and few if any critical works can pretend to do merely this—in so far, that is, as he seeks not merely to induct the reader into the experience but also to "elucidate," to "explicate," to "clarify" the work of art, the critic is actually taking the work in quite the opposite way, not as an object to be reintegrated in the mysterious world of words, but as a mysterious "word" which must be made tractable by explanation of at least a quasi-scientific, objective sort. One does not elucidate or clarify a work of art in so far as it is an object, but rather in so far as it is a word. For we do not elucidate or explicate an object—a quartz crystal, for example, or a fish. We elucidate or explicate words or remarks (which may, indeed, be "about" objects). But if to "elucidate" or "explicate" a poem or a painting is thus to regard it as a word, it is at the same time to ambition moving it in some sort out of the world of resonance and voice into space. For in so far as one aims to "elucidate," to "explicate," to "clarify," one aims to process one's knowledge through considering it by analogy with a space-and-light world of vision, not a world of sound. Concepts of this sort—elucidate, explicate, clarify—are all based on this visualist analogy.

Thus, between Scylla and Charybdis, the critic is caught in the dia-

lectic of object and word in which the work of art has its being. He
can take the work as an object and attempt in some sort to verbalize
it—or if it is a piece of literature already, to verbalize it still more—
or he can take it as a word and attempt to objectify it, to exploit
its likeness to "things." Generally he does partly the one and partly the
other. In either case he advertises its limitation—or, we might say, the
limitations of all human perception and intellectual activity, or for
that matter, of all finitude, of finiteness. For in this universe of ours all
objects are in some sense words, and all our words invite maneuvering
as objects. Like the poet himself, the critic can encode the object in
words or decode the word into a quasi object. He cannot do both at
once. To gain ground in one sector is to relinquish it in another. And
yet the over-all loss is never so great as the gain. For the critic can
overcome the impasse in which he finds himself at least to the extent that
he realizes that it is an impasse. The mind cannot get outside its
limitations absolutely. But it can get outside them to this extent: it can
recognize its limitations as limitations. Combined with an awareness that
indefinite progress in both empathic criticism and explicatory criticism
is possible, we must cultivate an awareness of the limitations within
which both types of criticism must ineluctably operate and we must develop techniques of talking about these limitations.

Finally a more explicit recognition of the oral-aural world in which
literary works, and in their own way other works of art, have their
being makes it possible to deal more directly with the all-important problem of history and artistic tradition. Philosophies or world views which
consider all human knowledge, wittingly or unwittingly, by analogy
with sight-knowledge (abetted more or less by tactile perception of
spatial relations) to the exclusion of sound-knowledge, have no place
for history, and are helpless to deal with evolution, cosmic, organic, or
intellectual. For history they tend to substitute cyclicism. It is a commonplace that the early Hebraeo-Christian tradition, which has been
the great well-spring of mankind's genuine historical awareness, as the
late Erich Auerbach has so masterfully shown in the first chapter of his
book, *Mimesis,* is a heritage rooted in an oral-aural notion of knowledge, not in the more visualist Hellenic notion.

The growth in the reflexiveness of human thought and in explicit and
deliberate attention to the individual, unique in his interiority, which,
despite many spectacular and disheartening setbacks, is the dominant

pattern in the intellectual history of man over the ages, is another manifestation, at a higher level or pitch, of this same interiorizing economy which marks, so it seems, cosmic developments taken in their larger phases. It is this increase in interiority which makes history possible and which governs artistic tradition. Only when mankind has become pretty thoroughly reflexive, not only individually but socially on a large scale, does history as a subject take form and begin to dominate in a specific way man's outlook on the world. At this same stage, art and literature become intensely conscious of their past, not as outside the artist and his works, but as in them, and the age-old dialectic is intensified between tradition, claiming more and more attention as historical lore deepens, and the individual, courted with growing fervor as philosophies of personalism come into being.

So far, no way of philosophizing about history has arisen to compete with that which sees the movements of history as analogous to those of dialogue—to what happens when one inviolable interiority or human person sets about communicating with another. In the primacy of this analogue for the handling of history, a late-comer in the evolution of the cosmos, the interiorizing momentum which seems to dominate large-scale developments asserts a kind of ultimate claim. If literary history is to be more than a sheer enumeration of befores and afters, more than, quite literally, a surface treatment proceeding by likening works of art to discrete objects apprehended by sight rather than, in a mysterious way, to persons themselves (for voice is an intensification of person), it will have to avail itself of this notion of dialogue more explicitly, although not quite in the Hegelian, much less in the Marxian way—for Hegel's dialectic is too little vocal in preoccupation, deflecting attention from the word as word to a visualist analogue of the word, the *idea*, the that-which-is-seen, reflected in an equally visualist (thesis-antithesis-synthesis) reduction of dialogue itself.

If it is difficult to consider literature under a definitively aural aspect, and if any such consideration must necessarily involve visualist references and analogies (as this present discussion, and this very sentence, certainly does), nevertheless it should be less difficult in this age than it has been in the past. It should even come rather naturally to us in an age dominated by figures such as Proust, whose work seeks to perpetuate in the hollows of the mind all the reverberations of the past; Joyce, whose work seeks to condense all the past, present, and future into the fathomless, echoing interior of one night's monologue; Faulkner, whose North Mississippi county resounds with the voices of four or five continents; and Pound, who presents in the *Cantos* an attempt at something like "pure" poetry which nevertheless consists in an echo and amplification of snatches of conversation salvaged from all over this world's history—snatches, that is, of what registered in the interiors of men and women since these interiors began that communication with one another within which we still live our conscious lives.

❧ THREE ❧

Metaphor and the Twinned Vision

I

METAPHOR, our generation likes to tell itself, is an omnipresent principle of language. What is the reason for the kind of primacy which metaphor enjoys in linguistic operations and which underlies its peculiar semantic effectiveness? No single answer can exhaust this fecund question, but I should like here to suggest a sort of answer which has hitherto not received the formulation it deserves.

Metaphor has many aspects, but for the present we may consider it, in a least-common-denominator definition, as the use of a term in a sense or signification improper to the term. Thus we include what all definitions or descriptions of metaphor somehow or other take into account: a kind of doubling, a bifocal quality. This twinning aspect of metaphor is implied as soon as we speak of an "improper" signification, which suggests a "proper" one. The term "improper" is not to indicate that the second signification is wrong, awkward, or only grudgingly allowed, although theories of metaphor have always suffered from a tendency to read this implication into the metaphorical situation. In metaphor, there is merely a signification, which has a kind of priority, a prescriptive or presumptive right to the term for the simple reason that, in the hurly-burly of semantic activity, it somehow got prior hold of the term. In this sense, the second meaning has some of the disadvantages of an intruder.

While this is not to say that metaphors are embarrassing in the linguistic situation, it is perhaps to say that the linguistic situation itself is embarrassing, that the human way of knowing, which gives rise inevitably to linguistic symbolization, is involved in an impasse in which it can find and maintain its sense of direction only by somehow escaping from itself.

It is a commonplace that in metaphor a term does not abandon one signification for another but rather stands related to two significations at once. When we speak of a certain man as a cur, the metaphor is effective in so far as we can keep the term "cur" attached primarily not to a man but to a dog. If the primacy of this original attachment is compromised, if the word becomes attached to the second meaning more or less directly so that the primary meaning is eliminated or at least is no longer effective—as when we speak of the foot of a mountain or the head of a table—the metaphor becomes spent, or even ceases to be a metaphor at all.

The doubling or twinning of two concepts which metaphor thus demands is a clue to the psychological and linguistic importance of metaphor. At the heart of the linguistic situation, there is another kind of twinning which human intellection must constantly seek to circumvent but which it can never succeed in escaping. This twinning is at the heart of all human operations of understanding. It is the judgment or enunciation or statement, the operation by which a subject is joined to a predicate to make a unit of discourse which has, as we say, *complete* sense.

Faced with an object, the human intellect is simply not equipped to assimilate it *en bloc*—not the object nor even any tiniest aspect of it. Man knows *componendo et dividendo*—by putting together and setting apart. Even after it has built up a reserve of symbols or concepts, if the mind is to get at the truth of a thing, it must always make two passes at it. One never suffices. The mind needs two items to set against each other. Looking at the object in the aquarium before us, "This," we say, laying hold of the thing intellectually in a sweeping, indiscriminate, unabstract way ("this" is a kind of pointing)—"This," we say, "swims," and with "swims" we have made another pass at the same object, caught it up again, only this time in a more precise kind of grip, one which clamps tighter the first, more haphazard, intellectual hold we had. We consider here only the simplest possible instance, but what obtains here always obtains: predicates specify, delimit, render more definite their subject, give it "form." By manipulating two items so that one thus for a brief instant controls the other we "know" in the full sense, we possess—for a brief moment—truth.

The object with which the intellect is concerned may be a huge disorganized landscape or a small, highly unified existent—our living, swimming organism. It makes no difference. The intellect must secure two separate footholds, one in the condition of subject, the other in the condition of predicate. In terms of a simple apprehension, a simple grasp, a simple concept, we cannot even pose the question of truth or falsehood. If a person says merely "star" or "arthritis" with no complementary subject or predicate even implied, it is impossible to broach the question as to whether what he is saying or thinking is true or not.

The fact that our decisive engagement with reality, the achievement of truth, is effected in some sort of twinning process throws light on the nature of concepts themselves—or, as they are also called, ideas or simple apprehensions. These things are destined to be coupled. They cannot stand on their own feet alone. They generate truth only by pairing with each other, as in the material world the most avanced form of generation is accomplished by the bipolarized sexes, for human concepts are drawn from this world and behave accordingly. Our concept of "tree" or of "color" or of anything else, including complex concepts, which may also serve as subjects or predicates, such as "a nation of free men," "freedom from all contagious diseases"—each of these concepts is so formed as to be joined with other concepts in our intellectual operations. For everything we represent to ourselves as a concept can only turn up as a potential member of a pair of concepts, a potential part of an enunciation or judgment.

Now, as an intellectual device, the enunciation or judgment presents real problems. Its binarism—the binarism endemic in human intellection—is awkward, and such is the curiously introspective power of intellect that it can sense its own limitations here. Intellection is polarized to simplicity. It yearns to reduce everything to one principle, one starting point, not two. This polarization is so strong that the intellect wants to cut back of the enunciation itself, a poor, two-membered thing. Over the ages we can actually observe the human intellect as, by a chronic compulsion, it beats about for a simple apprehension, a single concept, an idea out of which it can draw everything. It wants a plenary or elemental experience of truth which is absolutely simple, a one. Out of this compulsion, all the philosophies of idealism are born, from Plato through medieval idealistic philosophies, through Cartesianism, down to Hegel and our modern world.

The attempts to base truth not on a compound—which is the result of perception—but on a supposedly simple thing come into the mind from no one knows where, will doubtless continue to the end of time. And critics will not be wanting, as they have not been wanting in the past, to point out that the attempts are, however fruitful in many ways, ultimately involved in a fog of self-deception. Descartes' essay was indeed a dream, as it has been called, just as much, if not so overtly, as was Plato's theory of reminiscence. Any idealism is an escape from the real problem. Descartes pretends to develop an idea, but he does so, significantly, not by firing ideas one by one at his auditors but by firing enunciations or statements. His ideas, like everyone else's, come two by two. If the idea itself is primary, it is indeed strange that it needs explaining, needs clarification, in what is supposed to be a series of secondary or derivative operations known as enunciations in which ideas turn up as dependent on one another, not as absolutes but as parts, as pieces in a construct.

The critic will indict Descartes of "angelism," reminding him that he is trying to project into the human cognitive situation conditions which philosophical speculation has better associated with cognition by "separated intelligences" or angels. In a world of "pure intelligence," where intellect was not embedded in material existence, there would, indeed, be no necessity for the composite thing called enunciation or judgment: understanding would be effected immediately by a simple concept, an intellectual monad, not a dyad. But of a concept such as this, one which expresses truth in one sole grasp, we can have no direct experience. We can talk of it, for we can envision it as the limit which our intellection moves toward but which it is incapable of achieving. We can dream about the whole science of field physics, let us say, as summed up in one word. But to us, the word is quite ineffable. We cannot conceive it, let alone express it. Were we instructed by some strange illumination how to form such monad concepts, we should perhaps be destroyed by the travail which their conception would entail. For us, relativity physics, however awe-inspiring its conclusions, will remain like everything else we understand: a series of principles and conclusions expressed in the composite structures called enunciation or statements. If and when the more simple and generalizing mathematical formulae now being sought are found, they will be, like their predecessors, mathematical formulations figuring in enunciations, too.

About the further criticism of idealism, we need not be concerned, but only with the persistent attraction of idealism for the human mind. A finite being with an intellect is always too smart for himself. Inevitably, the human intellect becomes acquainted with its limitations and hankers to circumvent them. Intellect has at least this much edge on nonintellectual knowledge, that it can know that it has troubles when it has them. It thus develops a curious nostalgia for something it has not really known, for the greater unification of which its own activity bears a negative imprint.

II

At this point metaphor offers its tantalizing consolations. Metaphor, as has been seen, is a doubling or twinning of intellectual vision, and as such decidedly reminiscent of the double grasp at the heart of every enunciation.

Here we are taking metaphor in its simple form, as when I say of a man, *That cur should not be allowed to continue in office.* It must be understood that we are not considering the instances when metaphor is applied to a subject by means of a verb, as in the sentence *That man is a cur,* where there are questions extraneous to that of the metaphor itself. It is in the metaphor itself, independently of expressed predication, that the doubling here spoken of occurs. By the very fact that it occurs independently of a predicate, by a simple operation involving only one term, the metaphorical kind of twinning has from the point of view of simplicity and unification an advantage over the kind found in the full statement or enunciation. It suggests this latter twinning without being so overtly complex. It seems to do the work of an enunciation but it also seems to be simpler in structure.

Actually, the metaphor does imply a kind of predication. We imply a proper term and implicitly predicate the improper term of it. It is as though I said, *That man, who is a cur, should not be allowed to continue in office.* But, since "cur" is predicated of man only by implication —for in the simple metaphor the "man" does not openly appear—the mind feels the impact of the two terms as practically one. This creates the impression of extraordinary unity or condensation, and it accounts for the brilliance, the glow of resplendent intelligibility which we sense in metaphor and which Quintilian long ago referred to as "light." Since the metaphor must be based on some similarity, however elusive, the impression of unity rests on more than a pure illusion. Often on not much more, for the similarity desirable here is of a curious kind, since the same term which unites the two concepts must also keep them distinct. Thus it is that the most farfetched or unexpected metaphors can be the most effective, provided that somehow the distance between the widely divergent meanings can be effectively bridged. Their divergence can then suggest the separation of subject and predicate terms without the actual complications which an expressed subject and predicate would necessitate.

The metaphor is thus an intellectual monad and dyad all at once. In it the mind senses the twinning suggestive of the enunciation, by which it is best equipped to lay hold of truth intellectually, but it senses this twinning in one single term, so as to suggest that the mind is, for once, functioning with single, not with double vision. The mind is pretty well eating its cake and having it, too. Which is only as it should be, for in nonmetaphorical apprehension of truth, it never manages to eat to its complete satisfaction.

III

The explanation advanced here, which sees metaphor as a kind of economical or condensed judgment, suggests intimate connections between metaphor and poetry. For in some profound sense, poetic apprehension involves a condensed and simplified awareness, too. The vistas opened at this point are too extensive to be gone into fully here, but a brief example may be to the point.

"The Phoenix and the Turtle" has long seemed to me a poem in which metaphor rules with particular insistence. The economy of the poem comes so far under the control of metaphor that, in a twinkling, by a simple flick of attention, the theme of the poem converts into a metaphor of metaphor itself. The cardinal metaphors at work can be discerned at once. The phoenix, as suggesting change which is both death and birth, and the turtle, symbol of devotedness moved by love, can be considered each as a metaphor with a particularly wide range of applicability—as potentially multiple metaphors. Like the archetypal symbols of Jung, these are capable of engaging reality at all sorts of levels simultaneously and indeterminately. They weave through the analogies of being, where "the dance along the artery/The circulation of the lymph/Are figured in the drift of stars." The exact reference of the phoenix and the turtle will depend on where you choose to pull them up for the moment by arresting your attention momentarily. They can be metaphorical terms for persons, for philosophical abstractions such as love and death, for mind and body, for Christ and the Church.

We cannot go into the means by which these and all the other possibilities are kept in agitation within this poem in a way such possibilities seldom enough are. We must note only the fact that the possibilities *are* kept alive, are not killed off by the disasters which can overtake a poem less well managed than this. Here the reader is not distracted by irrelevancies but encouraged to let the metaphor grow and extend its range of applicability without particular limit.

It is while letting the metaphor grow that we may suddenly become aware that the phoenix and the turtle can fly off as symbols into a still further dimension and become a metaphor of metaphor itself, for the union of these two divergent terms—the "mutual flame" in which they are united—lends itself with surprising readiness to being taken as a symbol of the union of two terms which is the precise thing that metaphor realizes.

> So they loved, as love in twain
> Had the essence but in one;
> Two distincts, division none:
> Number there in love was slain.
>
> Hearts remote, yet not asunder;
> Distance, and no space was seen

The way the symbolism accommodates itself here to metaphor should be no surprise, for, if what we have said of metaphor is true, the union of the two meanings in one term, the unity of the twinned vision, is as intimately and deeply involved in the meshes of being as are the kind of symbols here operating.

Metaphor, in its strange double focus, brings us quickly to the quest for unity with which the phoenix and the turtle are preoccupied and which conditions their appearance in this poem—the quest for unity set in motion by the mysterious structure of a composite being, man, nostalgic for a simplicity which he cannot find within his own consciousness, resentful of everything short of this simplicity, ultimately discontent with his grasp of truth in statements, which are poor divided things like man himself, bearing the mark of their own destruction within themselves. Even when they contain no margin of error, when everything they assert is absolutely true, our statements have a way of leaving us unsatisfied by not meaning so much as we had thought ourselves on the point of uttering. "One has only learnt to get the better of words/For the thing one no longer has to say."

The difficulty goes deep, for it lodges in the structure of human cognition itself. Hence it is not surprising that among the elemental, archetypal symbols he is operating with, Shakespeare encounters human reason itself, nonplussed by the divided unities and the united divisions with which it must deal:

> Reason, in itself confounded,
> Saw division grow together,
> To themselves yet either neither,
> Simple were so well compounded,
>
> That it cried, How true a twain
> Seemeth this concordant one!

Although more explicitly focused on something else, this last phrase hits off the metaphorical situation to prefection, because it touches the depths of the human situation out of which the need for metaphor grows.

Voice as Summons for Belief

LITERATURE, FAITH, AND THE DIVIDED SELF

> Memory believes before knowing remembers. Believes longer than recollects, longer than knowing even wonders.
>
> —WILLIAM FAULKNER, *Light in August*

> Everything that we believe, we believe either through sight or through hearing. Sight is often deceived, hearing serves as guaranty.
>
> —ST. AMBROSE, *Commentary on St. Luke*, Book IV, Chap. v.

> A Presence is never mute.
>
> —PIERRE TEILHARD DE CHARDIN, S.J., private notes.

I

ANY discussion of literature and belief must at some point enter into the mystery of voice and words. In a sense every one of man's works is a word. For everything that man makes manifests his thought. A dwelling or a spear tip communicates even when communication is not particularly intended. A building or a tool, we say, "shows" thought. In this, it is a kind of word, a saying of what is in one's mind.

In the fine arts, communication is even more intense, for the *raison d'être* of works of the fine arts is some sort of communication. As a "word," a painting may be polysemous and mysterious. Yet it remains something that some person has projected outside himself and made accessible to others. It externalizes something conceived within the artist —although not fully conceived, indeed, until it was in some way externalized—in order that this something may be assimilated into another or others, or at least may be available for such assimilation.

In this a painting is both like and unlike a word. For, if a word is an externalization, it is not so external as this. A word can live only while actually issuing from the interior, physical and psychic, of the living individual. As soon as it has passed to the exterior, it perishes. Returning toward its speaker, a word is not a word, but only an echo. "Words, after speech, reach/Into the silence." No spoken word can exist in its entirety all at once, but only bit by bit.

On the other hand, in so far as words are formed within us, they are destined for externalization. One might conjecture about intelligences with ineffable private words which remain forever media of interior contemplation and cannot be projected to the exterior. But the fact is that our natural interior words or concepts are not of this sort. If we can conceive a thought within ourselves, it is the sort of thing our fellows—the more perceptive ones, anyhow—can enter into. If we can think it, others can, too. Depth analysis has made it more evident than ever that there is no private language, even of inarticulate symbols. In so far as we speak to ourselves in any way, others are capable of sharing our thoughts. To conceive something interiorly is to process it for externalization.

If a painting is in some sense a human word, an exterior saying of something conceived interiorly, much more is a work of literature a word. For it is not only, as a totality, a word, but the stuff of which it is compounded is words. The canvas and oils and ground clays and salts with which a painter works are not of themselves means of expression, although they can be made so. But the words with which a speaker or writer works are themselves means of expression, and, no matter what we do with them, this they must remain.

This fact, banal enough in itself, is occluded by our present tendency to think of literary works as objects. Under one of their aspects, they are objects, of course. As a painting or sculpture or even a dwelling, while essentially an object, is also in a more subtle sense a word, so a literary work, while consisting of words and being in its own totality a word, is also in a more subtle sense an object. But it is well to remind ourselves how subtle this sense really is. Would an illiterate society, where verbal expression could be given no vicarious existence in space through writing or printing, be able to think easily of songs or orations as objects?

In a society where the only known word is the pure, evanescent spoken word it is easier to think of objects as words than it is to think of words as objects. This is the mentality revealed in the Old Testament and even in the New. It is the mentality of the primitive peoples studied by Benjamin Lee Whorf and others. Even in John Donne's day, when typography was established but had not laid so tight a hold on society as it has in the days of neoscholasticism and the New Criticism, a poem, circulated in manuscript, was associated with rhetoric rather than with an artifact. Literature was expression. "The play's the thing," says Hamlet. But it is not a "thing" in the sense of an object. It is a "thing" to move the "conscience of the king." Moving or persuading was one of the offices of rhetoric.

II

When we say a literary work is a "word," we mean that it is some thing which is said or spoken. In our typographical culture, of course, this saying or speaking must be understood in a special sense. For in such a culture the greater bulk of literary production never finds its way out of the silence of the manuscript or the printed page. Probably the only persons who actually pronounce aloud the words of novels or of most poems written today are proofreaders, whose experience while reading proof, whatever else it may be, is hardly literary; and, alas, most of what is written never gets so far as the proofreading stage. Nevertheless, in an acceptable sense silent writing is a form of speaking, as silent reading is a form of hearing.

Speaking and hearing are not simple operations. Each exhibits a dialectical structure which mirrors the mysterious depths of man's psyche. As he composes his thoughts in words, a speaker or writer hears these words echoing within himself and thereby follows his own thought, as though he were another person. Conversely, a hearer or reader repeats within himself the words he hears and thereby understands them, as though he were himself two individuals. This double and interlocking dialectic, so beautifully described by Louis Lavelle in *La parole et l'écriture,* provides the matrix for human communication. The speaker listens while the hearer speaks.

The fact that the speaker listens to himself and the hearer speaks to himself shows that communication is not effected between individuals related to each other as we might imagine a broadcasting station and a receiving set to be. In wireless transmission there is a center of emission and a center of reception, one active, the other passive, and there is movement of impulses from one to the other. Because it has this simple structure, broadcasting is not at all communication in the human sense. It is an aid, a tool of communication. In the human situation, matters are quite different. The center of emission is a kind of receiving center, too, and cannot emit its words properly unless it is at the same time receiving them. Similarly, the receiving center has to be a kind of center of emission, for it receives its words by imagining them as emitted. One consequence of this is that it is fallacious to imagine that words are capable of being reduced to impulses.

Every human word implies not only the existence—at least in the imagination—of another to whom the word is uttered, but it also implies that the speaker has a kind of otherness within himself. He participates in the other to whom he speaks, and it is this underlying participation which makes communication possible. The human speaker can speak to the other precisely because he himself is not purely self, but is somehow also other. His own "I" is haunted by the shadow of a "thou" which it itself casts and which it can never exorcize. In "The Secret Sharer," that strangely existentialist story from a preexistentialist age, Conrad's hero is painfully aware that the refugee from justice whom he has secreted on board his ship is his double, a symbol of his own interior division and of his alienation from himself. The stranger-double is somehow there in the captain's own cabin because the captain himself feels himself a stranger on his own ship, and this because he is a stranger to himself in his own soul. The same double is party to the captain's conversations with other men. When a visitor from another ship, come aboard to look for the refugee, speaks too low, the captain explains, "*As . . . I wanted my double* [concealed in the cabin] *to hear every word,* I hit upon the notion of informing him [the visitor] that I regretted to say that *I was hard of hearing*" (italics added). It was essential that the double participate secretly in the conversation. But to effect this participation, the captain had to attest a deficiency in his own powers of communication.

Conrad's profoundly symbolic tale is a kind of allegory of human existence. It reveals a rift, a limitation inside our own beings, but a rift which opens its own way to salvation—for it is a rift which comes from our bearing vicariously within ourselves the other with whom we must commune, and who must commune with us, too, and thereby compensate for the rift, the limitation, in our persons. The other within must hear all, for he already knows all, and only if this other, this *thou*, hears, will *I* become comprehensible to myself.

A literary work can never get itself entirely dissociated from this I-thou situation and the personal involvement which it implies. For a literary work to exist in the truest sense, it does not suffice that there be code marks, which we know as letters, printed on paper. A drawing can exist on paper, in space, in a way in which a literary work cannot. A drawing can be assimilated in an instant, at a glance. For a literary work to be what it really is, words must move in sequence, one after another, in someone's consciousness. The work must be read or heard, re-created in terms of communication touching an existent person or persons over a stretch of time.

The manner of this literary communication is, of course, complicated in the extreme. As compared with real dialogue between two persons, a literary performance—a story or a poem or a play—has a special objective quality, signalized by the fact that the author himself stands outside the work, as Shakespeare's own person stands outside his plays. In this way the literary work is like a drawing. It is in a sense something that the author has extruded and thereupon left. This same impression is not given by the words spoken in a personal conversation in which persons find themselves actually involved through the process of daily living. The words in such conversation are less exteriorized.

The symbol of the exteriority of a literary creation is the mask, for in such a creation the author does not communicate directly but through a kind of covering or disguise, fictitious persons or characters, who are more or less in evidence and who speak his works. As T. S. Eliot remarks, poetry "is not the expression of personality, but an escape from personality." A literary work is a sign of special alienation, for wherever we have literary creation some sort of mask inevitably appears. In *The Sound and the Fury* Faulkner nowhere emerges as Faulkner in the way he does in his Nobel Prize speech. The bard who sings the ballad is not the same person who sits down to eat afterwards. The courier who brings news by word of mouth is. The orator, being partly creative, both is and is not the same.

In the case of the drama, the communication is still more complicated by another echelon of persons coming between the writer and his audience, the actors themselves. Actors are real persons, but they perform not as the persons they are, but as persons they are not. They have at times worn masks, to show that they are not themselves, but something other. Yet, is it not highly indicative that the word for mask, *persona* (that-through-which-the-sound-comes), has given both to the ancients and to us the word for person? It is as though this ability to take on the rôle of another shows the actor's own humanity, shows that the other is already within him, and is, indeed, the shadow of his most real self. Ortega y Gasset points out that the brute animal is pure *alteración*, pure "otheration," in the sense that he cannot enter into himself. Man is not pure "otheration," because he can enter into himself—and yet, by the same token, he can find in himself and recognize by contrast the echoes of the personal other, the "thou," the alientation or *alteración* which is there. Thus acting a rôle, realizing in a specially intense way one's identity (in a sense) with a someone who (in another sense) one is not, remains one of the most human things a man can do. No brute animal can act a rôle. Unable to recognize himself, he finds it impossible to recognize what by contrast with self is other. By the same token, he has nothing against which to set a rôle so that it is a rôle.

III

Voice is the foundation for rôle-playing among men in the sense that the use of voice and its understanding, as we have seen, forces man to enter into others. From this point of view, it is not strange that as literature develops in the course of history, rôles become more manifold and more complex. Homer's Odysseus plays a great many rôles, but how many more are played, and played designedly, by the modern Ulysses, Leopold Bloom? And how many more, still, are played by the voice whom the reader hears—it does not matter here whether or not he knows that the work is by James Joyce—narrating the story *Ulysses?* Over and beyond all the other rôles in which it is involved (those of Bloom and of all the other characters) is the voice playing the rôle of mocker, making fun of itself?

Whatever the answer, a rôle cannot exist outside a context of belief, and it is my purpose here to discuss how it is that, since voice demands rôle-playing, taking the part of the other within who is not ourselves, it demands belief as well, and how it is that belief is thus not something superadded to communication and thought, but something endemic to all human thinking, so that the question of belief and literature is really a specific variant of the general question concerning belief and communication in general, and ultimately concerning belief and human thought itself. All human intellectual activity implies belief because it implies faith in the possibility of communication and faith in someone with whom we can communicate.

Here one must make the well known distinction between belief as opinion and belief as faith. Essentially, as Gabriel Marcel points out, belief as opinion is belief *that* and faces toward what is concerned with as toward an object or "thing" or "fact" (a truth considered as a thing), as when I say, "I believe that tomorrow will be rainy," or "I believe that this book would sell well." Belief as faith, on the other hand, is belief *in* and faces toward a person or persons, as when I say, "I believe in Matthew," or "I believe in God." Belief as opinion is impersonal and should be impersonal, for its whole rationale is its "objectivity." Even if it is concerned with a person, it treats the person "objectively," not as someone to commune with but as an object to be measured. Thus, "I believe that Matthew is a competent reporter." Belief as faith, on the contrary, is personal in cast, and must be.

However, despite these contrasts between opinion and faith, it is no accident that the term "belief" is used for both, since opinion and faith are indissolubly related by the commerce they carry on with each other. Thus, although belief as faith basically is belief *in* a person, it is also possible to believe *in* a thing or an object by giving it a personalist cast. Thus, "I believe *in* this book" erects the book into more than object. It makes of it a cause, with all the personal issues which this involves. It throws down the gauntlet on behalf of the author, whereas "I believe that this book would sell well" does not necessarily do so. Conversely, to believe *in* a person (belief as faith) involves a certain belief *that* what he says (in so far as he understands and controls it) is true.

Moreover, it appears that any belief *in* (belief as faith) not only is directed toward a person but also involves in one way or another his truthfulness, his "word." This is shown in part by the fact that one cannot believe in a liar as a pure liar (if such a man can exist). But something more profound than this negative example is involved. For belief in a person is ultimately an invitation to the person to respond. As Gabriel Marcel has pointed out in *The Mystery of Being*, belief in a person may include all sorts of beliefs *that*, varying from mere conjectural opinion (thus I believe that my friend will act considerately) to the acceptance of the truth of something of which I do not have direct knowledge (thus belief in God includes the acceptance of the existence of God as a truth, belief *that* God exists). But belief in a person includes also much more than this. To believe *in* God is to look for a response from Him. The construction of our expression and thinking with the term "in"—a construction found in many languages other than English —is significant here. It suggests that somehow in believing *in* someone, we enter into him. He is not merely an "object" of belief with whom our belief terminates. He is an interiority into whom our belief penetrates and with whom it enables us to commune. The expression suggests the same interpretation of I and thou which, we have seen, underlies all human communication.

This brings home to us the fact that all communication—and, indeed, all our thinking, which is learned and developed only through communication with others—goes on in a context of belief. For when we speak, we invite response. If I expect no response, no Yes, no No, no riposte of any sort, at least internal, I do not normally speak at all— unless I am losing hold on myself, am distraught, or am not in my right mind. Now, any expectation of response is in some way a declaration of belief in the person or persons to whom I address myself. It is recognition of a presence to whose word I can, in turn, attend, and in whom I can thus believe through the acceptance of what he has to say.

Since belief, either as opinion or as faith, includes some sort of acceptance or commitment without full "objective" evidence, belief as faith, or belief *in*, surpasses belief as opinion, or belief *that*. Belief as opinion moves toward knowledge of objects, but, since it has not sufficient contact with objects to amount to full knowledge, it is essentially deficient and vulnerable. Belief as faith moves toward knowledge and love of persons, and since persons cannot be known as objects at all, no matter how intimately they are seized, the lack of "objective" evidence here is not the liability that it is in the case of belief as opinion.

This situation can be restated in terms of the way in which belief as opinion and belief as faith differ with regard to their relationship to words. Belief as opinion tends to do away with words in so far as it is ordered to "objective" knowledge, which has to do with things which do not speak. Belief as faith, on the other hand, since it has to do with persons, tends not to eliminate words but rather dwells in words and feeds on them, since they are manifestations of persons. Furthermore, in so far as communication with persons is better, more human, and, we might add, holier than contact with objects, belief as faith outclasses belief as opinion. Opinion is styled belief because it can be thought of as analogous to belief as faith. But belief as faith is simply belief in its purest form. For, short of direct observation, the best contact we can have with objects and "facts" is not opinions about them gleaned from imperfect evidence but faith regarding them—that is, knowledge derived from our acceptance of the word of other persons who have this knowledge by direct observation.

Of the knowledge which individual men have today, almost all of it is grounded in faith. The knowledge of scientists themselves is almost all grounded in faith, well founded and rational faith in the reports of their fellow scientists, but faith nevertheless. Of the scientific knowledge which any man has, only a tiny fraction has been achieved by his own direct observation. For the rest, he has good reason to believe *that* it is true because, within the limits of their competence, he believes *in* his fellow scientists reporting on their work or reporting reports of the work of others. Thus, even in the most "objective" of fields, in actuality the word of persons is more pervasive than factual observation. Science itself cannot live save in a network of belief. Even in science, where fact is more determinative, presence is nevertheless more pervasive than fact.

IV

Against this background, the question of belief in literature can be raised. A survey of current writing in English on this question shows that it is pretty well all concerned with literature as involving belief *that*. The grounds of the question are staked out in terms of Coleridge's "willing suspension of disbelief," so that the problem becomes, as in Richards's *Practical Criticism,* How can one who does not share Donne's Christian faith enter into his sonnet "At the Round Earth's Imagined

Corners Blow"? Or, to adapt Richards's terminology, How can one share Donne's beliefs emotionally while not sharing them intellectually?

This focus of the question of belief in literature is legitimate. However, we must remember that it considers belief as concerned with a kind of object or "thing," excised from any personal context. The notion of response to a presence, manifested by voice, drops out entirely, although such response seems intimately a part of literature. Objects cannot elicit response to a voice in the way in which persons can, and when we treat belief in terms of the object of belief exclusively, response becomes attenuated to behavior, and its correlative is not voice but stimulus in the Pavlovian pattern of stimulus-response. It is significant that Professor Richards not only concerns himself with "willing suspension of disbelief" but also, perhaps not entirely out of line with Coleridge's thinking even here, regularly discusses literature in terms of the way words "behave," as though words were not cries but "things," visible objects. We have a right, of course, to speak of words in terms of this analogy, but let us not forget that it is an analogy.

Without attempting to deal with the question of belief on these grounds, I should like to set it up on other grounds and to examine it there, not with a view to providing utterly conclusive answers but to improve our perspectives and to reveal how limited some of our common views of this problem really are. Let us recall that in the last analysis, any utterance, even a scientific utterance, is the manifestation of a presence, which cannot be "grasped" as an "objective" of knowledge can be, but only invoked or evoked. The most abstruse mathematical theorem remains always and inextricably within this framework of utterance, for it originated as something communicable and remains always something which someone *says* to others or, in special cases, to himself. But, since in the case of scientific utterance the vocal element is minimized, we can treat such utterance readily as an object and speak with ease of "grasping" or "not grasping" it, as we might an object. Thus, we grasp or we do not grasp the meaning of the formula $E = mc^2$. But we know how difficult and unconvincing it is to apply the notion of "grasp" to a poetic work. The notion can, of course, he applied to some extent. We can speak of "grasping" *Hamlet* or *The Marriage of Heaven and Hell* or *Absalom, Absalom!* But so to speak is not very satisfactory, not convincing. It seems much more real to speak of the response which these works evoke from us. The "evocative" quality—which is to say, the "calling" quality—is paramount in a work of real literature. Literature exists in a context of one presence calling to another.

This is a context of faith, no matter how much there may be in an individual work which, outside the work, we can know by direct evidence. Indeed, here faith achieves a special intensity (and simultaneously a special attenuation) in so far as the voice which invokes us as present and evokes our response is in a way more a pure or self-subsistent voice because of the "objective" quality of the literary work as such, its detachment from the poet, who as an individual is disassociated from the work by his literary mask. There is a special kind of dialectic at work here. In so far as the work is objectified, set apart from the existent writer who gives it being as a kind of well wrought urn is detached from its creator, its evocative effect becomes more poignant. Thus Yeats went to the Japanese Nō plays for "more formal faces," explaining that "a mask [even taken metaphorically] . . . no matter how close you go is still a work of art." Joyce's progress from *Stephen Hero* through *A Portrait of the Artist* to *Ulysses* and *Finnegans Wake* is progress from personal involvement to artistic detachment, and, as the masklike detachment grows, the evocative quality of the work, its pull on the sensibilities of the reader, grows. Because Poe can never achieve so great a detachment, because his personal problems and neuroses show through—to those, at any rate, for whom Poe's English is their native language, as it was not for Baudelaire and Mallarmé—the evocative quality of his work remains less poignant than that of Joyce or, to take another American, that of Faulkner.

We might ask why this is. If voice is an invitation to response, in what sense can the invitation become more insistent when the speaker wears a mask? To see what is involved in this question, one must consider the peculiar conditions of person-to-person communication, which is implemented by the use of voice. Human persons are of themselves distant from one another in the sense that they cannot enter entirely into one another's consciousness. The sense of distance attending on personal or I-thou relationships has been elaborated by recent writers such as Lavelle, Heidegger, and Buber, but once it is stated it needs no great explanation, for we live with this sense all the time. In dealing with another person, I am always dealing with one whom I cannot entirely fathom and with whom I cannot enter into direct communication quite like the communication I enter into with myself. His sense of self remains outside my direct awareness, and yet I can feel its aura and know that there is some interiority with whom I am dealing.

My contact with this interiority is mediated by exterior phenomena which implement commerce between interiors. This commerce is most readily maintained by voice. Voice is the least exterior of sensible phenomena because it emanates not only from the physical but also from the divided psychological interior of man and penetrates to another physical and psychological interior where, as we have seen, it must be re-created in the imagination in order to live. Unlike a picture, it lives by its contact with these interiors—when they are gone, it is gone.

Still, for all this interior orientation, even a voice is an exterior something. It achieves its effect through an exterior medium. Our way of hearkening to one another, and thus our sense of presence, necessitates a kind of breakthrough. We penetrate into a "thou" through a something which is neither "I" nor "thou," through a medium over which the action emanating from one person exercises an effect on another. Even direct physical contact involves an externalizing medium, for our body is, in a sense, not so much ourself as is our consciousness. Even in its interior, our body is somehow the "outside" of us.

The exteriority attendant on communication is what gives point to the mask in dramatic performance and, analogically, in all literature. Although it modifies the presence which manifests itself most poignantly in voice, of itself the mask is not vocal, but a medium manifest in space. It does not modify the voice of the character (presence, person) as the mute modifies the sound on a violin. Even though masks may occasionally affect voice projection, to do so is not the mask's primary function, for it is patently objectified as a visual phenomenon and produces its characteristic effects by being seen. It stands for that in the person-to-person situation which is nonvocal, noncommunicative, nonpersonal, remote, alienated.

In the preliterate world, where the eye is especially subservient to the ear, masks themselves are felt as belonging rather more to the world of voice than they are today, or perhaps are caught up more thoroughly into the world of voice, and aesthetic distance tends to disappear. For the Wintu, Dorothy Lee has noted, Coyote, Buzzard, and Grizzly Bear are bewilderingly man-and-animal. Although the wearer of a wolf mask among primitives is not a wolf, he somehow really participates in wolfness. In this situation, where the object-world is not clearly differenti-

ated from the world of voice and person, belief has not the depth of
meaning it enjoys in a civilized society, for the same reason that science
itself has not: the two are confounded with each other, for the dialectic
which sets them apart with some precision has not yet sufficiently pro-
gressed.

This seems to have been the state of affairs with the very early
Greeks in their ritualistic use of masks. Later, with the great tragedians,
real characters appear, and the masks worn become devices establishing
aesthetic distance, *alteración,* limited more definitely to the universe of
space. For space separates, whereas voice unites. As this evolution takes
place, the number and complexities of rôles, and of literary forms,
proliferate. The means of controlling and differentiating characters and
forms have been developed as the tension between the vocal and the
visual grows. For this tension the mask is the symbol, or in a later day
costume and make-up, a mitigated form of mask.

As the tension between visual and vocal grows, and with it the use
of the truly dramatic character and the formalized separation of drama
from life, there grows also, paradoxically, an awareness of the foundation
in real human existence for dramatic character. A character in a drama
is a person set off, advertised as other. Yet this state of being-set-off, this
remoteness in the midst of intimacy, is found in real life, too, and experience of drama teaches us to recognize the fact. Each man is always in
some degree a mask to other men, more consciously so today because of
the progressive reflectiveness which mankind develops in its passage
through history.

The sense of being-set-off is not annihilated by intimacy. Indeed, it
is heightened and realized in its fullness through intimacy because of
the very interiority which makes possible intimacy between persons. As
a unique and induplicable individual abiding in the depths of your own
interior consciousness, you are in a way more other to me than even
inanimate objects are; and this despite the fact that I can carry on a
dialogue with you and cannot carry on a dialogue with inanimate objects. For in assuring me of my closeness to your consciousness, this
dialogue assures me also of the uniqueness of your consciousness and of
its ultimate inviolability—of the fact that, naturally speaking, I can
never know what it is to be you, can never share this ultimate experience
of yourself with you. Of course, I cannot know what it is to be an
object either—a rosebush or a canary—but neither can the object know

what it is to be itself, so that this lack of knowledge on my part does not prevent a quite full knowledge of the object. Object-being includes no experience of self to be shared. What uniqueness the object has is reflected from the outside. In the case of a person, however, his experience of his unique self is constitutive of his most intimate self. Yet it is this very experience that intimacy cannot share.

V

These considerations throw some light on what happens to the personal charge carried by a voice in the case of a work of literature—of poetry, let us say, to take a relatively pure instance of literature. In a poem, the voice is there, but "objectified" in such a way as to mask the real person who uttered it in the first place and any other real person who utters it after him. A poem thus advertises the distance and remoteness which, paradoxically, are part of every human attempt to communicate, and it does this in so far as it is under one aspect "objective," an "objective correlative," objectlike, which is to say, nonvocal. But under a certain aspect only, for under another it is not objectlike since it is attempting to communicate very hard indeed.

Given the effective drive toward communication, the more the remoteness between the voice which, working within this drive, really creates the poem (that is, the voice of the writer) and those who hear or read it, the more evocative the work becomes. The drama is the most evocative and personal of all literary forms. In it living persons on a real stage really speak to one another; and yet, here the remoteness between point of origin and point of assimilation has actually been increased because the number of masks has been increased: in a performance of *Othello,* besides the mask or masks which Shakespeare as author wears, there is the mask of a character which each performer wears and which makes him precisely a *dramatis persona,* a person or mask in the drama. The reason for the corresponding heightening of effect seems to be the fact that all communication takes place across barriers, or is an attempt to crash through barriers, namely, the barriers which bar the ultimate compenetration of the "I" and the "thou." Provided that communication is going on, the interposition of further barriers has a tantalizing effect. It teases us to more vigorous attempts, sharper alertness, greater efforts at compassion or sympathy. One thinks of the poignancy achieved by the device of the wall in the story of Pyramus and Thisbe.

But certain other parallels might be adduced to show the intensification of the personal charge by the interposition of a mask or other barrier. A major one is in the religious history of Judaism and Christianity, where, moreover, the connection becomes evident between person and mask on the one hand and faith on the other. Compared with Aristotle, who thought it impossible that God should concern Himself at all with human affairs, Hebrews and Christians know God in a highly personal fashion. Yet they know Him by faith, which is in a kind of mask, "through a glass darkly." Moreover, in the Christian dispensation God reveals Himself more personally to man when the Second Person of the Trinity, Whose personal name is the Word as well as the Son, takes to Himself a human nature which masks His divinity. His passion, where even His human nature is seen through the mask of death, is memorialized in the Eucharist, where the human and divine natures of the Word are both masked under the appearances of bread and wine, which also, by symbolic separation of His Body and Blood, masks His human death itself. But this "masking" only heightens the personal relationship between God and man, for through the Eucharist the personal union of Christians in the Person of Christ and thence in the other two Persons of the Godhead is realized and perpetuated. Although not applied to what we are discussing here, this sense of the Eucharist is highly operative in Christian tradition. It accounts for a favorite name of the Eucharist, Holy Communion, that is, Holy Togetherness. Its implications are elaborated by St. Thomas Aquinas and other theologians, who point out, moreover, that the consecration of the elements in this sacrament of sacraments is effected not by any sign in space, but by *words* given us by the Word of God. The whole setting for this series of masks is one of communication of the most personal sort, in a universe of words and of faith, where sight is always at one or more removes from full reality.

VI

The masks in literature are generally assumed by one party to communication rather than by both. The playwright and the actors, who are the communicators, assume the masks—the playwright a metaphorical one and the actors real ones or their equivalent in costume and make-up. By contrast, the hearer is present in his own person. Were he to put on a mask, he would become a part of the play, a *dramatis persona*. As it is, although the actors and the play may enrapture him, carry him somewhat out of himself, they do not make him into a quasi-other person. The act on his part which corresponds to the masking on the part of the communictors is simply his act of belief, in the sense of faith; and belief here is not at all tantamount to opinion. One has no "opinion" that Sir Laurence Olivier is Hamlet, and no "opinion" that Ophelia's death is real. Belief *that* is relatively meaningless here. This belief is more radically belief *in,* and such belief is not pretended.

But belief in whom? In whoever are the persons behind the masks. In the actors and the playwright all together. The act of faith, or belief *in* is an invitation to them to respond as persons, to give themselves in and through truth. While there is also a certain faith in the audience which playwright and actors both have, a belief *in* the audience, an invitation to the audience to respond—for this faith, as we have seen, accompanies all human communication—nevertheless this faith of the playwright and the actors is less obviously faith than that of the audience. The reason is the curious one-way nature of artistic communication, the fact that no real dialogue takes place, that the audience itself has no occasion or opportunity to speak. The audience's response is hidden, as the act of faith on the part of the playwright and actors is correspondingly hidden. The response of the playwright and actors, on the other hand, to the audience's faith is the play itself, which is far from hidden since the audience's act of faith is quite obvious.

In response to the audience's act of faith the playwright and the actors give themselves in and through truth. How the truth is contained in the words of the play—or, *mutatis mutandis,* in the poem or other piece of literature—and, indeed, what the truth in question really is, may be a very mysterious matter. This is to be expected. The truths arrived at by faith, natural as well as supernatural, are not noted for readily admitting of clear-cut statement or of clear-cut assimilation nor for being entirely evident to everyone, even to those of good will. They often submit reluctantly or not at all to full articulation, for they have to do most intimately with persons to whom we address ourselves. If they are neatly articulated, they are taken not on their own evidence but on the evidence of a person to whom we address our act of faith; and it is hard to articulate a person. For a person whom we are addressing nature provides us no distinctive word while we are addressing him save the strange noun-substitute or name-substitute or pro-noun "thou," which is not a name at all but changes its entire meaning with each different person we apply it to.

Our belief in a play or a poem is thus an invitation to the persons involved in composing it and presenting it to us either to say something worth our while or to betray our trust in them as persons. It involves a kind of openness to them and to their meaning at all levels, to what Professor Philip Wheelwright in *The Burning Fountain* styles "depth experience." If certain details of a poem seem unacceptable to us in terms of belief *that,* the voice of the poem, coming through the mask of its speaker (as well as through the masks of any characters he may have introduced) teases us on, so that beneath any disagreement with detail there persists the conviction that something worthy of assent is being said, into which the otherwise unacceptable detail may somehow be fitted. If we cannot believe in Prospero as a real magician, we can believe that the playwright is using him to convey some further word or truth to us.

In *La parole et l'écriture* Louis Lavelle makes much of the "world" as language. For communication to be possible there must be a world shared by our individual consciences so that by naming the objects in this world we can break through our solitude and communicate with one another. When a child believes that he knows something as soon as he can name it, he is not entirely wrong. For when he can name it, he can use it for what it is worth, as a means of communicating with others. That which is neither you nor I, once it is known, becomes a link uniting you and me. This is true not only of the natural world which we apprehend through our senses, but also of poetry and of literature in general. Poetry is often involved and mysterious, but by its very existence within our ken it is destined to communicate. Indeed, its communication is in one sense communication par excellence, the most intimate communication. John Stuart Mill's notion, romantically rooted, that poetry is something which is overheard is a not too happy attempt to deal with the intimacy which poetry can effect: so intimate is the union of hearer and poet that it is as though the hearer as other were not there. The opinion sometimes expressed that poetry or art in general is basically not communicative at all is connected with the dialectical situation in which estrangement (the mask of the poet) and intimacy (achieved when the mask is somehow penetrated) are so strangely compounded.

If a poem is likened to an object in the world, it must be likened to an object already named, processed for purposes of communication, if named with a quite mysterious name. "Poetic truth," which seems so difficult to bring to earth, to isolate, to state clearly, and which is also so strangely intimate, has its roots in a sense of communion with other persons, persons perceived through masks, yet somehow decidedly there, who have believed in us enough to invite us to this uncommonly intimate response and in whom we, in turn, are called on to believe.

We come to the conclusion that any belief *that* involved in literature is subservient to belief *in*, that the most basic meaning of belief in literature has to do not with belief in the sense of opinion, which regards objects and facts (truths treated as objects), but with belief in the sense of faith, which regards person-to-person relationships, invitations and response, and truth with reference to these relationships. This conclusion is, I believe, nowhere more strikingly evident than in the situation which has obtained for some years in twentieth-century poetry. The withdrawal of the serious poet (or of the serious artist generally) has been commented on *ad nauseam*. Withdrawal from what or into what? Into himself, we are told. Yet we are faced with the striking fact that serious readers of poetry today favor no other type of poetry so much as this poetry of withdrawal. The conclusion would seem to be that readers like nothing better than to follow the poet into his retreat. Everybody wants to be alone together; and this is not strange. There is no doubt that in our age, which has evolved, among other things, a mass culture and mass media of communication, intimacy is also in many ways better served than it has ever been before. Certainly the human race is more conscious of itself as a whole and has developed its dialogue about intimacy and communication more than at earlier periods in human history. We have a more highly perfected vocabulary and more advanced means of articulation about this subject than ever before. However aware earlier man may have been of persons and of the "I-thou" situation, the philosophy known as personalism is a twentieth-century creation, just as thoroughly a product of our age as technology or television commercials. In this climate belief *in* becomes very meaningful. In terms of belief as we have viewed it here, the serious modern reader wants to believe in his poets more than ever before. This would seem to indicate that in the age of television voice is in some ways regaining a prestige over sight, that we are at the end of the Gutenberg era.

FIVE

System, Space, and Intellect in Renaissance Symbolism

I

ONE way of looking at the Renaissance is to regard it as a time when the world was flooded with sound. This was the melodious age of poetry and rhetoric, following on the vocally impoverished, cacophonous Middle Ages. The ancient tongues found voice again, and the vernaculars came into their own, spurred by the renewed attention to rhetoric, the art of speaking, that is to say, of speaking aloud.

Today we are especially aware of the aural emphasis in Renaissance culture through the work of scholars such as Lucien Febvre and through the exhaustive treatments of the rhetorical tradition which has become an American specialty at the hands of Morris W. Croll, C. S. Baldwin, Donald Lemen Clark, T. W. Baldwin, Rosemond Tuve, Douglas Bush, Richard McKeon, Maurice B. McNamee, Sister Miriam Joseph Rauh, George Williamson, and others. But there is another series of phenomena which marks this same period and of which, largely through our growing knowledge of the history of science, we are becoming more aware. For the Renaissance is also the age out of which modern mechanics and modern physical science grow. It is the age not only of Poggio and Erasmus, but of Copernicus, Vesalius, and Galileo as well.

The outlook which terminated in the mathematical transformation of thinking and yielded the world of modern science has roots which are much older than the age of humanism and are exceedingly ramified. Recent studies have underlined the fact that the humanists in general exercised a retarding influence on the physical sciences and have stressed the fact that the prehumanist scholastic age was the great seedbed of modern scientific habits of mind. Since Duhem, the role in the development of modern science played by the impetus theories elaborated in medieval Paris and elsewhere has been studied in detail, and the more recent work of A. C. Crombie, Anneliese Maier, and a host of

others has filled in our knowledge of many other aspects of physical
and optical theory. Panofsky has pointed out certain fascinating analogies between the aims and performance of Gothic architecture and
scholasticism,[1] and has further described the evolution in painting which,
by the High Renaissance, resulted in the assertion of a kind of infinite
pictorial space, through which the beholder looked and in which he felt
himself situated, and to which all other interests of the artists had finally
to yield: no longer could a floor be tilted up to display its parquetry
nor the animals in a hunt treated each as a thing interesting in itself,
enveloped in its own particular space more or less independent of its
"real" position in "modern" or "infinite" perspective.[2] This dominance
of geometrical considerations in man's response to reality has obvious
scientific implications, and Benesch has suggested certain connections
between it and the new cosmology.[3]

However, these various shifts in emphasis are further involved with
something more pervasive than architecture or painting or even the new
science. In the present study I should like to draw attention to a series
of developments in the history of ideas which specifically relate the
shifts in symbolization and conceptualization observable in the physical
sciences to another series of shifts in the ways of representing the field
of knowledge and intellectual activity itself. This latter series of shifts
is observable in the three *artes sermocinales,* or arts of communication—
grammar, rhetoric, and most particularly dialectic, or, as it came later to
be styled, logic. At present, it seems best not to go into the question of
causal relationships between these shifts, to decide whether the way
one thought about knowledge brought on the changes in ways of thinking about the world, or whether the converse was true. The sequence
could be either way, or better, both ways. The psychological operations
involved in the shifts are so subtle and concern so many people over so
great a period of time that it is impossible to discover in full detail which
new way of symbolization preceded which. The important thing is that
the two shifts work in concert, that man's view of the universe and his
view of his own mind are in great part correlatives.

II

In many ways, the greatest shift in the way of conceiving knowledge
between the ancient and the modern world takes place in the movement

from a pole where knowledge is conceived of in terms of discourse and hearing and persons to one where it is conceived of in terms of observation and sight and objects. This shift dominates all others in Western intellectual history, and as compared to it, the supposed shift from a deductive to an inductive method pales into insignificance. For, in terms of this shift, the coming into prominence of deduction, which must be thought of in terms of visual, not auditory, analogies—the "drawing" of conclusions, and so on, not the "hearing" of a master—is already a shift toward the visual and a preparatory step for induction, from which deduction was never entirely separated anyhow. Stress on induction follows the stress on deduction as manifesting a still further visualization in the approach to knowledge, with tactics based on "observation," an approach preferably through sight.

The remote origins of the auditory-to-visual shift need not concern us in detail here. They have been traced to the difference between the Hebraic concept of knowledge, auditory and consequently personalist and existential, and the Greek concept, based on analogy with vision.[4] For the Hebraic (as perhaps for the present-day Arabic world still), to know (*yadha'*) meant to know one's way around, to "know what's what," to "be in the know," whereas for the Greek, to know (γιγνώσκω) meant to see, to intuit, to envision intellectually.

However, compared to the modern world, even the Greek tended to set knowledge within an auditory frame. Only with the slow development of scientism out of the Greek tradition have the promises or possibilities latent in the visualist orientation of the term γιγνώσκω been finally realized. Socrates's technique, if not his objective, had been real, oral dialogue. Plato retained this dialogue perforce in reporting Socrates's teaching, but he reduced it to the visualist medium of writing and, in his own mind, allowed concern for dialogue to be eclipsed by the visualist notion which obsesses him, that of the "idea," a term used originally to designate the look or appearance of things. Following Plato had come Aristotle's search for sciences which were "objective"—objects being items in a visile's universe, as persons are in an audile's.

Even Aristotle, who thought of himself as the inventor of what we should today style logic, is far from decisive in dissociating this science from dialectic, that is, from implication with dialogue and sound. He uses the term λογική to refer to dialectical reasoning, with its suggestion of dialogue, and generally equates λογικῶς and διαλεκτικῶς, contrasting both with the term ἀναλυτικῶς, which refers to scientific procedure, and with συλλογισμός, which refers to formal reasoning or inference. Most significant of all, his notion of predication is based on "saying" or vocal assertion. Aristotle's categories or predicaments are radically things said of, or accusations brought vocally against, a subject.

This kind of inability to dissociate an art of thinking from an art of speaking is passed on, directly or indirectly, through Cicero to the Middle Ages, and thence through John of Salisbury[5] and, more equivocally, through Peter of Spain, until it floods into the Renaissance, where it rekindles interest in actual dialogue[6] and crosses with other tendencies to generate curious offspring such as Ramism.

Compared to the ancient world, the world of scholasticism is a visualist age. The ancient educational ideal of the orator here yields to a less auditory ideal as rhetoric is superseded by dialectic, and dialectic itself begins to lose the two-sided character of genuine dialogue and attenuate itself into a teacher's monologue under the lecture system of the teachers' unions which we call universities. Isidore of Seville's kind of encyclopedism in his *Etymologies,* drawn out of the ancient world and organized around words, is replaced by the new encyclopedism of Vincent of Beauvais's *Speculum,* a concept which is so typically medieval as to furnish the Mediaeval Academy of America with the name of its journal —and which seeks to concentrate man's knowledge in the visile's symbol of a mirror. But most of all, the visualist tendency is fed from within scholastic dialectic or logic itself.

Studies matured within the last decade are beginning to bring out the startling advances over Aristotelian logic made by the medieval logic which has four centuries lain almost completely unknown, even to those —or especially to those—who think of themselves as neoscholastic philosophers, but who profess a logic which is not at all that of the main medieval current, as represented in Peter of Spain, Ockham, Buridan, Burleigh, Tartaret, and the rest famous as old scholastic logicians. As against Aristotle's logic, medieval logic is, like modern mathematical logic, highly quantified[7]—which means, for our present purposes, that it is a logic with a very high visual component.

This logic, I should like to suggest, is best viewed not as the prelude to or as the accompaniment of Thomistic metaphysics, with which it has almost nothing to do, although it is in its own right and on its own terrain quite as respectable an achievement, but as the prelude to modern mathematics and mathematical physics. In this historical perspective, medieval scholastic logic appears as a kind of premathematics, a subtle and unwitting preparation for the large-scale operations in quantitative modes of thinking which will characterize the modern world. In assessing the meaning of scholasticism, one must keep in mind an important and astounding fact: in the whole history of the human mind, mathematics and mathematical physics come into their own, in a way which has changed the face of the earth and promises or threatens to change it even more, at only one place and time, that is, in Western Europe immediately after the scholastic experience. Elsewhere, no matter how advanced the culture on other scores, and even along mathematical lines, as in the case of the Babylonian, nothing like a real mathematical transformation of thinking takes place—not among the ancient Egyptians or Assyrians or Greeks or Romans, not among the peoples of India nor the Chinese nor the Japanese, not among the Aztecs or Mayas, not in Islam despite the promising beginnings there, any more than among the Tartars or the Avars or the Turks. These people can all now share the same common scientific knowledge, but the scientific tradition itself which they share is not a merging of various parallel discoveries made by their various civilizations. It represents a new state of mind. However great contributions other civilizations may hereafter make to the tradition, our scientific world traces its origins back always to seventeenth and sixteenth century Europe, to the place where for some three centuries and more the arts course taught in universities and parauniversity schools had pounded into the heads of youth a study program consisting almost exclusively of a highly quantified logic and a companion physics, both taught on a scale and with an enthusiasm never approximated or even dreamt of in the ancient academies.[8]

In the scholastic arts program as registered in the Chartularium of the University of Paris and in other such documents, the quantified formal logic of the Middle Ages, it is to be noted, is a companion piece, not so much of metaphysics, as might be popularly imagined, for metaphysics as such amounted to little enough historically in scholastic philosophy, but rather, chiefly, of the physical or natural sciences. In this, as well as in its own internal preoccupations and structure, it shows itself the medieval correlative of modern formal logic or mathematical logic, which also appears conjointly with an interest in physical science.

In these perspectives, which can only be suggested here, certain phenomena characteristic of the Renaissance can be regarded as the culmination of a quantified, visualist drive more concerted than the world had ever before known. This drive is marked by an increased sensitivity to space and a growing sophistication in ways of dealing with quantity and extension, which comes to a climax not only in the neutral Copernican cosmic space that supplanted the less abstract, more crudely physical space of "favored directions" in Aristotelian cosmology,[9] but also in even more subtle psychological shifts felt through the whole of society and affecting man's entire outlook on reality. The sensitivity to space is obvious in the whole medieval, and even more the Renaissance, cultural complex, and is seen, for example, in the artist's attitude toward the world which he projected from his consciousness. "Of all artists," remarks György Kepes, "the Greeks alone reveal space concepts limited by Euclidean geometry."[10] With the Middle Ages, the artistic sensibility was already more spatially sophisticated, even when its relationship to the extended universe seemed more simple:

The finite universe of late medieval times found a pictorial counterpart in the limited, shallow, "abstract" spaces of Giotto. Stage by stage, art kept pace with developing cosmological concepts. . . . The past seven centuries have given us the "symbolic" space of early Flemish masters; the "rational" space of fifteenth century Renaissance Italy, deep and clear; the "ideal" space of Raphael and the High Renaissance, in which a clear foreground, continuing the spatial characteristics of the world in which the observer finds himself, converges upon a spatially mysterious, other-worldly realm; the soaring, levitational space of Gothic cathedrals; the poised and balanced spatial volumes of the High Renaissance church of San Biagio at Montepulciano; the "exploding" space of the German Baroque at Vierzehnheiligen; the pervasive space of the Impressionists, dissolving all solid form; the laminated, time-bound space of the later Cubists.[11]

The mind has its spaces, too, and at the time of the Renaissance, nothing is more evident that the rôle which spatially oriented conceptualizations begin to play in the notion of knowledge itself. The general stage had been set, as we have seen, by the quantification of medieval logic, which gave occasion to think of mental operations less by analogy with hearing and more by analogy with more or less overtly spatial or geometric forms. The central strategic operation in the procedure of visualizing knowledge at this time was undoubtedly the exploitation of letterpress printing. I believe that there is no doubt of an intimate connection between the mental habits encouraged by medieval logic and the emergence of printing, which is a curious phenomenon in the extreme, for the reason that all the elements necessary for its use had been known from antiquity—lead castings, brass dies, paper or its equivalent, ink, and presses, none of these were new. However, the reasons for the interest in and final development of successful printing techniques cannot be gone into here. But the psychological implications of the process must be looked at.

Basically, the new procedure was a technique for giving permanence to sound by transmuting it more perfectly into silence, a technique for fixing the word in space more adroitly than ever before. Not only was it now possible to have an unlimited number of paper surfaces on each of which words were set in exactly the same spatial relationship to one another, but the very technique of producing this spatial organization was itself an adventure in local motion such as the parts of words had never before seen.

Writing had reduced the sound of words to visual equivalents, and the alphabet had further dismembered these equivalents in visual parts. But printing from movable type cast from matrices struck from a die or punch—the essence of the achievement perfected by the Fust-Schöffer-Gutenberg combination—had spatially unmoored these parts themselves. Letters thus acquire local motion. More than that, their manufacture had been reduced to a matter of simple local maneuver. With one set of punches, one could move over bits of softer metal and strike out whole boxfuls of matrices. Casting from one set of matrices, one could produce whole fonts of type. With one font of type, one could set up an indefinite number of lines and compose an indefinite amount of type for making up an indefinite number of printing forms. From one form, one could print an indefinite number of pages simply by moving the paper into contact with the type and pressing it. Space had become pregnant with meaning, not only in the orderly arrangement within the book itself, but even more in the font of type, and still more in the little box of punches, in whose tiny compass were imprisoned more pagefuls of words than in a pre-Gutenburg inkwell the size of the Heidelberg tun.

This advance in the way of dealing with knowledge could not but affect the notions of what knowledge itself was. Curtius has examined the ways in which writers, in the Middle Ages and later, exploit the book and activities associated with the scribal art as symbols.[12] But in this connection the evolution of the very notion of what a book is deserves closer looking into. With the invention of printing, this notion itself undergoes metamorphosis. Rather than a record of something someone had said, a book now became an object, belonging more to the world of things and less to the world of words. Silent reading now began to replace the older oral habits of the manuscript age, when even a scholar reading privately to himself habitually picked the words off the page one by one and aloud.[13] Book titles change from addresses to the reader to become labels like the labels on boxes, for, with the spread of printing, books became items manufactured like tables and chairs. As objects or things, they obviously "contained" knowledge. And, since knowledge could be "contained" in books, why not in the mind as well?

At this point, the whole intellectual world goes hollow. The mind now "contains" knowledge, especially in the compartments of the various arts and sciences, which in turn may "contain" one another, and which all "contain" words. Discourse contains sentences, sentences phrases, phrases words, and words themselves contain ideas. (It is hardly necessary to remark that "sentences" or "periods," "commas," and the other paraphernalia of syntactical analysis were quite other things than this to the ancients and to the medieval man.)[14] What is more, ideas contain other ideas, for the Ramist and Kantian notions, as well as the Renaissance scholastic and most neoscholastic notions of "analysis" are bound up with this outlook.[15]

What you are thinking is now less than ever what you are holding converse with yourself about. It is simply what is "in your mind." The new orientation is as ineluctable as it is subtle, rendering ineffectual the very efforts to escape it. Thus, when the humanists attempt a retreat into classical antiquity, their very reason for doing so and their way of conceiving their maneuver reveals them as men of the Gutenberg era. Erasmus' and others' assertion that all the knowledge possible to man is contained in the writings of the ancients clearly manifests the spatialized understanding of knowledge typical of postmedieval man.

The use of printing need not be regarded as the cause of this shift of the focus of knowledge toward spatial analogies, but rather as a spectacular symptom of the general reorientation going on. This reorientation is far-flung in its implications, being connected on one side with the emergence of the topical logics (logics of commonplaces or "place"-logics, and thus in effect space-logics) of Rudolph Agricola and Peter Ramus and their half-successful bid to replace the predicamental logics (statement-logics); on another side with the interest in plotting the surface of the globe which makes this same Gutenberg era the great age of cartography and exploration; and on still another with what is probably the most fundamental stylistic difference between ancient writing and modern writing—the immeasurably greater exploitation today of visualist metaphors and of imagery which in one way or another admits of diagrammatic analysis.

III

The related visualist phenomena which appear in such riot are all, to a certain extent, subsumed or summarized in the changed way of conceptualizing the field of knowledge as a whole. The stepped-up visualism which reaches its initial climax in the Gutenberg era and thence moves on to still greater conquests was having consequences in man's way of picturing the universe of the mind quite as real as its consequences in man's way of thinking of the physical universe. No "field" of knowledge was spoken of yet—that was to come later, as field physics was to come later, too—but the ways of thinking about mental activity had grown increasingly spatial in the Middle Ages.

One of the great climaxes in scholastic philosophy is the wave of interest in what we call today the "structure" of a science (the term was to come into use in the late Renaissance period). By the late sixteenth century, this interest had become an obsession in the discussions on method and related matters which Ramus, Descartes, and Francis Bacon do not at all initiate—as it is sometimes taken for granted that they do—but rather bring to a climax. Well before these men, the method discussions are big with diagrammatic symbols: "method" itself (a "way after" or "way through"), *ascensus* and *descensus*, *analysis* and *synthesis* (a mathematical notion used by Ramists, and by others after them, to replace the more elusive, less diagrammatic *genesis* which had been the term Aristotle himself paired with *analysis*), and the like.[16]

These concepts derive from antiquity and are to be accounted for basically by the fact that any attempt to *explain* mental activity tends to deal with the activity in terms of analogies with the sense of sight, since reduction in terms of one or another type of sense knowledge is inevitable, and reduction in terms of other senses, notably of hearing, while enhancing the mysterious and existentialist implications of knowledge, serves little to satisfy the demand for some sort of explanation, for "clarification." However, despite their presence in philosophy from the beginning, nothing in antiquity or in the Middle Ages matches the clatter which such terms make from about the 1540's on. At Cambridge in the 1580's, as at Paris three or four decades earlier, the method disputes threaten to set all the university dons and a great many of the students at one another's ears, first in the philosophy courses on the arts faculty, and thereafter by a kind of chain reaction up through the other faculties of medicine, law, and theology.

The method disputes had been initiated in an age which could not yet differentiate philosophies from one another with the adroitness which we feel we can command today, for it had as yet no "-isms" at all in its conceptual apparatus. When the early sixteenth century speaks of what we should today glibly call "Thomism," "realism," and "nominalism," it habitually thinks not in terms of different philosophies but in terms of different persons—of "blessed Thomas," of the "reals" (*reales*), and of the "nominals" (*nominales*)—with their different approaches or "ways" (*viae*), or else of these persons' different "opinions" (*opiniones*).[17]

Needless to say, there is no talk of philosophical "systems," for the application of this particular concept to philosophy is a relatively late product of epistemological visualism, tied up directly with the transit from Aristotelian to Copernican space.

IV

The notion of a philosophical "system" or of philosophical "systems" is so well established today that it is hard for us to believe that it has a history at all. *Systema* is, of course, an ancient Greek term, translatable perhaps as "setup" or organized, composite whole, but its application to the realm of the mind, and in particular to philosophy, becomes current only after the medieval experience terminating in the methodological disputes, which give unequivocal evidence of the penchant of the time of viewing knowledge with the help of visualist, quasi-diagrammatic constructs.

Conceived of as a "way through" a problem or investigation, or as a "way after" a desired answer, method is patently a concept based on a visualist analogy, which takes up the concept of "way" and further visualizes it by conferring on it a fuller implication of direction. This fashion of dealing with the notion of "way" contrasts strikingly with the Scriptural use of this notion when Christ asserts, in an obviously personalist and existentialist context, "I am the way"—the "I" being here not only a Person, but One to Whom the audile's rather than the visile's world is particularly relevant, the Incarnate Word of God, Who is also the Truth and the Life.

By setting the term "way" in this context, the biblical text, recognizing the general validity of the "way" metaphor, in effect discourages attempts to elaborate on its visualist or spatial implications independently of auditory or oral connections. For, while the work of the Incarnation, in Christ's own earthly life and as continued by His Church, takes place in space, and while notions such as "mission" can apply to it, it is always the work of One to Whose Person the auditory-oral notion of Word particularly belongs. The work of Christ's visible Church is carried on in space, but by means of preaching—*fides ex auditu*—as well as of the sacraments, which are visible signs, to be sure, but, as Aquinas long ago pointed out, which differ from the quasi sacraments of the Old Law by having words (or, in the case of matrimony, the equivalent —a consent) as their determining "form." The very Sacrifice of the New Law, unlike those of the Old, is effected by words. In this context, it becomes impossible to interpret the "way" which is the God-Man in terms of crude visualist constructs alone. And in the interior life, although "the Kingdom of God is within you," Catholic spiritual writers find little ascetic value in the contemplation of mandalas or other semidiagrammatic constructs associated with Yoga and Buddhism, but a great deal of value in an auditory-oral directive: silence.

The "way" of the methodologists, on the other hand, was free or gradually freed itself, from auditory or oral commitments as it was elaborated in terms of ascent (*ascensus*) and descent (*descensus*), division, partition, distribution, induction, deduction, analysis, and the rest of the psychogeometrical apparatus used to describe the intellectual processes. Here we are in a definitely spatial universe. Its psychic space is like that of the Aristotelian physical cosmos. The Aristotelian cosmology, as is well known, did not operate by purely geometrical laws such as Copernicus, Galileo, and Newton were to favor, but rather in terms of favored directions, up and down, the directions presumably followed by substances seeking their natural levels in the universe. Horizontal motion was, in this scheme, difficult if not impossible to account for intelligibly. This universe was directional, as against the Newtonian universe, which was to be more purely geometrical, directionally neuter. Now the space which figures, by analogy, in the method literature is directional, too, for the very notion of method is highly directional. Method proceeds to an end through median points or "means." The axiomatics associated with methodology is thought of as concerned with ascent to the first principles or axioms or *dignitates,* and with descent from them to conclusions.[18]

One trouble with this directional universe was that the ends toward which or away from which it moved often, if not always, proved to be unattainable limits such as those in calculus rather than readily ascertainable points. Once one moved away from generalized discussion to particulars, it was very difficult to produce genuinely first principles. Each of the various arts or sciences was nominally connected with its first principles, but, although one could intuitively discern the order which a science ideally should have in relation to its first principles arrived at inductively and thereafter functioning deductively to give the interior structure of the science its consistency, no one could actually produce a complete science fully rigged out with its first principles and all their conclusions. From this point of view, all the sciences were imperfect, and most of them little more than shambles.

Peter Ramus was to protest this before the University of Paris and the whole world, and, although there was violent resistance to Ramus's own notions on method and although many of his opponents were beyond a doubt intellectually abler men than he, no one could take up his challenge and produce even one thoroughly "methodized" art or science, logically consistent from start to finish.[19] Some few cited Euclid's *Elements,* but Ramus insisted that this, too, was not properly "methodized" or reasoned out. Ramus was, as we know today, to some extent right about Euclid, whose geometry is not quite so complete a deductive system as it has been taken to be.[20] However, Ramus's strictures against Euclid give evidence of impatience more than of genuine insight, and his own attempts to remedy the intolerable situation in which he found all the arts by "methodizing" not only geometry but all the other arts as well, are the amateurish works of a desperate man who is not a thinker but merely an erudite pedagogue.

With the method discussion at this point and the visualist tide running strong, an important shift took place in the whole notion of space, signalized if not caused by the publication of Copernicus's *De revolutionibus* in 1543, the year of Ramus's own first published works. Copernicus's astronomy approaches the universe from the point of view of purely geometrical space, in which no direction was more favored than any other, since neither up-and-down motion nor any other directional motion had priority over other kinds, any more than it does in a geometrical abstraction. This new approach had the effect of highlighting the notion of system (*systema*).

Although this term had always been applicable to the Aristotelian or Ptolemaic cosmos, it was not particularly exploited in this connection for the reason that this cosmos was conceived as one unique system without even an imaginable competitor. The notion of wholeness was so inevitable that it was not particularly attended to. Hence the notion of system, an organized *whole*, was a rather uninteresting one. It was not even practicable to imagine the parts of the Aristotelian universe as lesser wholes, for this universe had no really detachable parts forming little systems of their own. The earth-moon relationship could not be imagined as a system comparable to the sun-earth relationship, because neither was conceived of in the purely geometric terms which invite such comparison. The sphere of the moon was a *special* part of the cosmos which belonged in its own altogether particular place among the celestial spheres, as the spheres of the sun belonged in its own place. Neither was thinkable as being anywhere but in its own orbit.

The Copernican hypothesis changed all this. The newly proposed explanation encouraged thinking of even the Aristotelian system as a system or organized whole by proposing another system to supplant it. It was a case now of one whole against another. Moreover, the Copernican cosmos itself was a system involving an incalculable number of minor systems: not only that of the earth and sun, but that of the moon and the earth, of Jupiter's moons and their mother planet, of the rings of Saturn, and, as was later to appear, of whole solar systems and whole galaxies outside ours.

V

How much the advent of Copernican geometrical cosmic space depended upon the unsatisfactory status of the Aristotelian explanation of the external universe and how much upon more subtle pressures due to the general build-up of the visual sensibility symptomized by the emergence of printing in the West, by the phrenetic interest in method, and by many allied phenomena which mark the Copernican period but which are too abundant and complex to be gone into here, no one at present can say. It is certain that Copernicus's new approach was in some measure tied up with subtle psychological forces, for it depended on no new discoveries—these were to come later as corroboration—only on a new way of thinking about what everyone already knew. However this may be, the notion of system, given its new currency, took hold in connection with the universe of knowledge quite as quickly as it did in connection with the physical universe, and exactly in those areas where the method agitation had been strongest. Methods of knowledge give rise to systems of knowledge. Thus we find the Ramist Johann Heinrich Alsted, author of several famous "methodized" encyclopedias,[21] publishing at Herborn in 1610 his *Double Mnemonic System* of knowledge (*Systema mnemonicum duplex*) and his *Mnemonic System of the Liberal Arts and of All Curriculum Subjects* (*Artium liberalium ac facultatum omnium systema mnemonicum*). This was twenty-one years before the first appearance of Galileo's *Dialogo . . . sopra i due massimi systemi del mondo*. Galileo's work was to give the notion of system an urgency and currency which it had never known before, but the welcome for the notion had been well prepared outside the field of astronomy in works treating the cosmography of the mind.

By the end of the seventeenth century, the habit of thinking of philosophy itself, the quondam love of wisdom, in terms of a "system" had become well established, and with it the habit of thinking of theological systems and of systems and orbits of other sorts of knowledge as well. Indeed, as early as 1620, a philosophical system, explicitly so called, had been launched by Alsted: Philosophy, he says, as viewed in the mind is a *habitus,* as viewed outside the mind, a *systema.*[22] But if he anticipated Galileo, Alsted—teacher of the important educational reformer Jan Comensky or Comenius, who wrote the *Orbis pictus,* a visual education system—does not anticipate Copernicus. The system of philosophy which he envisions is conceived by analogy with a free-wheeling Copernican universe in a neuter geometrical space, for throughout this period system or *systema,* used absolutely and without qualifications, means a celestial system. Having once conceived of various "systems" of philosophy. Alsted and others deal with these "systems" by "harmonizing" them, making use of a conceptualization indubitably associated with the old harmony of the spheres.

What it all came to, or comes to—how far what we call philosophy or theology or history or any other kind of knowledge can be related even analogously to a twirling set of bodies free-wheeling in space—is a matter which no one ever explained. The concept of system simply took unquestioned hold of the mind, applying itself everywhere.

By the early eighteenth century, there is a real epidemic of systems. *The New Intellectual System of the Universe* by Ralph Cudworth has by this time become famous, together with a thousand other systems: book titles announce systems of medicine, systems (that is, school courses) of physics, systems of geography, systems of divinity, metaphysical systems,[23] Bartholomew Keckermann's *System of Rhetoric* (or course in rhetoric), *A New System . . . for a General Peace* (London, 1746), and *A New System of the Gout and Rheumatism* (5th ed.; London, 1719). The fad which Copernicus had loosed was coming into its own.

Anyone could now envision a system. Application of the Aristotelian "system," if anyone had troubled to advert to it as a system, to the field of knowledge would have been difficult in the extreme. Conceived along Copernican lines, system was a much more maneuverable concept, quite as visually satisfying as method was, and without some of the annoying disabilities of this other earlier favorite. Even as popularly conceived, a method or "way through" suggested patience and painstaking labor—the inability of anyone, except perhaps Euclid, to produce even one perfectly organized or methodized science was embarrassing and discouraging in the extreme. There was difficulty about the very notion of "end" in method, the goal toward which the "way" led, for the great problem of method, at least since Aristotle, had always been this: How is it that in an investigation we can set a methodical procedure, when the method must depend on understanding what we are looking for, and we obviously cannot understand what we are looking for until the investigation itself brings us to it? Thinking of knowledge as governed by the diagrammatic, easily imagined, and only loosely applicable notion of system was more satisfying than thinking of it in terms of method and these conundrums. It was comforting to think of oneself, or of one's enemy, as possessing a philosophical "system," something which whirled dazzlingly around a center in the mind like the Copernican spheres around the sun, a whole self-contained and independent of the rest of reality. Such pictures could cover intellectual situations of which one knew really very little. The very looseness and inadequacy of the system metaphor was and is one of its greatest recommendations.

VI

The rise of the notion of system as applied to the possessions of the mind is only one in a whole kaleidoscope of phenomena which mark the shift from the more vocal ancient world—truly an audile's world—to what has been called the silent, colorless, and depersonalized Newtonian universe. This is no place to settle whether the shift is to be applauded or regretted. It is here presented simply as a historical fact in the evolution of human thought. As a fact, it deserves to be approached with a humble curiosity out of which we can hope to mature understanding both of ourselves and of external reality.

Certain advances and certain losses connected with the shift are discernible enough. Out of it has come modern science, with the possibility it offers for increasing the subjection of matter and impregnation of matter by spiritual forces, in so far as these spiritual forces can orient themselves within their own spiritual realm. Out of the same shift have come the more contestable advances in human relations themselves, with the possibility of greater social justice which is, if by no means realized, at least ambitioned with conscious concern by far more people today than ever before. For social planning, human engineering, managerial revolutions, and, on the other side of the ledger, the welfare state, are all part and parcel of the "objective" approach to even human existence which, if not initiated, was at least furthered by the new scientism coming out of the Renaissance as by nothing else before.

The new world was a world of objects as nothing before had ever been. An "object" in its basic conception—something thrown against, thrown in the way of—is obviously a formulation with visualist roots, and one predestined to dominate scientific thinking. (One recalls St. Thomas Aquinas's insistence on the "object" in his approach to knowledge and to psychology, for he was a visile if there ever was one.) In this sense, object is opposed not to subject, but to person. Inasmuch as the world of science is a world of objects, which are exteriorities or surfaces, conceived of by analogy with the data of visual apprehension, it is not a world of persons, or interiorities manifesting themselves by a word. For even in this sublunar world, sound or voice comes from the interior of things, not so as to exteriorize this interior but to enable it to communicate with other interiors. Little wonder that in the post-Newtonian object-world, God's voice, too, is silenced, that revelation becomes meaningless, and that the Creator—a visile's God—becomes no more than a kind of mechanical brain. You need no person to run a machine. But you need a person to utter a word. You also need a person to elicit from you an act of faith. For there is no way to believe an object, or even to believe "in" an object in a purely objectified, impersonal context. By definition, objects as such in the sense of impersonalizations should be dealt with by being seen. That is why above the sensible world there are no longer any mere objects, only persons.

These matters are objects for reflection, not for reform. It is impossible for us to abrogate the history which has shaped our minds and our sensibilities and made us fit for twentieth century existence. We are committed to being intellectual visiles in ways in which earlier men were not, by the very fact that we are irrevocably explainers, cultists of the clear and distinct, reasonable men. The ideals of reasonable men and scientific explainers need not be repudiated, irrelevant as they have sometimes been and perhaps still are to types of minds and types of approaches other than our own. However, such ideals do need to be complemented by a return to something larger than a merely visile, scientist's view. The history of philosophy itself has largely been the history of a search after more and more adequate visualist or spatialist analogies by which to represent and deal with the real universe and the universe of the mind, but we are living in an age today which has begun to feel uneasy about this quest.

The uneasiness is shown in the growing or recurrent suspicion that such notions as system may, in the last analysis, prove to be philosophical mare's nests. This suspicion need not lead to a new irrationalism at all. It should mean a recurrence of certain other approaches to knowledge which marked the Renaissance, the approach through voice and sound, the Hebraic rather than the Greek approach. Here knowledge is contained not in a system, but in discourse, in conversation which has been going on since man appeared on earth. This point of view submerges the visualist, explanatory approach and with it science itself in something more ultimate and more transcendent, in the existentialist situation, with which our most immediate contact is through voices and persons rather than through observation and objects. In this more living and vocal view of reality, which represents a symbolization the polar opposite of that whose evolution has been discussed so briefly and inadequately here, science is only arrested dialogue of man with man, and an echo of the interior dialogue in silence of each soul with God.

NOTES

[1] Erwin Panofsky, *Gothic Architecture and Scholasticism* (Latrobe, Pennsylvania: The Archabbey Press (1951), esp. pp. 30-67. Cf. the same author's *Studies in Iconology* (New York: Oxford University Press, 1939), pp. 172-73.

[2] Erwin Panofsky, *Early Netherlandish Painting* (Cambridge, Massachusetts: Harvard University Press, 1953), I, pp. 3-20, 57-61, etc.

[3] Otto Benesch, *The Art of the Renaissance in Northern Europe* (Cambridge, Massachusetts: Harvard University Press, 1947), pp. 124-43.

[4] See R. Bultmann, *Gnosis*, trans. by J. R. Coates (London: A. and C. Black (1952), pp. 1-6, 15-18.

[5] John of Salisbury, *Metalogicus*, Lib. I, cap. x, in *Patrologia Latina*, CXCIX, 837 BC.

[6] Eugenio Garin has reaffirmed the preeminence of dialogue as a literary form typical of the Renaissance in his *Medioevo e Rinascimento, Studi et ricerche* (Bari, 1954), II, 1; see André Chastel, "L'épître et le discours," *Bibliothèque d'Humanisme et Renaissance*, XVI (1954), p. 381.

[7] See Philotheus Boehner, O.F.M., *Medieval Logic* (Manchester: Manchester University Press, 1950); Joseph T. Clark, S.J., *Conventional Logic and Modern Logic: A Prelude to Transition*, with a preface by Willard Van Orman Quine (Woodstock, Maryland: Woodstock College Press for the American Catholic Philosophical Association, 1952); Ernest A. Moody, *Truth and Consequence in Medieval Logic* (Amsterdam: North-Holland Publishing Co., 1953). Father Clark's work gives explanations of quantification in logic—see the index.

[8] See Louis John Paetow, *The Arts Course at Medieval Universities*

(Urbana, Ill.: University of Illinois Press, 1910); also Stephen d'Irsay, *Histoire des universités* (Paris: Auguste Picard, 1933-35), Vol. I, *passim*.

⁹ See H. Butterfield, *The Origins of Modern Science,* 1300-1800 (London, G. Bell and Sons, Ltd., 1949), Chap. V.

¹⁰ György Kepes, *Art and Science,* in *Explorations* (University of Toronto, Toronto, Canada), I (1953), p. 82.

¹¹ *Loc. cit.*

¹² Ernest Robert Curtius, *European Literature and the Latin Middle Ages,* translated from the German (*Europäische Literatur und lateinisches Mitlelalter,* 1948) by Willard R. Trask, "Bollingen Series," XXXVI (New York: Pantheon Books, 1953), pp. 302-47.

¹³ See H. J. Chaytor, *From Script to Print: An Introduction to Medieval Literature* (Cambridge: Cambridge University Press, 1945), pp. 13 ff.

¹⁴ See Walter J. Ong, S.J., "Historical Backgrounds of Elizabethan and Jacobean Punctuation Theory," in *Publications of the Modern Language Association of America,* LIX (1944), pp. 349-60.

¹⁵ Father Peter Hoenen, S.J., reports on notions of analysis among Renaissance and more modern scholastics in his "De origine primorum principiorum scientiae," *Gregorianum,* XIV (1933), pp. 153-84.

¹⁶ Some of these terms are discussed in John Herman Randall, "The Development of Scientific Method in the School of Padua," in *Journal of the History of Ideas,* I (1940), pp. 177-206; R. I. Markus, "Method and Metaphysics: The Origins of Some Cartesian Presuppositions in the Philosophy of the Renaissance," in *Dominican Studies,* II (1949), pp. 356-84; Walter J. Ong, S.J., "Peter Ramus and the Naming of Methodism," *Journal of the History of Ideas,* XIV (1953), pp. 235-48; etc.

¹⁷ Thus we find Juan de Celaya's *Expositio . . . in librum Predicabilium Porphyrii cum questionibus eiusdem secundum triplicem viam beati Thomae, realium, et nominalium* (Paris, 1516—copy in the Bibliothèque Nationale, Paris), or the same author's *Expositio . . . in librum Predicamentorum Aristotelis, cum questionibus eiusdem secundum viam triplicem beati Thomae, realium, et nominalium, novissime . . . revisa . . .* (Paris, 1520—copy in the *Bibliothèque Nationale,* Paris). The use of *opinio* for what today would be called "a philosophy" is very common, and it connected with classical usage. Thus one finds "Expositio magistri Georgii . . . nominalium opinionum recitatoris . . . ," fol. 1 in *Interpretatio Georgii Bruxellensis in Summulas Petri Hispani . . .* (Paris, 1946—copy in the Bibliothèque Nationale, Paris). For other similar instances of the term, see the list of titles in Joseph P. Mullally, *The* Summulae logicales *of Peter of Spain* (Notre Dame, Indiana: Publications in Mediaeval Studies, 1945), pp. 145 ff.

¹⁸ See Markus, *op. cit.;* Randall, *op. cit.*

¹⁹ A complete check list of the Ramist disputes is to be found in my *Ramus and Talon Inventory* (Cambridge, Massachusetts: Harvard University Press, 1958) which gives the nearly eight hundred editions (some 1100 separately printed titles) of the works of Peter Ramus and his literary lieutenant Omer

Talon, with locations of copies in European and American libraries. See also my conjointly published volume, *Ramus, Method, and the Decay of Dialogue.*

[20] See George Henry Forder, *The Foundations of Euclidean Geometry* (Cambridge: Cambridge University Press, 1927).

[21] J. H. Alsted (Alstedius), *Cursus philosophici encyclopaedia libris xxvii complectens universae philosophiae methodum serie praeceptorum regularum* . . . (Herborn, 1620); *Encyclopaedia septem tomis distincta* . . . (Herborn, 1630); etc. Someone among his contemporaries discovered that an anagram of Alstedius is *sedulitas.* This might be called a very modest anagram.

[22] "Philosophia est comprehensio disciplinarum liberalium inferiorum: et alias dicitur encyclopaedia . . . Comprehensio illa spectatur in mente ut habitus, extra mentem ut systema."—Alsted, *Cursus philosophici encyclopaedia* (Herborn, 1620), p. 2.

[23] Early instances of the appearance of the term "metaphysical system" are: Rudolph Göckel (Goclenius) the elder (1547-1628), *Isagoge in peripateticorum et scholasticorum primam philosophiam, quae vulgo dicitur metaphysica, cum alio novo systemate metaphysico [Magistri] Constantini Cnirimii* . . . (Frankfort-on-the-Main, 1612, copy in the Bibliothèque Nationale, Paris); Clemens Timpler (Timplerus), *Metaphysicae systema methodicum . . . per theoremata el problemata selecta concinnatum* [with note and scholia supplied by Göckel] (Hanau, 1616, copy in the Bibliothèque Nationale, Paris). In devising systems, Ramists or circles where Ramists predominated, such as that at Frankfort and Hanau, were in the lead.

🎕 SIX 🎕

Wit and Mystery

A REVALUATION IN MEDIEVAL
LATIN HYMNODY

I

In a recent article Professor J. S. P. Tatlock pointedly remarks that "not all moderns to whom what is Latin is remote, see that before the late middle ages what is Latin was immediate."[1] He points out that our tendency unwittingly to make too little of the immediacy of medieval Latin results in misconceptions concerning the role of medieval vernacular literature, which was essentially a supplement to the literature in Latin. The situation on which Professor Tatlock so pertinently remarks has other unfortunate results as well. It readily enough induces an insensitivity to the Latin literature of the Middle Ages itself. Overlooking its immediacy to the medieval mind, we fail to approach this literature in terms of the sensibility in which it had its being and tend to regard it as a detached mass of material which we handle rather freely in terms largely of our own prepossessions.

The understanding of much medieval literature has suffered from this tendency, and perhaps none of the literature more than the Latin hymnody. The ordinary evaluations of medieval Latin hymns and sequences with which one meets give one not so much the impression that one has a balanced consideration of what is in the records as the impression that the corpus of medieval Latin liturgical verse has been made a sounding board for nineteenth and early twentieth century notions of religious poetry.

It is worth noting how most evaluations of medieval Latin hymns come around sooner or later to eulogize two pieces, the *Dies Irae* and the *Stabat Mater Dolorosa,* as unmistakably the finest of the lot.[2] This is significant because interest in Latin hymnody has grown up within the past hundred and fifty years,[3] and, while these two most praised hymns are not by any means representative of all medieval Latin hymnody, they are on the other hand both highly representative of that specific development within this hymnody which coincides remarkably with the temper of the age in which the study of Latin hymnody took form. The wave of enthusiasm for these hymns is quite datable: of the fifty English translations of the *Dies Irae* turned up for an article published in 1883,[4] only eight antedate 1805, and of the one hundred and thirty-three translations listed in *A Dictionary of Hymnology*, only nine antedate 1819.[5]

The *Dies Irae* and the *Stabat Mater Dolorosa* are notably alike[6] in that they both feature the tender and haunting melancholy, the awesome and plaintive foreboding, and the plangent pathos inevitably associated in the romantic era with serious poetry—or, indeed, with anything beautiful. The highest manifestation of beauty is inseparable from sadness, Poe had averred for his age.[7] And his poetry shows that the sadness he had in mind was not simply the tragic note common to a great deal of literature, but something more distinctive, plaintive, a little tearful, and hypnotic. Persons in quest of this sadness would take readily enough to the *Dies Irae* and the *Stabat Mater Dolorosa* while they gave pretty short shrift to great numbers of other medieval Latin hymns and sequences.

However, one section of medieval Latin hymnody which does not so well fall in with romantic notions of serious poetic achievement can today hope for a better hearing because of current interests which have resulted in the now matured appreciation of the once disreputable "metaphysical" poetry of seventeenth century England.[8] The age before the present was notably deficient in its ability to respond to such poetry —the worth of which has been a genuine discovery even in scholarly circles—and the resulting coldness toward the considerable quantity of medieval Latin hymns which have much in common with this poetry has been one of the great deficiencies persisting to the present in evaluation of the corpus of these hymns.

Present-day requirements for poetry will have their own limitations, but in this particular instance contemporary interests enable us to apply to earlier appraisals a badly needed corrective. So long as wit was taken only as an elaborate, if sophisticated, horseplay, religious poetry which employed it was *ipso facto* hardly worth consideration, for worth-while religious poetry must, in one way or another, maintain a texture basically serious. To discover, as the past few decades seem to have discovered, that wit can be a vehicle for serious expression is to open the way to long neglected preserves of medieval Latin verse.

But it is to do more than that. The trail of wit leads to one of the most vital centers of medieval literature. Here Christian teaching does more than merely supply the matter for poetry, and more than merely suggest an "architectonic" framework for literature (such as one finds often remarked in Dante or Milton and such as provides the basis for obvious, sometimes elaborate, but in the long run rather uneventful comparisons between grosser details in things like the *Divine Comedy* and the *Summa Theologica*). Rather, at the point to which the trail of wit leads, the very texture of poetry itself—the element which makes literature—is seen to come into functional contact with the heart of Christian doctrine, the mysteries distinctive of Christianity as these lie in their own distinctive way within the human mind.

The present study is an attempt to develop in connection with this fact a more comprehensive sense of values concerning medieval Latin liturgical poetry through examination of the work of two important authors to whom wit in the spirit of the "metaphysicals" was quite congenial: Adam of St. Victor (d. by 1192) and St. Thomas Aquinas (1224/5-1274). The combined lives of these two span a period particularly favorable to the emergence and development of a poetry of wit.

We can here identify wit poetry sufficiently for the present purpose as that poetry which characteristically employs conceit, that is, paradoxical or curious and striking comparison and analogy, and which favors the development of word-play.

II

Adam lived at St. Victor's at the end of the period in which the Parisian monastery enjoyed its greatest theological achievement, under Hugh and Richard, who died respectively in 1141 and 1173. Adam's poetry therefore quite naturally reflects definitely theological interests. It is in connection with these interests that much of his wit emerges.

> Infinitus et immensus
> Quem non capit ullus sensus
> Nec locorum spatia,
>
> Ex aeterno temporalis,
> Ex immenso fit localis,
> Ut restauret omnia.[9]

We find this in a sequence or prose for Christmas ascribed to Adam. The combination of apparent disparates here as the Incarnation is made to unfold itself in paradox is of a piece with the theological world that Adam knew. Hugh had written:

Dubium non est quin coelestium gaudiorum, et aeternae dulcedinis miram atque inerrabilem suavitatem Virgo ipsa conceperit, quando illud aeternum lumen cum toto majestatis suae fulgore in eam descendit: et quod non capit mundus, totum se intra viscera virginis collocavit.[10]

Paradox carries for Adam from the beginning to the end of Christ's earthly career. In an Easter sequence of his, the poet finds the strangely vivifying quality of Christ's death a paradox, too:

> O mors Christi vivifica
> Tu Christo nos unifica;
>
> Mors morti non obnoxia,
> Da nobis vitae praemia.[11]

More complex is the following, which Adam works out of the mystery of Christ's sacrificial death:

> Per mortem nos indebitam
> Solvit a morte debita:
>
> Praedam captans illicitam
> Praedo privatur licita.[12]

The last two lines are the more intricate: the robber (death) for taking illicit plunder (Christ) is deprived of his licit plunder (mankind).

In these passages Adam uses rather straightforward paradox; but there are ways of cutting paradox apart so that it can be inspected in cross section. Thus, in a sequence for the feast of the Holy Trinity, Adam writes:

> Trinae sit laus unitati,
> Sed et simplae trinitati
> Coaeterna gloria.[13]

Explications of the simple doxology ('Glory be to the Father and to the Son and to the Holy Spirit') such as this, duplicated in scores of conclusions to liturgical hymns written by many others besides Adam, do not resolve paradox but dissect it into pieces each of which is itself paradoxical: the threefold Unity, the simple Trinity (i.e., the Trinity with no parts in the strict sense), etc. The frame on which the paradoxical sections are stretched for exhibit is often, as here, provided by word-play.

Any number of examples could be adduced to show that Adam's word-play is not mere virtuosity of verbal figure. In a sequence for the Assumption one finds his lines:

> Verbum patris sine matre
> Facta mater sine patre
> Genuit in tempore.[14]

The wit here is engaged with the dogmatic truth that in the Godhead as manifested to man through revelation, the Second Person (called by St. John at the beginning of his gospel the *Verbum* or Word), and only the Second Person, has an origin, which, although eternal, is nevertheless a generation analogous to that by which a son proceeds from a human father. To this dogma of the eternal generation of the Son, His incarnation in time through a human mother but without a human father is no adventitious accretion but rather a kind of converse corollary, granted the fact that He was somehow to become man. For, as St. Paul had explained in *Ephesians,* III, 15, human paternity, and indeed even paternity in animals and plants, is a participation of the divine paternity of the Father, the First Person of the Blessed Trinity. Since the Father, being Infinite God, is Father in an infinite way with regard to His Son, Who is also Infinite God, it is rather to be expected that Christ would have no human father. The role of father in His case would seem to be filled in a supereminent degree from all eternity by His Father in heaven.

The father-mother paradox of Adam's, then, traces directly into theological discussion. Adam's fellow monk Richard had treated expressly the question as to why Christ did not have a human father. It was not that there would have been anything wrong in the sexual relations this would have implied. The difficulty is with the nature of the divine paternity, although Richard apparently agrees with later theologians who will not say that this rules out absolutely the possibility of a human father: rather it only makes it more suitable that Christ should not have one.

Certe, si Emmanuel noster de utroque sexu nasci voluisset, et hoc ratio exigeret, utrumque ad mundam prolem seminandam mundare potuisset. Sed, si de utroque carnem assumeret, utique et a proprietatis suae similitudine longius recederet, et ad nostram minus appropinquaret. Proprietati enim suae esset dissimile, si patrem et matrem haberet in humanitate, qui solummodo patrem habebat in divinitate.[15]

But Adam's lines and the theological speculation back of them reach beyond Richard of St. Victor: they are too deeply embedded in Christian dogma to have taken so late an origin. The material for Adam's paradox had been part of theological equipment at least since St. Augustine, who wrote in a sermon:

Denique natus est Christus et de patre, et de matre; et sine patre, et sine matre: de patre Deus, de matre homo; sine matre Deus, sine patre homo. *Generationem ergo ejus quis enarrabit* (*Isai.*, LIII, 8): sive illam sine tempore, sive istam sine semine.[16]

In the same hymn for the Assumption just mentioned, the dual nature in the single person of Christ is the occasion for more of Adam's tropical treatment:

> O Maria, redemptoris
> Creatura, creatoris
> Genetrix magnifica.

These examples do not quite involve punning, but Adam is not reluctant to exploit puns when the occasion presents itself. In the sort of contexts with which Adam is concerned, puns are used, as the English metaphysicals and others were later to use them, for serious effects—that is, puns are used to another purpose than that of giving a *prima facie* startling appearance to essentially drab fact. Puns are used where semantic coincidence penetrates to startling relations in the real order of things. Among seventeenth century "metaphysicals," for instance, Donne was to write "A Hymne to God the Father" in this vein:

> Wilt thou forgive that sinne which I did shunne
> A yeare, or two; but wallowed in, a score?
> When thou has done, thou hast not done,
> For I have more.[17]

He rings the changes on his own name in disconcerting seriousness, as he had earlier in a wry little tour de force when his marriage seemed to be heading for disaster: "John Donne—Ann Donne—Undone."[18] In both cases the similarity of *Donne* and *done* is more than merely vocal.

Donne is facing the finality and irrevocability of human action as embodied in himself. Donne is really the kind of being to whom the word *done* can be applied. His name is very relevant: it concurs, by chance indeed but none the less really, in the expression of a truth.

Similarly, Adam of St. Victor writes in a sequence in honor of the Blessed Virgin:

> Jesus, verbum summi patris,
> Serva servos tuae matris,
> Solve reos, salva gratis.[19]

Here again phonetic similarities do more than produce an illusory and quickly spent flutter of interest. *Serva* (save, rescue, deliver) and *servos* (slaves, servants) do more than resemble one another phonetically. The notions themselves which they represent are curiously intertwined in the Christian economy, where Christ the Saviour is the Master but becomes the servant in order to save His servants.[20] *Solve* (untie) and *salva* (save, redeem—connected with *salvere* = to be in good health) are likewise concepts woven together in the Christian theology of redemption, where Christ's work as Saviour is to loose the bonds of sin.

This poetry would of course have its own special predilections for metaphor, and in his use of this piece of equipment Adam shows industry enough. With the love for symbolic interpretation inculcated by medieval preaching and animadversions on Scripture,[21] Adam ransacks the Old Testament for figures to exhibit the mysteries of Christianity under various aspects. Thus an Easter sequence of his explains the Resurrection as the new leaven, the despoiling of the Egyptians, the liberation of the Hebrew youths from the fiery furnace, of the Hebrews from the "mud, bricks, and straw" of Egypt, the delivery of Joseph from the cistern, vengeance on those who taunted the bald Eliseus, Samson's victory at Ramath-Lechi and his carrying off the city gates from Gaza, and very many other things besides.[22]

From this welter of metaphor to the elaboration of an individual metaphor into an "allegory" after the manner of the later metaphysicals, the step is not far to take, and Adam takes it. Thus we find one of his Christmas sequences comparing Christ to a nut:

> Nux est Christus: *cortex* nucis
> Circa carnem poena crucis,
> > *Testa* corpus osseum,

Carne tecta deitas
Et Christi suavitas
Signatur per *nucleum*.[23]

These are only samples of Adam's techniques. Instances of the sort here discussed can be multiplied out of his works almost indefinitely. It is noteworthy, however, that most of his conceits are elaborated on distinctively Christian and dogmatic themes (the significance of this will be discussed later)—but not always. Sometimes the same techniques occur in connection with matters not directly dogmatic at all. For example, in a sequence commemorating the reception of the relics of St. Victor of Marseilles, he develops a conceit on the theme of the general jubilation:

Nostri cordis organum,
Nostrae carnis tympanum
A se dissidentia
Harmonia temperet
Et sibi confoederet
Pari consonantia.[24]

III

Perhaps the most familiar instance of wit in St. Thomas Aquinas's poetry is a couplet in the vesper hymn *Pange Lingua* written for the office of Corpus Christi, where it still occurs in the Roman breviary:

Verbum caro panem verum
Verbo carnem efficit.[25]

This multidimensional conceit is a variant of one of the paradoxes consequent upon the Incarnation of the Word of God, and in availing himself of it, Thomas is tapping a source which lies at the innermost heart of Christian doctrine.

Thomas is here concerned with the fact that it was not God the Father nor God the Holy Spirit, but the Second Person, God the Word, Who became flesh, and that this same Word, when He wishes to convert bread into His flesh uses *words* as the instruments for His action. This is a coincidence startling enough and too good to be missed, the more so because the use of words in connection with its sacramental ritual was plainly distinctive of the New Law inaugurated after the Word had entered the material world as man: the Paschal Lamb which in the Old Law prefigured the Eucharistic sacrifice, had, like most other "sacraments" of the Old Law, no special verbal formula connected with it.[26] It is difficult to regard all this as mere coincidence. It teases the theologian for some explanation: examine it, keep turning it over in your mind, and you may find in it some clue to God's plan of things.

This is the same theology of the Word which has proved a limitless source of conceits not only for medieval theologians but also for patristic rhetoricians, for seventeenth century Englishmen, and for contemporary poets interested in the metaphysical tradition. St. Thomas is moving over ground to which wit poetry has never relinquished its claim. One conceit, for instance, is to be found in all the three groups of writers just mentioned. St. Augustine uses in a sermon the paradox of the *Verbum infans*, Who was not only the infant Word, the child Jesus, but, to take the Latin *infans* in its full etymological force, the unspeaking Word.[27] A strange and startling paradox, but an unmistakable dogmatic fact, that the Word of God initiates His personal mission among men in the inarticulate rôle of a child. The identical paradox is remarked later by Lancelot Andrewes in a sermon on the Incarnation: "What, *Verbum infans*, the Word of an infant? The Word, and not to be able to speak a word."[28] And from Andrewes' world, that of the English "metaphysicals," the same conceit makes its way into Mr. T. S. Eliot's *Gerontion*.[29]

Corruptions of the text had until recently obscured the fact that in his hymn commonly known as *Adoro Te Devote* Thomas Aquinas is preoccupied with the identical notion of the concealed and silent Word. As proposed in the opening line, the theme of this hymn is the hidden *Truth* ("Adoro deuote—latens ueritas—"), not the hidden divinity ("latens deitas")[30] of the more familiar reading, in which, no doubt missing the force of Thomas's thought and feeling, someone has piously watered down his concept to a different one admitting of a more indiscriminate sort of response.

Thomas goes on in the same hymn to develop another conceit from the theology of the Word:

> Credo quicquid dixit dei filius:
> Nichil ueritatis uerbo uerius.[31]

Here he draws on the analogy between the intellectual generation of the Son or Word by the Father and the generation of the Son's own human knowledge in His human intellect, together with its manifestation by His human voice. More than this, the implications of the connection between *verum* (the true) and *Verbum* (the Word or Truth of God) are exploited to the full as the similarity of sound between the two words is brought out in the peremptory verse pattern. For the truth of things derives properly and primarily from their being known to God when He knows Himself by His divine Intellect: and in this act of knowing, the Father or First Person generates the Second Person, the Son or Logos, Who *is* the term of the divine knowledge.

These are capital passages. They illustrate how word-play can in the same context both grow directly out of distinctively Christian doctrine and be put to effective literary use. It is a mistaken notion of a past age disowned by current criticism to think that word-play must involve only abstract notions and must be deficient in emotional drive. As a matter of fact, all sorts of psychological and even physiological activities can be implicated in the development of a witty context, particularly when it exhibits the rich organization in evidence here.

We have here in St. Thomas an excellent example of what is often found in the English Renaissance writers, to take them again as a useful term of comparison: in connection with the manipulation of thought on an abstract plane, and running up to this plane and down from it, operations on a physiological, muscular level which engage the whole human organism in relevant perceptions and feelings. The repetition of the *verum* and its cognates in these passages, reinforced with *verbum* (*verbo*), dramatizes the insistence of truth by suggesting a reiterated "True . . . true . . . true!" Truth is inexorable. It keeps coming back, pounding itself not only into the intellect but into the nervous system: "True . . . true . . . true." To a sensibility on the *qui vive* for ever new connections and associations, such effects will not be lost.

This is the kind of psychological effect, operating upon and moving back and forth over various levels of awareness, in which Renaissance wit was later to deal. We recall Thomas More's "Yet for as much as if no man should dooe it, but he that might sufficiently dooe it, no man should dooe it: and better it wer to be vnsufficiently done, then vtterly undone."[32] The repetition builds up considerable physiological pressure, inducing the physical sense that action is imminent and urgent, and thereby conveying on a lower, concrete level the very point More's thought is making on the rational plane; "Do . . . do . . . do!" Moreover, spaced irregularly here as in the *Adoro Te Devote* passage, the beat from the iteration keeps the auditor a little on edge. In *Macbeth* Shakespeare employs the same device:

> If it were done, when 'tis done, then 'twere well
> It were done quickly.[33]

If, as has been pointed out above, word-play can be more than mere phonetic tinkering and become a fertile ground for intellectual activity when the crisscross of sound represents a genuine complexity of real relations, so, as passages such as these last show, play with words can also gain additional richness by moving off to other planes besides that of abstraction, gaining for itself further dimensions as it sets in motion forces at other levels.

Despite the small bulk of Thomas's poetry we have, there is in it no dearth of examples of this same poetic word-play. The *Pange Lingua* cited from above, has in its first stanza:

> Sanguinisque pretiosi,
> Quem in mundi pretium.

Here two words of the same derivation—the former in the sense of *precious*, the latter, with a slightly different turn, in the sense of *price* or *ransom*—are being used as foils against each other. The hymn continues:

> Fructus ventris generosi
> Rex effudit gentium.

Generosi carries its more original meaning of *noble by birth* as well as the later notion of *generous* or *lavish*, and careful reading of the present selection in context shows that the root meaning of the cognate *generare* (to beget) is being played upon so that the word *gentium*, another cognate, is made to ring several changes at once: for instance, the root meaning inherent in *gens* is brought to the fore, and we are reminded that the *gentes* or Gentiles are born also in Christ, now the *Rex gentium* as well as the *Rex Judaeorum* of *John* XIX, 19.

To say that poetry such as this moved through the minds of its readers or hearers in this elaborate array is not to say that all these details were to be apprehended in full consciousness and in all their minuteness. But there they were. And the medieval affection for etymologies, real or fanciful, certainly made a great mass of such detail quite assimilable, both in the case of passages such as the last two and in the case of the *verbum-verbo-verum* motif.

So, again, in the case of the *Lauda Sion* sequence, which offers further evidence of the sophistication of Thomas's wit:

> In hac mensa novi regis,
> Novum pascha novae legis,
>   Phase vetus terminat.[34]

The *phase* is a Vulgate form from the same Hebrew word as *pascha*—the *passage* or *passing*.[35] On this table of the new King (we recall the association of the old monarch of Egypt with the Pasch), the new Pasch (passage, passing) of the New Law—the Sacrifice of Calvary prefaced by the Last Supper, by which sacrifice Christ, and ultimately His Church with Him, passes from this world to His Father—marks the passing of the old passing. The hymn continues:

> A sumente non concisus
>
> . . . .
> Sumit unus, sumunt mille,
> Quantum isti, tantum ille,
> Nec sumptus consumitur.

In this stanza *sumere* and its cognates are used five times; in the next the root crops out in three more places:

> Sumunt boni, sumunt mali,
>
> . . . .
> Mors est malis, vita bonis;
> Vide, paris sumptionis
>   Quam sit dispar exitus.

The various meanings of the root *sumo* enrich these passages with the interplay of various concepts: to take, to lay hold of, to take for use, to put on, to begin, to assert or maintain—with which latter meaning is connected that of *sumptio* as the premise of a syllogism.

Paradox continues on through the seventh to the tenth stanzas of the same hymn, and many other examples of conceit can be found in St. Thomas. Like Adam of St. Victor, he saw the life of his Master as beginning with paradox.

> Verbum supernum prodiens
> Nec patris linquens dexteram,

and ending with paradox, as the Word, Who goes forth without leaving Him wherein He resides, finds the whole of life concentrated in death:

> Ad opus suum exiens
> Venit ad vitae vesperam.[36]

IV

Comparing poetry of the sort just examined with what one finds in the *Dies Irae* and the *Stabat Mater Dolorosa,* one soon becomes aware that the textures of the two sorts of work are quite different. The *Dies Irae* and the *Stabat Mater Dolorosa* both come into being within a distinctive current of medieval piety which may, for want of a more definitive characterization, be designated as the Franciscan school—both hymns are, as a matter of fact, attributed to Franciscans—although the school includes many non-Franciscan representatives, running back, as it does, to Bernard of Clairvaux and down into the Renaissance *Following of Christ.* This school, whose piety is generally described as affective, characteristically finds the source of its rhetoric in the commonplaces of ordinary life—the love of son for mother, of mother for child, of brother for brother, St. Francis of Assisi's love of animals—encouraging the effort to transfer these or similar emotions to higher and nobler objects. This kind of piety seldom turns to theological elucidation in the effort to grow by a fuller and deeper explication of divine Reality. In reference to Christ, such piety concentrates on His human nature, which provides it with a kind of bridge over which it can transfer to His Person responses, principally affective, with which it is familiar from elsewhere.[37]

The existence of a Bonaventure shows that this school is not entirely averse to theological explanation; still, in fostering piety, far more readily than it takes to its theologians' findings, it takes to the conscription of popular notions and fashions which happen to be at hand. It loves to contemplate Christ not uttering mysteries but speaking of fish and sheep to His fishermen and shepherd friends. The most characteristic note of the *Dies Irae* and the *Stabat Mater Dolorosa,* the anguish and plangent tenderness which they feature, is intimately connected with this tendency of the Franciscan school to draw upon popular themes. For anguish and plangency, dealing as they do in elemental and, so long as they last, quite enthralling emotions, are always popular enough responses, and their appeal was not diminished by the courtly love tradition of medieval society.[38] Just as St. Francis could effectively sublimate a concept from the romancers by developing the notion of a *Lady Poverty*, so here the writers avail themselves of feelings of the sort focused in Chaucer's "loveres maladye of hereos" and displayed in his *Troilus and Criseyde* or in Boccaccio's *Filostrato* or in scores of other places. No need for striking juxtapositions, for the stimulus of insights freshly arrived at, establishing intricate connections between realities apprehended in all sorts of ways and at all sorts of levels simultaneously—no need for wit in any form. Here the business is that of calling up familiar blocks of feeling and transferring them to a higher plane. Simply exclamation and conspicuous parallelism will do:

> O quam tristis et afflicta
> Fuit illa benedicta
> Mater unigeniti!

> Quae maerebat et dolebat
> Et tremebat, dum videbat
> Nati poenas incliti.[39]

Or simple narration or panoramic display in a loose scriptural setting:

> Dies irae, dies illa
> Solvet saeclum in favilla
> Teste David cum sibylla.
>
> . . . .
>
> Tuba mirum sparget sonum
> Per sepulchra regionum,
> Coget omnes ante thronum.[40]

The air of "mystery" here may readily prove deceptive. The term suggests Adam's and Thomas's theological interests, yet the "mystery" here is quite different from theological mystery. The air of "mystery" which fills the *Dies Irae* or the *Stabat Mater Dolorosa* is derived not so much from the dogmatic content of revelation, from the mind's being in contact with truths which it finds too massive for its grasp, as from the somewhat hypnotic repetitiousness and parallelism commonly available for popular incantations. It is the "mystery" of the eerie, like that in the witches' charms in *Macbeth*:

Round about the cauldron go;
In the poison'd entrails throw.
Toad, that under cold stone
Days and nights hast thirty-one
Swelter'd venom sleeping got,
Boil thou first i' the charmed pot.
Double, double toil and trouble;
Fire burn and caldron bubble.[41]

This weird diablerie, which here also in Shakespeare is seen, interestingly enough, to assimilate itself readily to themes involving the sweep of time (thirty-one days), burning, and so on, is in the *Dies Irae* and the *Stabat Mater Dolorosa* used indeed legitimately enough and to good purpose. It is quite effectively diverted from its magical uses to help convey the portentous air inseparable from the Last Judgment and Crucifixion themes. But once again the effect is not got *out* of Christian teaching: rather, effects at hand from elsewhere are detached and applied—in so far as possible in an intensified form—to the Christian ethos.

Generally speaking, the poetry of this other tradition is simply uninterested in the complexity of the Adamic-Thomistic style. In the course of a comparison made in a recent study vindicating Aquinas's claim to the authorship of the *Adoro Te Devote*,[42] one sees what happens to the close compression of Thomistic conceit in the hands of a typical representative of the Franciscan school, Jacopone da Todi. Thomas had written:

Visus, gustus, tactus in te fallitur;
Sed solus auditus tute creditur.—
Credo quicquid dixit dei filius:
Nichil ueritatis uerbo uerius.[43]

In a poem echoing this passage out of Thomas, Jacopone quickly short-circuits Thomas's high-tension conceit and carries through only the thought that one sense opposes the other four:

Li quattro sensi dicono:
Questo si è vero pane.
Solo audito resistelo
Ciascun de lor fuor remane.
So eueste[44] uisibil forme
Cristo occultato ce stane;

Cusí a l'alma se dáne
En questa misteriata.

The theology of the Logos is not entered into. It would involve the poem
in a head-on approach to one of the "mysteries" of Christianity, and
such a thing is simply not desired here. The mysteries of Christianity are
indeed accepted in this tradition: indeed, the last line here makes the
note of mystery explicit. Nevertheless, it is symptomatic that this line
represents no more than a loose gesture toward the mysteries as such.
Precisely as mysteries, the teachings of Christianity do not have great
poetic interest.

V

In Adam and Thomas, however, they do. And this fact has a definite
bearing on the predilection for wit in the type of poetry which Adam and
Thomas write. In this poetry interest in word-play and witty conceit
goes hand in hand with concern for the genuinely distinctive "mysteries"
of Christianity. Moreover, the juncture is not accidental: here conceits
are simply a *normal means* of dealing with the mysteries of Christianity,
the distinctively Christian teachings, as well as a means of achieving a
successful poetic texture. How this is so will, I trust, be demonstrated
in the following pages.

Word-play in hymnody was, to be sure, not first employed in the
strongly theological milieu of the twelfth and thirteenth centuries.
Throughout the medieval hymnographers from the earliest times there is
ample evidence of word-play and witty conceit,[45] and such things, in
turn, must have been caught up from classical Latinity at many of the
manifold points of contact—a strong current out of the rhetoricians is
maintained through the constant use of St. Augustine—and must also
have emerged or received stimulation from all sorts of vernacular
sources. But despite its common occurrence much earlier, this wit in
the twelfth and thirteenth centuries has a special connection with the
great theological activity of the time. The connection becomes explicit
in the writings of St. Thomas Aquinas.

When he draws the line of demarcation between what Christian teaching has in common with any well-reasoned-out religion ("natural" religion) which man has arrived at or might arrive at and what it has

as distinctively its own, Thomas makes the significant observation that the *distinctively Christian* element *creates a tension in linguistic expression* and that *precisely this tension establishes a point of similarity* with poetry.

This observation turns up as Thomas discusses the fact that metaphor, which seems to be a device distinctive of poetry and foreign to the physical and mathematical sciences and to metaphysics and logic, turns up time and again in Christian theology. This fact would not have concerned Thomas had he been thinking of theology as some sort of whimsical expatiation on religious themes—as random, if impressive, talk. But he was concerned with a theology maintained as a strict science, and the question his discussion broaches is whether theology, if it is a strict science, can be justified in its employment of metaphor. He finds that it can:

> The science of poetry is about things which because of their deficiency of truth cannot be laid hold of by the reason. Hence the reason has to be drawn off to the side by means of certain comparisons. But then, theology is about things which lie beyond reason. Thus the symbolic method is common to both sciences, since neither is of itself accommodated [to the human reason].[46]

For Thomas, Christian theology and poetry are indeed not the same thing, but lie at opposite poles of human knowledge. However, the very fact that they are opposite extremes gives them something of a common relation to that which lies between them: they both operate on the periphery of human intellection. A poem dips below the range of the human process of understanding-by-reason as the subject of theology sweeps above it. In common with medieval scholastic thinkers and their age as a whole, Thomas shows little interest in poetic theory and even less in aesthetics generally, but what he does say here and elsewhere is interesting both intrinsically and in connection with his poetic practice.

The "deficiency of truth" in a poem is to be traced to the peculiar kind of existence which a poem exercises, to its inability to survive the abstraction which is the peculiar condition *sine qua non* of human understanding.

Although truth is founded on the real, is in touch with the real, we can get into intellectual contact with reality only by the peculiar operation known as abstraction. Abstraction—for all the weakness and inadequacy of the process itself—is necessary both because of the kind of being man is, and, conversely, because of the kind of being with which he is in immediate contact: being which includes in itself matter. The fact is that an individual existent of the sort we encounter, an individual whose being is grounded in matter, cannot in terms of its own being alone, make an understanding of itself available to the one looking at it or feeling it. This is simply a matter of observation. For understanding, which comes with science, we need to examine a multiplicity of individuals, or at least of individual instances.[47] Only when we have experience of a number of other things and manage to put together various charts and tables and laws or principles, all of them abstractions, can we hope to possess intellectually, to understand (*intelligere*) the very existents about us here and now.

St. Thomas was struck by the somewhat eerie fact that nothing man comes across explains itself, that nothing he encounters is self-explanatory: always everything depends on something *else* for its own intelligibility. Although an object may be bright as day, right in front of you, it will not yield understanding unless you can keep various abstractions —the charts or tables or laws or principles, which are not the thing itself—somehow in view. A child does not look at a dog and understand. He looks at a dog and is puzzled. He blurts out a string of questions. The child who, hypothetically, would once come across a dog and never anything else, not even, let us say, another dog—on simply having one dog register once on him—could never hope to understand the dog. And yet, there the dog is. A being with an intellect *is* in contact with him. But the fact remains that the dog, unabetted by other things, is intellectually opaque. He does not make sense, alone. He can be brought around to making sense only by our working with *other* things. So we must step back for the moment, apply instruments, view this being which impinges so immediately on our senses through something which is not only other than this being itself but derived from observations involving many other beings besides this being itself: through a science, such as biology; that is to say, through a structure of abstractions. In the end, we come to know the dog, all right, for it is items such as this dog, that dog, which in the last analysis we want to understand, since we want to understand not abstract problems but the world and what is in it. Yet we come to understand the dog only when we have got far enough off from him to see him in perspective, to view him at a distance through the findings of a science.

It is a matter of record that this is the kind of understanding of things men have. Regarding the chances for a science of poetry in a setting such as this, St. Thomas, never too sanguine about human intellectual prowess, is clearly aware that there are going to be difficulties.[48] He is aware of the unsatisfactory and inconclusive, not to say distressing, nature of discussion about any poem. Because of its peculiar insistence on remaining concreted within the act of apprehension itself, a poem resists the very abstraction by which we would understand it. Abstraction, in one way or another, destroys it, dissolves it away. So we must content ourselves largely with simply apprehending the poem by reading or hearing it read, and as for any strict understanding of a poem, we must content ourselves with thinking and talking *around* it. Thomas does not put it in exactly the same words, but when he speaks of its "deficiency of truth," he is concerned with the same thing about a poem which prompts Mr. Archibald MacLeish to observe that "A poem should not mean / But be."[49]

Yet it would be inaccurate to say that we have no understanding at all of poetry. We do find ourselves able to think about it, which means that somehow or other our understanding is concerned with it. What we are doing is approaching it by a kind of indirection—this fact is attested to by the constant resort to metaphor which the most rigorous discussion of poetry seems inexorably to demand. A poem seems unable to forego this minimum of concretion even in being discussed. And in so far as it will not submit fully to abstraction but must retain the concretion of metaphor, it escapes reason. Not that it is against reason, antirational. Reason is an imperfect way of getting at a thing: it implies a special approach, it produces understanding only under certain conditions, and those things which are not amenable to these conditions simply escape it. These special conditions would not be demanded by the intellects of purely spiritual beings, the angelic spirits and God, in whom understanding is generated simply by the direct contact with the spiritual objects which are the things they find themselves immediately facing (for the Divinity this is primarily His own Being, in Whose all-pervasive light created reality, too, is pierced through intellectually).[50] This sort of intellect understands things without resort to abstractions: but with this sort of intellect man is not gifted. He has only a rational or reasoning sort of intelligence. He understands the things that surround him only at the end of a reasoning process, which is not simply a looking at things, an intellectual gaze, but an intellectual journey, a spinning out of abstractions. Only at the end of such a journey does the light of understanding come, after one has plotted out the terrain with little markers, worked his way carefully through a layout of abstractions.

Hence poetry really demands too much of the reason in its insistence both that it be understood and that it be understood somehow without resort to abstractions. From this fact arises the strain, which Thomas supposes as a matter of common observation, the state of tension in which poetry leaves reason. Plato had some warrant, after all, for barring poets from his republic: they do violence to and unsettle the reason on which his political order was to have been based.

In this connection Thomas says nothing specifically about the use of conceit. But the implications of his view are plain. If poetry implies a sort of rational derangement, an unmanageableness, a nonintegration on the rational level in the face of a unity perceptible in other ways (the unity of impression, the unity of perception in a poem), *the superlative derangement inherent in the conceit*, which by operating through devices such as paradox maintains a sense of order in disorder and disorder in order, *stands as a kind of paragon of procedure in a poetic economy*.

Thomas's explanation of the use of metaphor in theology moves along quite another, but a similar line. In the science of theology based on Christian revelation, as well as in the science of poetry, the intellect must in a way come upon its objective by a kind of flank movement. It grasps it only by the periphery. The difficulty here, however, is that the human intellect is in contact with something too massive for it, whereas in the case of poetry the object was too fragile for it.

St. Thomas clearly points out that this difficulty is especially inherent in distinctively Christian theology. The difficulty he envisions is not one which arises when reason has to do simply with the One True God under those aspects which many non-Christians acknowledge. To be sure, to come to any knowledge of God at all demands some elementary intellectual activity, though it involves no difficulties that the ordinary, unhandicapped mind cannot readily surmount (here, as everywhere else, to arrive at a certain knowledge and to be able to recount in scientific detail *how* one arrived at it are two different things). Moreover, what knowledge of God we come to by the natural workings of our intellect will not be proper but analogous knowledge, and in this sense no living man can form for himself a concept of God as He really is. Yet the difficulty with which Thomas is concerned is one which the Jew or the Mohammedan will not encounter, although they submit to the same God as the Christians do. "There are some truths concerning God," St. Thomas says, "which exceed all power of the human reason, as the truth that God is three as well as one. And there are some truths to which even natural reason may attain, as the truth that God exists, that God is one, and other truths of this sort."[51] This second group of truths any number of men may have in common with the Christian. But truths in the first group, the Trinity and the Incarnation (which is to be understood in function of the Trinity, since it is the Second Person of the Trinity Who became incarnate), together with the dispensation of Providence for the world in terms of these truths,[52] are had only by the special divine revelation on which Christianity is founded. Truths in the first group are the "mysteries" of Christianity, truths with which the unaided reason cannot establish contact, which man would be quite justified in rejecting for want of evidence did he not have them on the word of God Himself. Although all the evidence proposed against these truths turns out to be inconclusive or even a hoax[53]—evidence which is in the last analysis beside the point—nevertheless the truths really cannot be explained on rational grounds: although one cannot show that they are false, one cannot show *how* they can be true.[54]

The reason is that these truths are not of a piece with the being with which man is surrounded. The same created things which give evidence of God's existence, His uniqueness, His eternity, and so on, provide no unequivocal evidence of the Trinity. The Trinity is a secret of the Godhead, too interior and peculiar to the divine life to leave betraying traces upon God's operations *ad extra,* so that the various "trinities" which men attempt to demonstrate from reason in the Godhead do not fit the Christian Trinity of Persons at all. And the other Christian mysteries are all involved in this one of the Trinity, for only in the Trinity is their full explanation to be found.

But if these truths in the first group, such as the Trinity, are to be revealed to man by the oral teaching even of Christ Himself, and if they are to continue to be taught, they must be put into language, the terms of which *are* of a piece with the being with which man is surrounded, since these terms are derived from the created material being which man knows. Charged with the task of expressing something for which they have no natural aptitude, these terms will be taxed beyond their natural powers. They will be aligned in strange and unaccountable ways. The concepts and consequently the language will be in a state of tension.

This tension does not mean that in a conceptual formulation of any one or of all the mysteries of Christianity a contradiction is involved. There is, for instance, no real contradiction in an accurate enunciation of the doctrine of the Trinity, such as, for example, "In God there are three divine Persons in the one divine Nature" or "In the one true God there are three subsisting Relations." Considering the content with which the terms in such statements are charged, one find that by virtue of this content, drawn from the natural world, the terms do not positively repel each other.

But they do tend to drop apart simply from want of anything to enforce cohesion. Taking the terms with all the content one can give them and all the evidence one can bring from the natural world relevant to such content, one cannot show that the doctrine contained in such statements must of itself be so nor even how it might be so. In the light of natural reason, the doctrine of the Trinity cannot be seen to be urgent at all.

This remains true even though the fact that this truth has been revealed by God can be established quite rationally on the basis of intransigent historical facts as well as on the basis of contemporary evidence such as miracles, which are indeed unpredictable events but matters of simple fact, often entirely verifiable, still occurring in the Church and attesting to the disinterested mind the Church's claim to the possession of a divine revelation. For the human mind, even when brought by inescapable evidence to the conclusion *that* a revelation has been made by God, still needs an altogether special gift from God, an enlargement of its natural powers, if it is to lay hold of the *content* of this revelation, concerned, as it is, with supernatural truth—that is, if it is to accept, to assent to, this revelation in a salutary way.

This gift from God, which is the gift called Christian faith, comes into play in every Christian and sets the mind to a task beyond itself. It thereby establishes the mind of the believer in a lifelong state of real tension. An acute awareness of the presence of this tension brought Thomas to examine in terms of a detailed study of human intellection the condition of mind consequent upon Christian belief.[55] Since this condition is radical to the entire Christian economy and of extreme importance to an understanding of the interaction of medieval theology with medieval poetry, Thomas's study is of prime importance and worth inspection for our present purposes, at least as a report by an intelligent believer upon his own state of mind.

Examining the nature of the Christian mysteries, Thomas finds that the basic reason for the need of a special gift from God, if the intellect is to lay hold of these mysteries, is the fact that although the terms in which the mysteries are stated are indeed joined to one another by predication in a formulation of the mysteries—one numerical Nature is joined with three Persons—this connection cannot derive from the things from which the terms themselves derive. When such a condition exists, the intellect is necessarily in a distressing state.

Thomas recognizes that understanding is the goal of all intellectual activity, and he interprets understanding by analogy with sight, as somehow intellectual "vision" or intuition. This means that not only concepts but all the connections we make of concepts must be validated by being "discerned" in the material reality about us. It is not without significance that when they understand, men commonly and without effort, say simply, "I see." To understand is not to reason or to consider or weigh. Reasoning is usually the way to arrive at understanding. But understanding is to look, to view. (The present treatment of understanding and belief in terms of vision should be compared with what is said about belief as related to hearing in the essay above, "Voice as Summons for Belief.")

Unlike certain other medieval thinkers, Thomas was a rigid experimentalist: his observation was that everything man employs in understanding is found out, discovered, observed, seen in things round about man by a process, usually far less deliberate and calculating, but essentially the very same as that of a modern research scientist in his laboratory—a process of collecting evidence. Even the principle of contradiction does not simply turn up in the mind. It is the product of experience. Like everything else, it, too, is *found out*.[56] Once an individual has a minimum of experience, he sees it at work in things.

Of the truths which man finds out, by no means all are immediately understandable, and some are more readily understandable than others. To find out the fact that the angles of a triangle add up to one straight angle is not to *understand* the fact. Once come upon, such a fact is found to be not entirely permeable to the vision of the intellect: the intellect sees the need of further inspection, further explanation. It is faced with a thing which does not admit of immediate intuition: such a thing must be worked over, reduced to something clearly visible.

Man does discover some such clearly visible things, although unfortunately they are not the material substances with which he is surrounded. They are not individual wholes. They are abstract principles—called principles or points of departure because they are the points of origin of understanding—such things, for instance, as the principle of contradiction. Once come upon, this principle is immediately and and totally permeable to the intellect. It is so clear, indeed, that when one states it, one seems to be saying almost nothing: the principle is almost completely merged with the intellect itself.[57] But this is the way real understanding should be, after all: knowing is identification of the mind with its object.

Man's intellection may be described as thin because it is only principles like these and not the real individual existent material wholes with which he is surrounded that are *in themselves* permeable to his mind. Individual spiritual existents—an angelic spirit, for instance—would be immediately permeable to the intellect were the intellect put in contact with them. A purely spiritual substance would be a self-evident substance, an object for intellection which would be lucid without being thin at all. But it is material things that *we* have direct contact with, and they are not such. One need only have experience of them to appreciate that they are not self-evident, *selbstverständlich*. They are evident, lucid, in the light of principles derived from them. These principles are the only sort of thing we encounter which are *selbstverständlich*. They are self-evident not in the sense that they turn up in the intellect automatically but in the sense that they are lucid, that when the intellect finds them out it penetrates immediately to their innermost core. It sees all at once everything there is in them.[58] There is nothing left to be explained in terms of something else.

Now understanding being vision, it must be carried on in function of what is immediately and totally visible, lucid. Therefore to understand material things is to find in them such principles, to discover the area in them in which such principles are located, for once the intellect can hit on such a principle, it will pierce deeply into the being it is trying to understand. The principle, being permeable to the intellect, will admit the intellect to the core of the being itself.

This illustrates what happens when one comes to understand, for example, the fact that the angles of a triangle add up to one straight angle. This fact itself is not immediately permeable to the intellect: it is not evident *in itself*. But there is the mathematical principle that the whole is greater than any one of its parts, and another that the whole is equal to the sum of all its parts, and so on. These are self-evident, intellectually lucid truths discernible in things: constructing a mathematical figure in the imagination as one has learned to do from experience and memory[59]—a triangle, for instance, divided into parts—by inspection of the phantasm one simply *sees* standing out there the principle that the whole is greater than its parts. Equipped with principles such as these—how many such principles there are we can transmit in the present discussion—one is prepared to *understand* the fact that the angles of a triangle add up to one straight angle. One demonstrates the fact in the light of such principles. Thus (complete) demonstration is a process of disclosing the relation of a truth to self-evident principles. One studies the angles in a triangle in such a way as to see the self-evident principles in this fact. Once they are seen there, we say we understand.

Here one can begin to appreciate the difficulty inherent in Christian faith. In the case of mathematics the principles which make the fact understandable come from the same material source as the fact itself. (The same is true of other sciences which are the ways to understanding.) One sees the principle that the whole is greater than its parts, etc., by inspecting the phantasm in the imagination. That is, to find the principles one inspects the same things which one had inspected to gather the notions in the truth one is trying to explain: the notions of triangle, angle, straight angle, and so on. The notions and the principles are intimately joined, destined for one another, flesh of one another's flesh and bone of one another's bone, derived from the same source, complements, components of the same realities.

Now any truth which the human intellect naturally possesses or contains, the intellect lays claim to because of the fact that the truth is reducible in one way or another to principles immediately self-evident. A truth is naturally in the intellect, is naturally intellectually possessed, in so far as it is faced toward such principles, in so far as within it self-evident principles are at least implicitly grasped. These form the points at which the intellect as intellect secures purchase on its object, the points at which the wider *knowledge*, which in man includes sense cognition and various mixtures of sense and intellectual cognition, becomes specifically intellection, the points at which intellectual penetration begins.

But the truths of faith, the mysteries as such, as these present themselves to the intellect, are not in themselves faced toward such principles. Here the notions in the truth which offers itself to the mind derive indeed from the material world: *person, one, three, nature,* and so on. But as for the truth itself *In the one divine Nature, there are three divine Persons,* alas! there is no principle from the material world to which this truth is reducible, which gives the intellect any purchase on it at all. Even the principle of contradiction will not work here in positive fashion. That is not to say that the principle of contradiction, or any other similar principle, such as the principle of identity, is not universally true. It is only to say that it is irrelevant to an understanding of the Trinity, not irrelevant in the sense that it has nothing to do with the Trinity (since the principle itself, like all reality, has its source in God, and since, moreover, it can be used to show that the Trinity has been revealed by God and thus indirectly that the Trinity must be true), but irrelevant in the sense that it does not make the Trinity any more permeable by, available to the human intellect. That is, although the principle of contradiction will not work to show that the doctrine of the Trinity cannot be or is not true, still neither will it make evident from intrinsic nonauthoritarian reasons that the doctrine of the Trinity is true. Here one is in the realm of absolute truth, put forth in its own immediacy and interiority, and the possibility of reasoning *to* it vanishes. There is nothing to which it can be reduced, nothing that could make it more luminous, for it is luminosity itself. This truth must be seen in itself or it will not be seen at all. Beside it, all things are dim—including the principle of contradiction and every other principle. Not in any principle at all, nor in any reasoning process, but "in *lumine tuo*," says the Psalmist, "videbimus lumen."[60]

During this life, while there is no vision of the Blessed Trinity, assent to the truths of faith therefore means that the intellect is called upon to grasp a truth not contsituted like those it is naturally fitted to grasp. Natural truths are so constructed that they not only admit of, but point to validation in the same matter as that from which are drawn the concepts which enter into them. This construction is what adapts them to the human intellect. The mysteries of faith are otherwise. In them the mind starts indeed from material reality in the sense that it derives from material things the concepts by which it grasps the mysteries. But here its movement is not circular, as it is in natural cognition, where the intellect returns to material things for completion. It is centrifugal. And this for human intellection is violent movement. Thus at the very heart of the Christian economy there exists a state of tension, of violence, of stress.

In a psychological setting such as this, it is plain that Christian faith is in no sense reducible to a satisfying feeling of confident trust which salves one's uneasiness concerning the outcome of life, nor is it a satisfying culmination of intellectual life, an intellectual or volitional ultimate. Rather, it is an essentially unsatisfying state, and Thomas attempts no hocus-pocus to convince himself that it is anything else.

Faith serves a purpose in Christianity precisely because man has no natural equipment to see supernatural truth and will not be given this equipment until after death. If during this life man is to have any intellectual contact at all with the supernatural, it will have to be an imperfect intellectual contact. Faith makes possible precisely this intellectual contact which does not progress beyond the imperfect stage. Faith makes it possible for supernatural truth to establish a beachhead, and only a beachhead, in the mind.

The state of mind induced by belief or faith is a normal enough phenomenon of human life. Belief forms a common principle of activity, and an intellectual principle at that, for what a man believes forms ground for intellectual operations and for intellectually directed action. But further, the state of mind resulting from belief or faith is imperfect. It certainly leaves much to be desired. It leaves the mind in one way or another restless and tense. Yet, although it is not an intellectually perfect condition, man must utilize belief often enough, for, to tell the truth, he is not really so thorough-going an intellectual as he sometimes likes to make himself out to be. His intellect cannot always achieve its goal perfectly. It has its limitations, and he has to make up for them by half-measures, by flanking operations.

Belief is one of these operations. Although it is not a direct approach to truth, it is often the only approach available, and it often works so well that it leads ultimately, if deviously and somewhat erratically, to understanding. Anyone with an eye open to the facts knows, for instance, that the child who believes his parents and teachers will do well to believe them, for although, of its nature, understanding does not depend on belief at all but on vision, on intuition, still belief is a very normal, and for practical purposes an indispensable road—or short cut—to the point from which vision becomes possible. Although understanding and not belief takes the real measure of being, and belief should be checked when understanding is arrived at, one must face the fact that the child who refuses to take anything on faith from his elders will remain at best badly retarded, and most likely a sheer idiot. Indeed, practically speaking, it would be quite impossible psychologically for a child to act in such a way.

Moreover, reliance on faith remains a permanent, if progressively less important, condition of intellectual activity throughout man's life. This fact is no anomaly: belief is imperfect contact with truth, circuitous contact, but that is only to say that here, as elsewhere, man's activity does not achieve its goal in one fell swoop but proceeds by little and little from the less perfect to the more perfect. Even in scientific research work, the first steps are less sure, less definitive than the last.

It is not difficult, therefore, to see why God should utilize belief as a means of introducing into the human mind *in a preliminary fashion* truths which are of themselves beyond its comprehension and for which it will be completely equipped only in a subsequent stage of its development. The divine plan for the supernatural simply avails itself of the natural processes of the human intellect, in which belief is often a preliminary to understanding—the less perfect contact which commonly enough precedes the more perfect.

In its relation to poetic tension, the tension associated with supernatural faith has a particular relevance of its own because it is more acute than that resulting from natural faith. There is accordingly a relevance to wit poetry quite special to Christianity.

But the superlative acuteness of the intellectual stress or tension accompanying supernatural faith is not contravened by the absolute certitude which Thomas finds investing the same supernatural Christian faith.[61] Indeed, both the stress or tension and the certitude are traceable to the same conditions.

Although in particular areas of fact or at particular times the human intellect may have to rely on report, on belief, for its contact with natural truth, it is never completely at the mercy of belief for such contact. Precisely because a report is set within the material world where other effects of the truth reported upon are registered and can often be found, natural faith—the belief of one man in the word of another—admits of being superseded in the usual course of natural events. If in an individual case the mind fails to replace faith by science, to carry belief on to a more perfect knowledge, this is solely because of limitations of time and space such as beset all its pursuit of truth.

Of itself, a truth which the mind knows by natural faith admits of being checked. The human mind has open before itself the possibility of perfecting its knowledge by multiplying in one way or another its contacts with a reality. In multiplicity lies its preservative against error. Thus in scientific procedure the mind employs experiments hedged around by "control" of a multitude of factors and thus exactly repeatable. In the case of natural belief the mind can multiply its contacts by obtaining separate reports about an event or even, to some extent, by considering the event in terms of the circumstances of the report, the character and motivation of the reporter, and so on. In so far as it does such things, it arrives at that certitude which one unvalidated report from man can never give, although, at the same time, in so far as it validates the reports which it receives, it ceases to believe and begins to know. But man can do this sort of thing precisely because the truths with which natural faith is concerned occur within the setting of the material cosmos with which he is surrounded and to which he has ready and manifold access. This means, too, that in the last analysis they occur in the setting from which he can induce principles by which to understand them.

By simply occurring within this setting, therefore, the truths which man believes by natural faith on the reports of his fellow men admit of being transmuted from their status of reports into something else: the mind can proceed from natural faith to something better, to knowledge and understanding. Although there are some borderline cases in which we cannot decide whether a truth can legitimately be reduced from faith to simple knowledge, just as there are borderline cases in which the scientist cannot determine whether he can infer a general principle, still there are clear cases in which accumulation of evidence leads to the disappearance of faith. One could hardly say, for instance, that an intelligent adult who had never been away from Paris *believed* in the existence of Rome. He *knows* Rome exists. So the historian knows that Julius Caesar lived, that Christ lived. The informed Christian, who must believe *what* God reveals, *knows that* God has given a revelation. The only ones who believe such things are those who have not availed themselves of the necessary information at hand to reduce their state of mind from belief to knowledge.

Thus the assents of natural faith come about in an area of reality with which the intellect already has a multiplicity of contacts enabling it to operate so as to verify at least some of the things it believes in. These contacts are what give the mind its real hold on what it assents to. Not so in the case of supernatural faith. Here the intellect is projected by the very act of faith itself beyond its own natural bounds so that only in the act of faith has it any contact at all with the truth it assents to. There is no possibility of its reaching out under its own power to multiply its contacts with this reality, for the supernatural is precisely that which the finite intellect cannot contact under its own power.

Moreover, the intellect needs certainty here, for it could hardly be said to be assenting to supernatural truth at all if it assented to it as merely probable. For how could such truth be probable? Probability involves the possibility of being referred to something else for verification. And to what could this be referred?

But, according to St. Thomas's report, the mind is not so nonplused as all that, for the object of supernatural faith is known on the word of God Himself and is therefore absolutely certain. Here and here alone one has absolute certainty conjoined with belief or faith. This never happens regarding faith in human reports, which, so long as it is sheer faith without an element of science—introduced by consideration of circumstances, etc.—remains at best a kind of "vehement opinion."[62]

Thus the crisis at the center of the Christian economy can be stated as the presence of *a maximum of certitude with a minimum of understanding*. This is a state which exists at the center of Christian life within man's highest and most vital—his intellectual—activity, and which is essentially inescapable and lifelong, which no man can hope to put aside for himself, and which will vanish only when in the next life belief gives way to understanding, when God opens the floodgates and pours Himself without stint into the soul,[63] giving the intellect that understanding—that vision, that intuition—which it is powerless to achieve for itself.

Meanwhile, till this final stage is reached, even taking God's absolutely inerrant word is not seeing the truth, not understanding, and the intellect remains restless: it keeps poking around, inquiring. Indeed, of this inquisitiveness theology is born. But when theology comes into being, it is as an abiding testimony to the tension to which the mind is subject when it accepts any truth on faith, even if this be a faith with supernatural powers trained on a supernatural object. For, although theology is a science, by this strange science the mind can never really free itself of the tension inherent in a life founded on belief. Theology will indeed give the mind something to do concerning its state, bring it to a knowledge of much it did not know before. It will in a way satisfy the restiveness of the mind, but only deviously, by setting the mind to the task of pushing the limits of reason to their uttermost bounds.

But beyond the limits it cannot go. Theology will never *solve* the mysteries of faith at all. In the last analysis the only satisfaction the natural mind gets from theology is to be able to say, "At least *this* isn't a mystery. This is clear. The mystery lies from here to here." But the distance from here to here remains always infinity.

Thus at the center not only of Thomas's religious life but also of his scientific life, this state of tension existed. And he knew it and consciously adverted to the fact. For deep within the science of theology the mystery remains. The science is founded on a real, but imperfect, grasp of its subject. Because of this, because its subject, as a modern theologian aptly puts Thomas's view, is *incontrôlable*,[64] always half-way out of bounds, theology, like poetry, resorts to metaphor. For in the case of theology, even abstraction is an inadequate means of managing its material. Abstraction is weak here not only by virtue of its inevitable departure from real, individual beings, but also because in this case, despite all it sacrifices of concreteness, in the last analysis it does not eliminate the blind spot at the very center of the puzzle, however brilliant it makes things around the edges.

The very thing which science ordinarily sets out to do by departing from concrete, individual, material, real existents, it has here in the last analysis failed to accomplish in the most urgent sense. Hence the intellect is justified in tacking back again, in seeking through the greater concretion of metaphor to make up for what it has lost through a journey on which reason has taken it without too great success. Of course, metaphor will not be entirely satisfactory either. But at least it is a compensation of a kind. And at this point, the parallel with poetry comes clear. There are great differences, but there is also a parallel. For both poetry and theology, metaphor is a last, and not quite satisfactory, resort.

It must be noted that this explanation of Christian faith and Christian theology is not a speculative joy ride undertaken as an escape from reality. Nor is it merely a self-consistent explanation which Thomas offers for a fanciful condition in which man might find himself—a pipe dream in the realm of pure theory. It is—a point of moment for our present purpose—an account of what the milieu in which he lived and breathed and wrote his poetry looked like to him. It is St. Thomas's considered explanation of what he found to be happening as men lived— that is, believed and acted upon—what was proposed to them by the Church. It sets forth Thomas's findings at the term of the investigation of a concrete set of facts. This is plain from a look at his sources, which are primarily the teachings of the Church as he found them proposed for men in his day, then and there, to believe and to act upon. This must be kept in mind, for the point under observation here is not merely the relationship between wit poetry and St. Thomas's speculation, but the relationship between such poetry and the reality from which Thomas's speculation took its rise.

Moreover, Aquinas's report is consonant with a centuries-long string of reports on Christianity from men who were eminently familiar with it. At the very beginning of the Christian dispensation, St. Paul had stated that his teaching contained elements of mystery[65] deriving from the fact that it manifested the intimate secrets of the divine economy governing the human race. Accepting the Christian faith, he freely stated, involves getting over a "stumbling block" inseparable from that faith.[66]

Patristic writings come back again and again to the same thing. The theme is persistent in Augustine, in whom the intellectual leap demanded by faith finds expression, not too satisfactorily, in statements such as "Intellige ut credas, crede ut intelligas."[67] And in the fourth century St. Hilary could write that the mystery of the Trinity was a thing "beyond the denotative power of speech, beyond the representative power of sense, beyond the conceptual power of the intelligence."[68]

Through the Middle Ages the same general mind prevails: there is something at the heart of Christian teaching which, while not anti-rational is still somehow transrational.[69] The paradox causes the theologians to vacillate in their attempts to formulate a description of the matter,[70] but Trinitarian explanations such as Abelard's, which sought to prove the Trinity from reason, are condemned as being false to the facts.[71]

In Adam's monastery of St. Victor, Richard and Hugh seem to have been a little uncertain in their theological formulations, but Hugh at least was acutely aware that, viewed in terms of the science of logic or natural reason, Christian revelation posited somehow a special condition for the human intellect: once revelation was a historical fact, not one, but "two representations were proposed to man in which he might see invisible [i.e., divine] things, one of nature and one of grace. The representation [in the order] of nature was the appearance of this world. And the representation [in the order] of grace was the humanity of the Word."[72]

With Thomas's development of the theorems of the natural and the supernatural to describe the state of affairs, theorems dividing the content of Christian doctrine into areas which could be traversed by reason and areas contiguous to these but out of reason's reach, explanation reached a theologically stable stage.[73] More accurately set forth than earlier explanations, Thomas's analysis makes explicit the condition of the mysteries of Christianity as these lie in the human mind, and in so doing brings out the fact that the impact of Christian teaching on the human being gives rise to a state of mind which not only exhibits certain special affinities for poetry—Thomas is, as has been shown, quite explicit on this point—but which also finds a poetry of "wit," rather like that signalized later in the English "metaphysical" poets, a natural expression of its tensions.

Moreover, Christian theology, as is illustrated in the case of St. Thomas, brings attention to bear on the very condition which gives rise to the relationship between Christian doctrine and poetry, particularly wit poetry, and so increases awareness of the condition, thereby intensifying its effects. It is therefore more than a coincidence that medieval Latin religious verse, of which Adam's and Thomas's works are only samples which have scores of counterparts elsewhere, should freely employ witty conceit as a standard poetic device. This fact is intimately connected with the dominance of theological speculation in the milieu in which these men moved.

It is quite true that by no means all of the paradox and metaphorical elaboration found in Adam or Thomas or elsewhere in medieval religious poetry is directly concerned with the real mysteries of Christian doctrine. But the liking for conceit, for farfetched allegorical and even fanciful interpretations, which runs so strongly through patristic writing as a kind of wit and finds its way into medieval religious poetry, feeds to satiety on the fact that the whole of the Christian economy is dominated by what may be called with all reverence superparadox.

For an adequate understanding of medieval Latin religious poetry, this fact and the consequent interaction of poetry with theology must be taken into account, for its leads to the depths of some of the richest poetic passages, and it shows that wit poetry is much more integral to the great central forces in medieval civilization than has commonly been suspected.

VI

By way of sequel, there remains one question to answer. Both speculatively, from the point of view of its own structure revealed by critical examination, and practically, from the point of view of its impact upon contemporary poetry, the wit poetry of the English Renaissance, which has been the wit poetry effecting in great part the current revision of sensibility, has been noted for a kind of insatiable omnivorousness which enables it to devour all sorts of experience in one gulp.[74] It is the polar opposite of poetry which fastidiously sniffs about for something "poetic" to assimilate. It is strong enough, we are told, to digest all experience, raw if necessary, and make something of it.

This omnivorousness is intimately related to the ability of wit poetry —an ability earlier adverted to—to move simultaneously on the highest levels of abstract speculation and in a relevant fashion on lower levels, too, integrating in one experience the whole complexity which is man.

Not only twentieth-century scholars and critics, but contemporaries of the metaphysicals themselves make a point of this omnivorousness. Thus Abraham Cowley:

> In a true piece of *Wit*, all things must be,
> Yet all things there *agree*.

. . . .

> . . . as the *Primitive Forms* of all
> . . . . lie
> In that strange *Mirror of the Deitie*[75]

This is an inclusive order.

Since the drawing of a parallel of any sort with metaphysical poetry can hardly avoid the question of this characteristic quality of omnivorousness, a few observations should be made concerning its relation to the Latin poetry which this study has considered.

First of all, it may be said with some truth that medieval Latin poetry lacks all idiom, that it is largely a hothouse linguistic growth, its contacts with reality artificially insulated. The vocabulary does not bear the same relation as a completely developed working vernacular would to the totality of things out of which medieval man was drawing his experience and his concepts. Large areas of fact and feeling were to some extent isolated from Latin: men usually did not cook in it or manage labor in it or swear in it either. In view of these facts, there can be no doubt that in comparison with any writer whose vehicle was medieval Latin, the English metaphysicals, using the later vernacular, could effect a more complete juncture with the manifold entering into a concrete experience.

Still, Professor Tatlock's point remains valid and applicable here. If not in the time of Donne and Cowley, certainly in the time of St. Thomas, the vernaculars labored under a very real limitation themselves—a limitation the converse of that of Latin. The vernaculars were insulated from a very real phase of life, the intellectual activity at the universities and elsewhere.

It is perhaps not so easy to re-create the entire experience which a Latin poem conveyed in the twelfth century with the adequacy which we can command to approximate an experience vernacularly recorded at the same time, or, at any rate, certainly in neither the medieval vernacular nor the Latin can our judgments ever arrive at the refinements of perception which they can achieve regarding the literature of the present day. Semantic irrelevancies and the vagaries of associations unknown in the originals relentlessly intrude—there is no use for the most devoted scholar to pretend they do not—and facile interpolations of shades of meanings which cohere satisfyingly without being quite true to the original make distortions hard to detect. Yet, allowing for the difficulties in experiencing all that was originally in the work, one suspects, even from an examination of Latin religious poetry alone, that in view of the cleavage of the realm of experience into a vernacular and a Latin sector, the Latin may well be able to hold its own with the vernaculars in terms of the immediacy it was able to convey. Adam of St. Victor seems almost as little limited as the English metaphysicals in his sources for analogies.

This much is also true, as the goliardics show: if medieval Latin suffered both from lack of the close continuity with certain aspects of everyday life available in the vernaculars and also perhaps from the dissipating effects of several vernaculars pulling, each with its own connotations for Latin words, in various directions at once, nevertheless the very noncommittal international character thereby given to Latin supplied the language with its own peculiar setting and became itself a substitute for a vigorous idiom. One might cite a well known goliardic to bring out the point:

> Jam fit magister artium
> Qui nescit quotas partium
>   De vero fundamento.
> Habere nomen appetit,
> Rem vero ne curat ne scit,
>   Examine contento.

> Jam fiunt baccalaurii
> Pro munere denarii
>   Quamplures idiotae.
> In artibus ab aliis
> Egregiis scientiis
>   Sunt bestiae promotae.[76]

This is grammar Latin, and yet it remains as untranslatable as any vernacular piece ever was. This is not quite the language of Donne or of Shakespeare, turgid with the washings of daily life. Yet the life of a whole continent, in however distilled a form, does flow here. We sense the international sophistication of medieval civilization, and the very lack of idiom becomes an idiom of itself. We must not forget how this kind of thing flows through such macaronics as the "Boar's Head Carol" to enter into the thoroughgoing raciness of Jonson or of Herrick's *Hesperides*. Nor how it toughens the lines of Adam's sequences and of Thomas's eucharistic hymns.

NOTES

[1] "Mediaeval Laughter," *Speculum*, XXI (1946), 290.

[2] A typical remark is that of Herman Adalbert Daniel, who introduces his textual sudy of the *Dies Irae* with the remark that it is 'uno omnium consensu sacrae poeseos summum decus et ecclesiae latinae κειμήλιον . . . pretiosissimum' —*Thesaurus Hymnologicus*, II (Leipzig: J. A. Barthius, 1844), 112. The same scholar maintains that the *Stabat Mater Dolorosa* is likewise so perfect in its own way that it is impossible to institute a comparison between it and the *Dies Irae* in terms of intrinsic merit—*ibid.*, 137-38. Other similar encomia by Philip Schaff, Abraham Coles, J. M. Neale, and others may be found quoted by H. T. Henry in his articles *"Dies Irae," Catholic Encyclopedia*, IV, p. 788, and *"Stabat Mater," ibid.*, XIV, 240. Verdicts still current that the *Dies Irae* is "the greatest of all Latin hymns"—F. Brittain, *The Medieval Latin and Romance Lyric to* A.D. 1300 (Cambridge: Cambridge University Press, 1937), p. 197—seem to be intended as reaffirmations of accepted opinions formulated some decades ago rather than as judgments passed anew.

[3] See Samuel Willoughby Duffield, *The Latin Hymn-Writers and Their Hymns*, ed. and completed by R. E. Thompson (New York: Funk & Wagnalls, 1899), pp. 401-15, especially p. 407.

[4] "Fifty Versions of 'Dies Irae,'" *Dublin Review*, IX (1883), 56-57 (the article is unsigned).

[5] John Julian, *A Dictionary of Hymnology* (London: John Murray, 1915), pp. 299-301.

[6] Cf. Daniel, *op. cit.*, II, 137. Daniel is at some pains to show that there are some dissimilarities between the two hymns—the reason for his pains being that the similarities are so urgent and inescapable, as he himself notes.

[7] "Regarding, then, Beauty as my province [in composing "The Raven"], my next question referred to the *tone* of its highest manifestation—and all experience has shown that this tone is one of *sadness*"—"The Philosophy of Composition" (first pub. in *Graham's Magazine*, April, 1846), *The Complete Works of Edgar Allen Poe*, ed. by James A. Harrison (New York: Thomas Y. Crowell and Co., 1902), XIV, 198. Cf. also Wordsworth's typical association of beauty and foreboding ("I grew up fostered alike by beauty and by fear") reflected in the preface to the *Lyrical Ballads* and discussed by C. H. Herford, *The Age of Wordsworth* (London: G. Bell and Sons, Ltd., 1928), pp. 147 ff.

[8] A survey of work done since 1914 concerning this poetry is given by Theodore Spencer and Mark Van Doren, *Studies in Metaphysical Poetry* (New York: Columbia University Press, 1939).

[9] *Thesauri Hymnologici Prosarium*, Part Two, ed. by Cl[emens] Blume and H. M. Bannister ("Analecta Hymnica Medii Aevi," No. 54; Leipzig: O. R. Reisland, 1915-1922), I, 150. I leave the Latin poetry and prose untranslated

here throughout, as they were in the original appearance of this study in *Speculum*. The point about the Latin is most often its elaborate word-play, and word-play in its fullness obviously cannot be directly translated from one language to another, but has to be explained by elaborate grammatical and semantic analysis and lengthy paraphrase. Enough of such analysis and paraphrase is already given in my text to make the general movement of my argument evident. The Latin will fill in detail in proportion to the reader's familiarity with the language.

[10] *Explanatio in Canticum Beatae Mariae, Hugonis de S. Victore Opera Omnia*, I, in *Patrologiae [Latinae] Cursus Completus* (referred to hereafter as *PL*), ed. J.-P. Migne, CLXXV (Paris: Migne, 1854), col. 415.

[11] *Thes. Hymn. Pros.*, Part Two, I, 221.

[12] *Ibid.*, I, 220. Cf. *Eph.* iv, p. 8 ('captivam duxit captivitatem') and *Psalm* lxvii, 19.

[13] *Ibid.*, I, 249.

[14] *Ibid.*, I, 327.

[15] *De Emmanuele Libri Duo, Richardi a Sancto Victore Opera Omnia*, *PL* CXCVI (1855), col. 620. In *De Beatae Mariae Virginitate, Opera Omnia*, II, *PL* CLXXVI (1854), col. 872, Hugh of St. Victor treats of the allied question of why the Holy Spirit is not Christ's father according to the flesh since it was He who miraculously brought about Christ's conception of the Virgin Mary (*Luke*, I, 35).

[16] *Sermo CLXXXIV* (In Natali Domini Nostri Jesu Christi, i), *Sancti Aurelii Augustini Opera Omnia*, V[1], *PL* XXXVIII (1845), col. 997.

[17] *The Poems of John Donne*, ed. by Herbert J. C. Grierson (Oxford: Clarendon Press, 1912), I, 369.

[18] *The Life and Letters of John Donne*, ed. by Edmund Gosse (London: William Heinemann, 1899), I, 103.

[19] *Thes. Hymn. Pros.*, Part Two, I, 384.

[20] See *John*, XIII, 12-17; *Philippians*, II, 5-12.

[21] See G. R. Owst, *Literature and Pulpit in Medieval England* (Cambridge: Cambridge University Press, 1933), pp. 56-109.

[22] *Thes. Hymn. Pros.*, Part Two, I, 227-28.

[23] *Ibid.*, I, 154.

[24] *Ibid.*, II, 376.

[25] *Hymnographi Latini*, II, ed. by Guido Maria Dreves ("Analecta Hymnica Medii Aevi," No. 50; Leipzig: O. R. Reisland, 1907), 586.

[26] *Summa Theologica*, Pars. III, q. 60, a. 6, esp. obj. 3 and *ad* 3. Quotations and citations from St. Thomas Aquinas's prose works are all made from the *Opera Omnia*, ed. Stanislaus Eduardus Fretté and Paulus Maré (34 vols; Paris: Ludovicus Vives, 1871-1880).

[27] *Sermo CXC* (In Natali Domini, vii), *Opera Omnia*, v[1], *PL* XXXVIII (1845), col. 1008: 'Quis est iste infans? Infans enim dicitur, quod non possit fari, id est loqui. Ergo et infans et Verbum est.' Cf. *Ennaratio in Psalmum XLIV Opera Omnia*, IV[1], *PL* XXXVI (1845), col. 495.

[28] Quoted by T. S. Eliot, "Lancelot Andrewes," *Selected Essays,* 1917-1932 (New York: Harcourt, Brace, and Co., 1932), p. 297.

[29] *Collected Poems,* 1909-1935 (London: Faber and Faber, 1936, p. 37):
> The word within a word unable to speak a word
> Swaddled with darkness.

[30] Dom André Willmart, O.S.B., 'La tradition littéraire et textuelle de l' "Adoro de deuote," ' *Recherches de théologie ancienne et médiévale,* I (1929), 159. The "latens deitas" is not, however, the work of by any means so thick a wit as the "latens hostia"! of one manuscript which Dom Willmart cites. The attribution of this poem to St. Thomas Aquinas hardly admits any longer of serious doubt: see F. J. E. Raby, "The Date and Authorship of the Poem *Adoro Te Deuote," Speculum,* xx (1945), 236-38.

[31] Dom Willmart's text, *loc cit.* In *Hymnog. Lat.,* II, 589, the lines are only slightly different:
> Credo, quidquid dixit Dei Filius
> Verbo veritatis nihil verius.

[32] "The Lyfe of Jhon Picus," *The Workes of Sir Thomas More,* ed. by William Rastell (London, 1557), p. 2.

[33] Act I, Scene vii, *The Complete Work of Shakespeare,* ed. by W. J. Craig (London: Oxford University Press, 1935), p. 983.

[34] *Hymnog. Lat.,* II, 584.

[35] "Pâque," *Dictionnaire de la Bible,* ed. by F. Vigoroux (12th ed.; Paris: Letouzey et Ané, 1912), IV^2, 2094.

[36] *Verbum Supernum, Hymnog. Lat.,* II, 588. Cf. St. Augustine's "Verbum . . . ibi manens, hinc procedens," *Sermo CLXXXVII* (In Natali Domini iv), *Opera Omnia,* v^1, *PL* xxxviii (1845), col. 1001.

[37] Pierre Pourrat, *La spiritualité chrétienne* (Paris: J. Gabalda et Fils, 1928), II, 229, 253, 275. The *Meditations on the Life of Christ* once erroneously attributed to St. Bonaventure but certainly written by a thirteenth century Franciscan under the influence of St. Bernard of Clairvaux are typical of this school. Of them Pourrat notes: 'Elles se proposent de faire aimer le Christ, moins par des élévations sur sa doctrine divine que par le récit de sa vie mortelle. Les considérations font place aux descriptions colorées. . . . C'est l'humanité du Christ qui est ainsi mise en un puissant relief' (pp. 282-83).

[38] On the "torment" associated with courtly love, see A. J. Denomy, "An Inquiry into the Origins of Courtly Love," *Medieval Studies,* VI (1944), 183-185. I do not, of course, mean to imply by this connection between courtly love and devotional life any of the facile connections between courtly love and Christian mysticism which have at times been attempted and which are dismissed in Father Denomy's excellent study (pp. 188-92).

[39] *Thes. Hymn. Pros.,* Part Two, I, 312.

[40] *Ibid.,* 269.

[41] Act IV, Scene i, *The Complete Works of Shakespeare,* p. 994.

[42] Raby, "The Date and Authorship of the Poem *Adoro Te Deuote," loc. cit.*

[43] Dom Willmart's text, "La tradition littéraire et textuelle de l' 'Adoro te deuote,' " *loc. cit.*

[44] Raby, "The Date and Authorship of the Poem *Adoro Te Deuote*," *op. cit.*, p. 237; "eueste" should apparently be "queste."—Beyond that furnished here by Jacopone, there is other evidence of the tendency on the part of those who follow Thomas to disregard the keenness of his perceptions: see the remarks made above (p. 96) concerning textual corruptions in the "Adoro Te Devote."

[45] A familiar instance would be the *Ave Maris Stella*, written between the sixth and ninth centuries, which uses the common witty conceit developed from the fact that the Blessed Virgin has been hailed by the Angel Gabriel with the word *Ave*, which is *Eva* reversed and by reason of this fact hits off Mary's role as the "Second Eve," the antithesis of the first woman: "Mutans nomen Evae"—*Thesauri Hymnologici Hymnarium*, I, ed. by Clemens Blume ("Analecta Hymnica Medii Aevi," No. 51; Leipzig: O. R. Reisland, 1908), 140. Or there is the sixth-century *Vexilla Regis* of Venantius Fortunatus, in which Christ, Who is Life Itself, undergoes death to make life available to man:

Qua vita mortem pertulit
Et morte vitam reddidit

—*Hymnog. Lat.*, II, 74. Instances could be multiplied indefinitely.

[46] "Poetica scientia est de his quae propter defectum veritatis non possunt a ratione capi; unde oportet quod quasi quibusdam similitudinibus ratio seducatur: theologia autem est de his quae sunt supra rationem; et ideo modus symbolicus utrique communis est, cum neutra rationi proportionetur"—*In Sententias Petri Lombardi Commentaria*, prolog., q. 1, a. 5 ad 3. Cf. *In I Posteriorum Analyticorum Aristotelis Expositio*, lect. 1, where Thomas places poetic as a logic below the strict logic of scientific demonstration and also below the other logics of probability realized in dialectic and rhetoric. In the case of poetic, he says, "sola existimatio declinat in aliquam partem contradictionis propter aliquam repraesentaticnem."

[47] "Ex hoc ipso quod intellectus noster accipit a phantasmatibus, sequitur in ipso quod scientiam habeat collativam, inquantum ex multis sensibus fit una memoria, et ex multis memoriis unum experimentum, et ex multis experimentis unum universale principium, ex quo alia concludit."—*In III Sent.*, d. 14, q. 1, a. 3, sol. 3; cf. *In II Sent.*, d. 3, q. 1, a. 2 sol.; d. 39, q. 3, a. 1 sol.

[48] See *In I Post. Anal.*, lect. 1, and cf. my article, "The Province of Rhetoric and Poetic," *Modern Schoolman*, XIX (1942), 24-7.

[49] *Ars Poetica*, in *The Oxford Anthology of American Literature*, ed. by William Rose Benét and Norman Holmes Pearson (New York: Oxford University Press, 1941), p. 1501.

[50] See St. Thomas, *De Veritate*, q. 8, a. 15. An excellent and unusually discerning treatment of Thomas's observations on the various intellective processes, together with the relevant texts from Thomas's various works, which it would take too much space to list and discuss here, is to be found in Bernard Lonergan, "The Concept of *Verbum* in the Writings of St. Thomas Aquinas," *Theological Studies*, VII (1946), 349-92, esp. 384 ff.

[51] "Quaedam namque vera sunt de Deo, quae omnem facultatem humanae

rationis excedunt, ut Deum esse trinum et unum. Quaedam vero sunt ad quae etiam ratio naturalis pertingere potest, sicut est Deum esse, Deum esse unum, et alia hujusmodi."—*Contra Gentiles,* lib. 1, c. 3.

[52] *In I Sent.,* prolog. S. Thomae. Thomas here opens with the quotation from *Ecclus.* XXIV, 40: "Ego sapientia effudi flumine; ego quasi trames aquae immensae de fluvio; ego quasi fluvius Diorix, et sicut aquaeductus exivi de paradiso. Dixi: Rigabo hortum plantationum, et inebriabo partus mei fructum." On the theme provided by this text, he elaborates the whole sweep of God's plan for created being in terms of the revelation of the Trinity and the consequent initiation of rational creatures into God's interior life, both effected by the Incarnation.

[53] *Contra Gent.,* lib. 1, c. 7.

[54] *Ibid.,* c. 8; *Sum. Theol.,* I, q. 32, a. 1.

[55] Thomas comes back to this subject time and time again; e.g., *In I Sent.,* d. 3, q. 1; *In III Sent.,* d. 23; *De Ver.,* q. 14; *Sum. Theol.,* I, q. 32; etc.

[56] For Thomas's observations on this point, see P. Hoenen, "De Origine Primorum Principiorum Scientiae," *Gregorianum,* XIV (1933), 152-84.

[57] In the plenary act of human understanding providing insight into a principle such as the principle of contradiction, experience itself gives direct content to the dictum "Intellectus in actu est intellectum in actu" (cf. *Sum. Theol.,* I, q. 14, a. 2; q. 55, a. 1 ad 2; etc.), although human intellection never achieves the perfect identification of intellect and object found in divine intellection. Cf. Thomas's way of speaking of first principles as "prima principia quorum est intellectus" (*In III Sent.,* d. 23, q. 2, a. 2, sol. 1): back of this expression lies the fact that to have these principles before the mind is simply to understand; they are in themselves totally perspicuous: cf. *Sum. Theol.,* I, q. 64, a. 2, resp.; *In Boetii de Trinitate,* q. 2, a. 1 ad 5.

[58] Cf. Hoenen, "De Origine Primorum Principiorum Scientiae," *op. cit.,* 179-84.

[59] It is in the imagination that mathematics is validated, St. Thomas points out, and not directly in the senses. See Jacques Maritain, *Science and Wisdom,* trans. by Bernard Wall (New York: Charles Scribner's Sons, 1940), p. 39, and Lonergan, "The Concept of *Verbum* in the Writings of St. Thomas Aquinas," *op. cit.,* 374-75; cf. Thomas's observations on the conditions of mathematical infinity, as in *Sum. Theol.,* I, q. 7, a. 3 ad 1. One might note that this implies that Thomas's notion of mathematics was quite open to non-Euclidianism.

[60] *Psalm* XXXV, 10; *Sum. Theol.,* I, q. 12, a. 2, resp.

[61] *Sum. Theol.,* I, q. 1, a. 5, resp.

[62] *De Ver.,* q. 14, a. 2, resp.: "a fide communiter accepta secundum quam credere dicimur id quod vehementer opinamur, scilicet vel testimonio alicujus hominis"; a. 8, resp.: "Per se objectum fidei veritas prima est. . . . Unde neque hominis neque angeli testimonio assentire infallibiliter in veritatem duceret, nisi quantum in eis loquentis Dei testimonium consideratur." Cf. *In I Post. Anal.,* lect. 1.

[63] II *Cor.* v. 6; *Sun. Theol.,* II¹, q. 4, a. 5, resp.

⁶⁴ Michel d' Herbigny, *La théologie du Révélé* (Paris: Gabriel Beauchesne, 1921), pp. 163-65.

⁶⁵ τὸ μυστήριον: *Eph.* iii, 8-12. For a discussion of "the mystery," see Fernand Prat, *The Theology of St. Paul*, I, trans. from the 11th French ed. by John L. Stoddard (London: Burns, Oates, and Washbourne, Ltd., 1927), 308-9, and II, trans. from the 10th French ed. by John L. Stoddard (London: Burns, Oates, and Washbourne, Ltd., 1926), 5-8, 42, 383-85.

⁶⁶ *Rom.* ix, 32-33. Cf. *I Cor.*, I, 23-24.

⁶⁷ *Epistola CXX, Opera Omnia*, II, *PL* XXXIII (1845), col. 453-54. See Etienne Gilson, *Introduction à l'étude de Saint Augustin* (Paris: J. Vrin, 1931), pp. 34 ff.

⁶⁸ "Extra significantiam sermonis est, extra sensus intentionem, extra intelligentiae conceptionem"—*De Trinitate*, lib. 2, n. 5, *Opera Omnia*, II, *PL* x (1845), col. 54.

⁶⁹ A historical survey of patristic and medieval thought on this matter is given by Henri de Lubac, *Surnaturel: Etudes historiques* (Paris: Aubier, 1946), pp. 328-94.

⁷⁰ Speaking particularly of Richard of St. Victor and St. Bonaventure, concerning this vacillation and the state of mind responsible for it Matthias Joseph Scheeben has an illuminating statement: "The procedure of these two kindred souls [Bonaventure and Richard] is attributable to their point of view, which is contemplative rather than analytic. Their ecstatic spirits take flight to the heights which faith points out to them: and when they look about them with their natural reason, everything seems as near and obvious to them as objects that reason actually perceives by itself. The arguments they adduce for the Trinity really prove, that is, they are objectively sound; and in the supposition of their truth the conclusion follows with evident necessity, at least to some extent. But when their glance travels back along the path of reason, they assert that the basis for the Trinity is a 'truth that transcends reason' (Richard, *Benjamin minor*, lib. IV, cc. 2, 3); and in one passage St. Bonaventure says expressly: 'The Trinity of persons is not knowable by a creature who ascends by way of reason from the creature to God' (*I Sent.*, d. 3, a. 1, q. 4). According to Richard (*loc. cit.*), the mind can attain to objects that surpass reason only when it is joined to faith: 'In the investigation, discussion and assertion of these objects, the human reason accomplishes absolutely nothing unless it is joined to faith.' "—*The Mysteries of Christianity*, trans. by Cyril Vollert, S.J. (St. Louis: B. Herder Book Co., 1946), p. 39, n. 19. This book has an excellent treatment of the Christian mysteries in general.

⁷¹ Council of Sens, 1140 or 1141 A.D.—*Enchiridion Symbolorum*, ed. by Henricus Denziger, Clemens Bannwart, and Johannes Bapt. Umberg (21-23d ed.: Freiburg-im-Breisgau, 1937), n. 368 (p. 179).

⁷² "Duo enim simulacra erant proposita homini, in quibus invisibilia videre potuisset: unum naturae, et unum gratiae. Simulacrum naturae erat species hujus mundi. Simulacrum autem gratiae erat humanitas Verbi."—*Commen-*

tariorum in Hierarchiam Coelestem S. Dionysii Areopagitae Libri X, lib. I, c. I, *Opera Omnia*, I, *PL* CLXXV (1854), col. 926.

[73] In 1870, when the Vatican Council undertook to formulate, in terms taken from the theology grown up around the question, a definitive description of the condition of Christian doctrine with relation to the human reasoning process, its declarations came to the same thing as Thomas's regarding the distinction between naturally known and supernaturally known truths, and, like Thomas, it declared that the deposit of faith contains "mysteria proprie dicta."—Denziger, Bannwart, Umberg (eds.), *Enchiridion Symb.*, nn. 1796, 1816 (pp. 496, 500).

[74] For a survey of recent opinion here, see Spenser and Van Doren, *op. cit.*, and Helen C. White, *The Metaphysical Poets* (New York: The Macmillan Company, 1936), pp. 70 ff.

[75] "Of Wit," in *The English Writings of Abraham Cowley*, ed. by A. R. Waller, [Vol. I], *Poems* ("Cambridge English Classics"; Cambridge: The University Press, 1905), p. 16.

[76] In Charles Sears Baldwin, *Medieval Rhetoric and Poetic* (New York: The Macmillan Company, 1928), p. 200, quoted from E. du Méril, *Poésies populaires du moyen âge* (Paris, 1847), p. 153.

SEVEN

The Myth of Myth

DIALOGUE WITH THE UNSPOKEN

I

WHEN literary and philosophical discussion join today, the subject of myth must be placed high on the list of agenda. Intellectual interests seem to develop in clusters; and myth is not only the nucleus of one of the larger clusters today, but is a peculiarly amoebalike nucleus which engulfs the discussions which gather around it. Questions concerning the nature of metaphor, image, and symbol, and of the very nature of poetry and of expression itself, tend to be reinterpreted in terms of myth. The cult of semantics which seeks to reform existence by a revision of symbols is a kind of projection of the mythological mind.

The voraciousness of myth in devouring related or adjacent subjects and converting them into its own substance cannot be better illustrated than by an actual occurrence at a scholarly meeting held not long ago. A professor in a well known university had delivered a paper with the avowed intent of cutting under the question of myth to secure other bases for treatment. (He had described himself as "a kind of pre-Paul Elmer More humanist.") As the applause trickled away, the chairman of the discussion arose.

"This brilliant disclaimer of myth," he announced, "has only served to bring out the inevitability of myth in a new light. It contests the existence of certain myths in Shakespeare, but you cannot do this, of course, without automatically supposing others. The most you can say is that myth in Shakespeare isn't the kind of myth we thought it was. Does anyone have anything to add to my remarks?" No one had.

Those who are familiar with the literature on myth worked over here, or with the discussion which weaves its way through avant-garde literary circles today, will know that the treatment given myth is often tortuous and groping, and occasionally loses its way. It is bewildered, and occasionally betrayed, by the confusion of interpretative theories which beset it on all sides. And yet, whether conducted under the aegis of the ritualist theory or as an attack on this theory, whether literary or anti-literary, the study of myth seems always to be pursuing pretty much the same game. The literature on myth is extensive and growing. A convenient résumé and bibliography can be found in the invaluable *Theory of Literature* by René Wellek and Austin Warren;[1] and some of the newer material is gone over in Stanley Edgar Hyman's "Myth, Ritual, and Nonsense" in the *Kenyon Review*.[2] If, as Mr. Hyman remarks at the opening of the article just cited, there is more than one way to skin a myth, it is also true that, no matter who does the skinning or how, myth skins all come from the same sort of animal. Beneath all the discussion and conflicting theory, there seems to be one central reality which has caught everyone's attention. There are regular hunting preserves over which the chase moves.

In terms of the conditions of the human intellect in its relations with the finite being toward which it is immediately faced, one can, I believe, plot the general area with which myth and mythology have to do. Such a plotting will not, of course, adequately settle all the questions agitated in the name of myth; but it will perhaps provide some insights into the question as to why the study of myth proves as intriguing as it does, and it will point to some of the connections between myth and current literary speculation. The attempt here will be to indicate a general framework for mythological discussion rather than to assign particular writers or theories to their place within the framework.

II

A prima-facie response to the term "myth" today would take the term as applying to a story having to do with religion which is circulated as true and taken as such by people who unfortunately are not so advanced as we are. This prima-facie meaning has a long history which need not be detailed here. It has evidently come far since the Greeks originally used the word *mythos* to signify a word, speech, or some sort of vocalized sound, and is only remotely related to Aristotle's use of the same term as signifying the plot of a play (but notice the parallel English "fable" for "plot").

Closely allied to this prima-facie meaning is the use of the word "myth" to signify a story featuring preternatural persons or personifications which is historically untrue. With this meaning, there grows another more sophisticated meaning: myth is such a story, which does not represent any truth of history, considered in terms of what truth it can be said to represent—that is, in terms of almost anything but historical truth. This concept involves, it will be seen, dealing with truth by a kind of indirection. The myth is told in the form of history —it is said that Prometheus did steal fire from heaven for man—though it is precisely as history that validity is wanting to myth. What is not is here employed after a fashion as a surrogate for what is.

This economy of indirection provides the real setting for what we may call the concept of myth in its quintessential form. As this term settles down in current discussion to a definitive meaning, it comes eventually to refer to the nonexplicit complement accompanying any body of expression, story or not, when this complement is considered as forming a whole. It is what is expressed indirectly precisely in so far as it is expressed indirectly. Myth in this sense is that which fills in the voids between man's abstractions.[3] It is, more quizzically and pointedly, what one says when one says something else. Exponents of myth do not always put it so outspokenly as this; but if a person holds this description in mind as he trails along through mythological treatises, particularly those of the more heady kind, he will find himself able to identify most of the game which will be disappearing into the bushes around him.

The concept of myth here is shaped by a condition of human knowledge. Large bodies of more or less general statements roughly connected with one another carry with them a kind of substructure of suppositions, unexpressed and even unformulated, but more or less definitely implied. For example, the more or less general statements centered about the "doctrine" of "progress" have beneath them a definite body of suppositions, many of them not yet conceptualized, not yet brought to light. So with the things that have been said in the name of democracy, of humanitarianism, and so on.

Such suppositions are hardly on the tip of everyone's tongue. They are discovered only slowly after a good deal about humanitarianism or democracy or what have you has been ventilated and acted upon. Before they are discovered and formulated, conceptualized, where are these suppositions? And what are they? They are not yet abstract statements, formally constituted truths. Yet one can consider them as forming some sort of whole, delimited by what has been explicitly said.

Indeed, it is in a sense this whole which bestows on "democracy" what unity it has; for the formally enunciated tenets of democracy or humanitarianism often seem in themselves at odds with one another, hard to reconcile with one another as they stand in themselves, unsupported by further explanation. The student of such a thing as democracy has often as his task the discovery of the unifying element. He seeks to formulate the underlying, as yet unconceptualized, but somehow unified body of "suppositions."

The fact that his work is often styled a search attests the fact that the suppositions are indeed somehow there before he "discovers" or formulates them. They have been in some way a coherent thing even before their discovery or formulation—we need not wait on this formulation in order to apprehend democracy as a unified thing. These suppositions are the "myth," *so long, that is, as they are not formulated.* For myth, in this ultimate sense, is the unconceptualized undertrussing or complement supporting bodies of human statement and conveyed in them precisely in so far as this undertrussing remains an unconceptualized but somehow intrinsically coherent whole.

One might make this theorem absolute and say, instead of "bodies of human statement," simply "any human statement," for it would seem that suppositions of the sort here styled myth accompany any human utterance, even the most simple. For the present, however, it will suffice to restrict ourselves to the more obvious cases of myth, those implied and defined in bodies of human statement of some extent, such as the myth of Shakespeare's *Macbeth* or the myth of democracy.

Those interested in myth in the sense just explained like to point out that such myth will never be completely formulated. There will always be a residue of unformulated myth after every formulation. Put another way, this sounds not so disquieting. It means that any body of connected human statement will, first, be limited, and, secondly, will have certain things implicit in it, no matter how far it is refined. Total human statement is impossible.

This does not at all mean that all human statement is enveloped in falsehood; much less does it mean that human statement—that especially which is concerned with ultimates—is devoid of content, although there is a temptation, often given in to, to falsify the records just a little bit and make things come out this way. What is does mean is that it is impossible to say something which does not run off at the margin into things not said. It means that it is impossible to put a statement so that nothing *about* it can be misunderstood. This is not the same as saying that I cannot make myself clear about anything; it is only to say that in making myself clear about one thing, I shall always be hinting obscurely at other things about which I am not clear.

Expression in human terms, in other words, is not all act, but is quite replete with potency. This is to say no more than that human statement, like all things finite, is not self-contained, not pure act, but is faced outward to other things—ultimately to God, Who is not this way because He does not in Himself admit of explanation, but is rather explanation itself.

III

The economy of indirection exploited by myth and mythology derives ultimately from a peculiar devotion to the potential coefficient as such in finite being.

The explicit and the implicit in human statement are related to each other as act and potency. Somewhat as man is what he is (his essence can be predicated of him directly), so a human statement is what is explicitly said. But this very "what" has a certain obliquity about it. What a man is (his essence) carries with it what he is not (for example, his intellect, which is a potency). Similarly, finite expression has about it an obliquity, an indirection. Each implicit statement carries with it something it is not, an implicit, which is a kind of potency. In devoting itself to this implicit something, to the indirect in human statement precisely as it is indirect, the study of myth is capitalizing on the potential coefficient in human expression.

Moreover, the study of myth exploits this potential coefficient in human expression in a curiously dramatic, all-out fashion. Myth admits of not only a scientific, but a mythological exegesis, an exegesis which is not explicit, as that of the philosopher would be, but implicit and non-abstractional. Asked what his myth means, the mythmaker may well answer by another myth. In doing so, he not only attends to the potential component in expression, but does so in such a way as to honor this potential component in the very process.

There is a way to attend to the potential coefficient in terms of act after the fashion of philosophical explanation, which makes the implicit explicit and then deals in the explicit as such. Even so, of course, the philosopher has attaching to his explanation so executed certain implicit and still-to-be-explained areas. But it is to the others, to the explicit areas, that he attends. He seeks increased explicitness.

The mythmaker does otherwise. Aware of the implicit areas which attach to human statement, he prefers to keep clear as far as possible of explicit statement as such. To be sure, as he refines his implicit meaning, he must resort to statement in some way explicit; but he keeps the explicitness as far as possible irrelevant. Prometheus did not really steal fire from heaven, as he is said explicitly to have done, and Pandora's box, historically and explicitly considered, is a hoax.

Such a retreat into implicitness may conceivably be tantamount to a denial of the right to philosophize, but it need not be so. The mythmaker may be hinting that his is the only way to possess truth (the term "truth" being thereupon given a curiously introverted and tortured meaning)—that is, that truth can be known not expressly at all but only implicitly. This is modernism, or something pretty close to it. It seems to be the ultimate position not only of Gnosticism, but also of much Protestantism, as well as of most unattached high-flown religious speculation today. As to whether it is doctrine or no, one can only say that in this matter it keeps a little o' the windy side of the law, being simply the assumption that there is no such thing as explicit truth, together with the refusal to state the assumption explicitly. Any deficiencies it may have are amply covered by sheer elusiveness. It rejects any sort of explicit statement, even of its own position.

But the mythmaker need not assume this pose and deny all right to philosophize. He may simply forego philosophical activity without denying its validity. If his retreat from explanation into further myth comes to this, it is of course unobjectionable. Everyone does not have to philosophize when requested to do so. And the mythmaker as such does indeed have access to reality in a fashion which the philosopher or other scientist as such is obliged to forego. Though it be good and even necessary, given the conditions of human intellection, explicitation is not an unmixed good, for human intellection is not perfect intellection. It might be remarked that whereas Christ explained some parables by making their reference explicit, others he explained by still further parables, and still others he let sink in without explanation.

Although myth as such dwells very much in the never-never land of potency between the *is* and the *is not,* and, although this land has its disadvantages and is, in its way, unreal, one must not pretend that it is a territory unknown to man or dangerous to him. It is the territory man has to do with directly; and if he has difficulty in exploring it, this is not because he has or should have nothing to do with it, but because it has limitations which he shares. It is not pure act, pure being.

IV

In terms of its preoccupation with the potential coefficient of reality, the connection of myth with philosophical and theological interests on one side and with literary interests on the other can be seen. One notes immediately that the study of myth rides along with the interest in evolution and development which has marked the philosophical thought of the past two centuries and which is an interest not directly in existence, but in potency and becoming.

Evolution may be considered as referred to the world of being or to the world of knowing. Within the latter world, one notes a close approximation between "myth" in the sense discussed here and the earlier, likewise baffling, expressions "spirit," "idea," or "ethos"—for example, the "spirit" or "idea" or "ethos" of progress, of democracy, of the machine, Newman's "idea" of a university or "idea" of Christianity or the other "ideas" which, in *An Essay on the Development of Christian Doctrine,* he instances as undergoing development. The term "myth" can be applied to all these items to which the earlier terms applied and today is actually so applied to many or most of them.

A too innocent idealism might like to suppose that these "ideas" and the entire Hegelian world with which they connect are matters of pure intellectuality and intellectual formulation, that one is here in a world of complete abstraction and hence of complete formulation—of act in this sense rather than of potency. However, as it comes down to us from the mechanistic and mathematical philosophies through the associationist, the "idea" does not represent a full-fledged abstraction as such at all, but a semiabstraction, a concept with its accompanying phantasm, or perhaps a phantasm regarded as prolific of concepts.

Hence it is that the idea can evolve. Maintaining a special rapport with matter, it can have a history suggesting its close connection with material beings, whose very essences are partly potency, a developmental history such as an entirely spiritual thing could not have.[4] It is no accident that the editors of the *Journal of the History of Ideas* have made this sort of "idea," and not the concept, the object of their study.

Discussion of being in terms of "ideas" is discussion which fixes as its ultimate division of being not potency and act, but rather mixtures polarized toward one or the other of these two ultimates. The characteristic result of this procedure, observable in the tradition of Hegelian dialectic, is a series of exercises on the theme of becoming, exercises which can be started from any point whatsoever and protracted in a potentially infinite series, operations in the realm of the still-to-be-realized—legitimate operations, be it said, provided the operator knows what he is operating with and is prepared to pay for startling insights the high, but perhaps not exorbitant, fee of constant intellectual feverishness and overstimulation.

As much as this is the world of Hegel, it is also the world of current speculation in myth, where explanation is always big with promise which it never quite brings to term. It is also the closely adjoining world of Freud, where explanation is oriented—not perversely or arbitrarily, but inevitably—toward sex, which is a set not toward existence, but toward becoming. It is an annoying world, and by definition and intent an incomplete one, but it is far from a fruitless world.

The "ism" mentality which rules much philosophical thought today finds in this same world its natural habitat. For the "isms" are of a piece with "ideas," putting in their appearance under the same auspices and becoming discernible only as interest in "ideas" gathered momentum. It is hard to believe that ancient languages, and even modern languages up to recent times, could be so devoid as they are of terms and apparatus for handling "isms." The "isms" put in their appearance late, for they are simply "ideas" considered less in point of their reference to knowledge and more in function of an analogy with real being. "Communism" is a fraction more substantial than the "idea of communist society."

V

The economy of indirection and ultimately of potency which is exploited by myth and determines its relationship with philosophical thought also governs the connections of myth with subjects of current literary interest. Several such subjects were mentioned at the beginning of this article: metaphor, image, symbol, the nature of poetry and of human expression, and the cult of semantics.

The fact that current literary theory has been so dominated by interest in metaphor is highly symptomatic. Metaphor is the rhetorical device of indirection par excellence, a kind of apotheosis of indirection as such (as its Greek etymology and the Latin term for the same thing, *translatio*, both attest), the use of a term which has been attached to one concept for another concept. The currency in all quarters of questions turning on metaphor has been both a symptom of the interest in indirection and a spur to develop the interest further.

Development of this interest naturally extended to consideration of the symbol and image, concerning both of which there is so great a bulk of contemporary literature. The symbol and the image are not only, like metaphor, variants on the theme of indirection played by myth; they are also the products of a movement away from abstraction toward a kind of implicitness and hence have an affinity with myth on a second score. Coleridge, whose discussion of the symbol still lives in literary theory and practice, sees the symbol precisely as a flight from abstraction, a relief from the sort of thing encountered in allegory. Allegory is merely "a translation of abstract notions into a picture-language, which is itself nothing but an abstraction from objects of the senses," whereas a symbol

is characterized by a translucence of the special [the others of the species] in the individual, or of the general [the diverse species of the genus] in the special . . . ; above all by the translucence of the enternal through and in the temporal. It always partakes of the reality which it renders intelligible, and while it enunciates the whole, abides itself as a living part in that unity of which it is the representative.[5]

In its ability to be representative while escaping after a fashion from being a genuine abstraction, the symbol can be regarded as a kind of universal concept in disguise. With its aid, the mythmaker can achieve a sort of universality by hinting, a universality a little less than explicit, just as he would wish it to be. When literary theory talks symbol, it is very much in the territory frequented by myth.

The relationship between myth and poetry which makes metaphor, image, and symbol standard equipment for both is established by the fact that poetry does not restrict itself to the conceptual ranges of human knowledge as such, but carries on a traffic with the infraconceptual as well. Hence discussion of the nature of poetry itself tends to cover the same sort of ground as discussion of myth.[6] The resemblances between poetry as such and myth are, indeed, remarkably close; for, as against other types of art such as music, poetry carries on its dealings with the infraconceptual by a kind of indirection. The materials with which it operates, words, are quite different from musical sounds in that they are explicitly vehicles for concepts rather than for the infraconceptual, with which they are concerned only obliquely.

But the interest in metaphor and allied subjects which feeds back and forth between myth and poetry feeds on out even further from the consideration of the nature of poetry into the treatment of discourse as such and into the knotty field of semantics. I. A. Richards and others after him have made their chief point concerning metaphor the fact that it should be regarded not as an "ornament" but as a device natural and inevitable in speech.[7] And so, indeed, it is. The result of Mr. Richards's insistence here has been to import into the entire field of communication or expression as such the emphases common to myth and poetry—the emphases on indirection and, ultimately, on the potential coefficient in human knowledge and expression. As has been noted earlier here, some sort of indirection can indeed be discovered everywhere if that is what you are after. There are analogies between the indirection of poetry and myth and the limited, finite condition of other forms of human expression. If there has been a tendency in some quarters to make things exciting, but just a little too simple, by expanding analogies into equations, by hinting that even with Basic English the communications system at the level of explicitation is at root an illusion—maybe the Chinese simply *never* understand what we are saying—this sort of heady speculation can perhaps be written off as sheer overenthusiasm.

Interest in the implicitness of language feeds also into most of the views which seek to find salvation for man in linguistic operations or attitudes and which ride the current of literary speculation rather high today. Such would be the views of Alfred Korzybski and his disciples, who propose the semantic solution for personal and cosmic problems, or of the earlier Richards, with his hopes in poetry as the instrument of salvation for man. Views such as these are generated by an awareness of the disorder which often lies not so much in explicit expression as in implicit suppositions. Korzybski proposes to operate rather directly on the suppositions.[8] Richards had looked for a more indirect approach: good poetry was to do away with the disorder at the infraconceptual level.[9]

VI

For all the wealth of insight it provides and for all its usefulness, it is quite possible for preoccupation with myth to become sterile and degenerate into an elaborate hoax. This it does when it pretends to preclude or to overrule the abstractive disciplines. When it does this, it will not do so explicitly, let alone theoretically, for the reason that there is no explicit mythical theory available *in terms of myth*. When myth precludes or overrules the abstractive disciplines, pretending that it is only the myth as such that can be true and/or ultimate, it will do so by implication, mythically.

This is the way the cult of myth operated in Nazi Germany. It is the way it operates in the Soviet Union, where an aberrant science is quickly brought to heel. It is the way it tends to operate in America when the myth of "Americanism" rather than fact is made the basis of the Ku Klux Klan or any of various other nativist movements. (It might be noted that the explicitation of its dogma and, even more basically, the fact that it is, and conceives of itself as, a concrete body of persons keep the Catholic Church as a reality essentially independent of any myth of "Catholicism" which might develop.[10] Significantly, the Apostles' Creed does not read, "I believe in Catholicism," but "I believe in . . . the Holy Catholic Church.")

Too complete devotion to myth which decries all explicitation is based on an obsession with a half-truth. It is one thing, however, to know that nothing is absolute, complete act, but God. And it is another thing to hint that no explicitation of expression can be a *participation* in the absolute, that it must be an illusion.

Myth should, to be sure, serve as a kind of corrective to those who want to make too much of explicitation. The foes of myth have been at times guilty of false emphases here. An insidious rationalism has wanted more ultimates than God Himself. Under the spell of this rationalism, it is possible to make too much of "eternal truths"—which in fact, only in so far as they are identified with God, are strictly eternal.

There is no rack of "eternal principles" alongside God where one can shelve the various sciences and all reality. Certainly, there are explicit principles; and these are true exactly as we know them. But it is not *as we know them* that they are eternal. They are eternal as God knows them. God knows the principle of contradiction in its cause, namely Himself. He does not see His existence in terms of such a principle, as we do. He sees the principle in terms of His existence, which is His essence, which is *the* eternal. Before creation, there was God and that was all.

When, in honoring the limitations and enigmatic character of our dealings with reality as this is carried out on the finite plane, the pursuit of myth works against the tendency to make a set of abstractions do for God, it does well. But it does entirely too well when it hints that all explicitation, any explicit participation in the absolute, is an illusion. In so far as it so hints, the study of myth is a hoax; for, whatever it may pretend, myth does employ explicit statement and thereby attests to the presence of the explicit in the world. For, just as there is no total human statement, no total explicitness, so *there is no total myth*, no total implicitness.

The total or pure myth would be a story, not without words, but one in which the words were devoid of any explicit meaning—each word, that is, quite undifferentiated from the others. This would be a sort of pure intellectual potency posing as expressive of something—in short, as act. Popularly, it might well be described as universal intellectual balderdash.

It is a lie to pretend that all the mythmaker does is hint, that in any given case *all* can be indirection. The myth operates in a world apprehended in terms of explicitation as well as of myth. The story of Prometheus is not a little influenced by explicitly apprehended truths about fire—for example, that it cooks things—though the influence of these truths is not felt in the same way as it is in scientific statement. Indeed, it is in function of the residue of abstraction of which it can never rid itself that one myth will fall back upon another for "explanation."

Practically speaking, literary study of myth today is often inclined to succumb to a self-intoxication, hinting that all explicitation is an illusion and that ultimately in myth alone is any meaningful apprehension of reality to be found. In this land of indirection, to steer clear of this position, it is hardly sufficient to avoid stating it explicitly—for here it is to what is *not* stated that one particularly lends ear. To keep clear of the implication—and, indeed, to keep oneself clear of the supposition—it is rather necessary once in a while to state the opposite.

Mythological study is in a peculiar position with regard to anthropology and psychoanalysis. These two disciplines have not only in various ways pursued the study of myth, but, in the popular mind, have become myths themselves. In the land occupied jointly by anthropology and psychoanalysis, it is felt that there sits some court of ultimate appeal, vaguely presided over by the dimly luminescent figures of Sir James George Frazer and Freud, flanked perhaps by Jung and Lévy-Brühl. Before this court of appeal, the popular myth has it, all human activities are somehow to be arraigned—those which have not been already tried and found wanting.

Current exploitation of myth is often, one senses, a response to the drives set up by this myth concerning anthropology and psychoanalysis. To precipitate discussion in terms of myth becomes, for those under the spell of this myth, largely a means of purchasing intellectual standing. Talking the court's jargon is reassuring. Moreover, the anthropology-psychoanalysis myth is peculiarly charming in the way in which such things are. It is a myth having to do with the very subject of myth itself and thus exhibits the curiously involuted character which myth assumes as one myth is validated by another ad infinitum.

But, as can be seen from the state of affairs here, to succumb to the self-intoxication of myth so as to seek to live by it alone is to give carte blanche to all sorts of drives indiscriminately. For myth, as myth, is blind and uncritical. Only in so far as truths are made explicit can they as such be put to the test. Without some explicitation, the question of truth and falsehood cannot even be broached, let alone settled. False myths cannot be told from true ones; and one is likely to end, as the Nazis and others have done, enslaved by an unreality which ultimately one has to set about enforcing.

When it yields to the self-intoxication and narcissism which constantly threaten it, the study of myth becomes a mere drill in the age-old antics of Gnosticism. Begging the question of truth and falsehood without ever being so gauche as to own it is doing so, such study can be merely an exercise in frustration. The key to the cabala is kept in a box locked with another key kept in another locked box, and so on.

One recalls how the Gnostic Manichees of St. Augustine's day kept putting him off: he would understand better when he had heard the exegeses of the next exegete, who was soon to speak his piece. Augustine finally heard him, as he writes in the *Confessions,* but all he had to add to the endlessness of former explanations was his rhetoric, which, Augustine had to admit, was superb. In the Gnostic chase, it is only the pursuit which intrigues. As the quarry digs in and the hunters delve deeper and deeper without stop—for to potency there is no bottom— one comes to forget after a while that there is a quarry, until, sooner or later, death or something similarly definite intervenes to pull us up with the realization that myth is not all.

For all this, the value of current discussions of myth is not to be made light of, let alone scornfully dismissed. Our knowledge runs off into the depths. Human intellection is spotty. Islands of conceptualized knowledge are joined by dark seas of knowing which, in one way or another, are still laid up in the senses. These seas have their beauty, too. Their content should not be suspect, nor should interest in them be so. And since they are dark, one can certainly be excused for talking about them a little darkly.

But, once aware of the submarine elements in the human pursuit of truth, let us not deceive ourselves with false hopes. Scrutinized by means of the narrow beam of light thrown from a discursive intellect such as man's, however piercing it be, however fast it move, these seas prove endless. The explorer will indeed always find plenty to do here. We need not grudge him a lifetime of work. But if he does not take his bearing occasionally by explicit, recognizable landmarks, he is liable to be lost, and his discoveries with him.

There are false hopes which interest in myth, as well as in many other things, may breed. There is not only the myth of industrialism or the myth of imperialism or the myth of democracy. There is the myth of the myth, too.

NOTES

[1] New York: Harcourt, Brace & Co., 1949.
[2] Summer, 1949 (XI, 455-75).
[3] Wellek and Warren, *op. cit.,* pp. 196-97.
[4] Hence it is, too, that the notion of "anlysis" comes into play in the area

around "ideas." St. Thomas Aquinas, considering things not in terms of "ideas," but in terms of concepts, described the origin of first principles as coming about in every case, in metaphysics as well as in the physical sciences, by a kind of induction, an insight into the phantasm—see Peter Hoenen, S.J., "De origine primorum principiorum scientiae," *Gregorianum*, XIV (1933), 153-84; Edmund H. Ziegelmeyer, S.J., "The Discovery of First Principles according to Aristotle," *The Modern Schoolman*, XXII (March, 1945), 132-43. But as the "idea" has gained in ascendancy within the past few hundred years, the tendency has been to explain first principles as produced by "analysis" of one or the other or both of the terms which constitute the principle. The inductive process—a process of emergence out of the material into the intellectual world—has been relatively neglected because the implications of an emergence of the purely intelligible out of the material have been passed over in favor of operations within a "mixed" order—a mélange of the intelligible and the sensible. "Analysis," which, like other things within the world of "ideas," involves a carefully sustained rapport with the material as such, seems to be an operation within such a mélange.

[5] *The Statesman's Manual*, Vol. I of *The Complete Works of Samuel Taylor Coleridge*, ed. W. G. T. Shedd (New York: Harper & Bros., 1884), pp. 437-38. Cf. Wellek and Warren, *op. cit.*, pp. 193, 330, where it is noted that Coleridge's distinction had been made earlier by Goethe. For a typical and discerning contemporary statement on the symbol, see Max Brod, *Franz Kafka: A Biography*, trans. G. Humphreys Roberts (New York: Shocken Books, 1947), p. 194: "The symbol stands on both levels at the same time, on the level which it describes by suggestion and on the objective, real level, etc."

[6] Mr. Hyman, in the article already cited (pp. 462, 467), objects, quite understandably, to Richard Chase's performance in the latter's book *Quest for Myth*, which Chase concludes with a chapter interpreting a half-dozen English poems as though they were myths. But Mr. Chase has had predecessors and will have successors. It might be observed that particularly when it is considered in terms of "poetic truth," poetry tends to be confused with myth.

[7] Wellek and Warren, *op. cit.*, p. 201.

[8] Alfred Korzybski, *Science and Sanity* (New York: Science Press, 1933), *passim*.

[9] See Walter J. Ong, S.J., "The Meaning of the 'New Criticism,'" *The Modern Schoolman*, XX (May, 1943), 208-9; Wellek and Warren, *op. cit.*, pp. 147, 201.

[10] One might mention that there could be a Christian "myth" in the sense of what is implicit and as yet unformulated in Catholic teaching and practice in so far as this implicit and unformulated complement constitutes a coherent whole apprehended (implicitly) in Catholic teaching and practice. Although, as applied to Christianity, the term is not often given this generous sense and, of course, tends to invite misunderstanding, still the state of current discussion can leave it open to such a sense.

❧ TEACHING

AND

COMMUNICATIONS ❧

EIGHT

Educationists and the Tradition of Learning

I

EVERYBODY today, it seems, wants to reform education. It would be interesting if this ambition were a mark of our times. But it is not, for an ambition to reform education is found in most of the ages of known civilization. The desire for educational reform may be an all-consuming fire, it may be a steady, quiet flame, or it may be a fitful flame easily extinguished. It may be a mere velleity. The drive for reform may push in any of various directions—toward new methods calculated to improve on the old, toward recovering purportedly successful old patterns, toward a better organization of existing operations. Indeed, the contrasting, and often conflicting, shapes it takes condemn the reforming drive frequently to ineffectiveness. But the drive is seldom wanting.

It is present even among the students in colleges and universities, where the more intelligent students—from whom we hope our educators are drawn—are normally highly critical of the education being meted out to them, whatever it is. This is as it should be. No educational pattern is perfect, and if a student is being educated at all he is being educated to judge. When he complains that something is wanting in the education he receives, his complaint is often some indication, paradoxically, that he has truly been educated and that the program he is criticizing was, to some degree at least, a success.

College and university students, and the teachers drawn from them, are not the only ones who become heated about what is wrong with the teaching processes or curriculum. A good friend of mine on the board of education in a large American city, who is himself a businessman, speaks frankly of other prominent businessmen of the city with whom his board has frequently to deal as "frustrated teachers." Many of them have very definite ideas as to just how teaching should be carried on and are quite vocal as to what reforms are necessary to get their ideas accepted.

We can be thankful for the drive to reform education, for when this drive ceases to operate, education is finished. Education must be in a constant state of reforming itself. However, it is important that the objectives of reform be realistically conceived. This means that that reform must be based on some knowledge of the history of education, for it is through studying its history that we learn more profoundly what education really is.

Among the various ideas noised about today for the reform of education, there is one in particular which merits careful examination in the light of history. It is the idea that education is seriously suffering from being in the control of professional educators or educationists, at least in English-speaking areas on this side of the Atlantic. This idea appears in various epiphanies in books such as Arthur Eugene Bestor's *Educational Wastelands* or Rudolph Franz Flesch's *Why Johnny Can't Read*, or in education programs such as the Great Books Program. Is this idea old or new? And is the threat that it envisions old or new? If the threat is old, what was done about it in the past? If new, how did it arise out of the past? For new things rise out of the past as surely as old things do. There is nowhere else for them to come from.

II

It is impossible to give an answer to these questions out of the whole of educational history, but in terms of educational history since the rise of the universities something can be said.[1] The university is, after all, a key to all formal education from the Middle Ages on. From the time of their rise in the twelfth and thirteenth centuries to the present day, universities have been more self-possessed and more tightly organized than any educational institutions which earlier ages had known. They have been the organs at the top of the educational structure, and consequently have had great influence on secondary and elementary educators, who have been, more or less, themselves the products of higher education. Moreover, the universities are unique in the sense that all the universities in the world today derive in some way from those of medieval Western Europe. There have been many modifications of the original pattern, but there has been no independent starting point. The universities of the United States are not European universities, and Canadian universities are neither one nor the other. Universities in communist countries are still another thing, and universities in Latin America another. Yet, for all their varying patterns, these universities all have links with the first European universities.

When we look at the universities in their origins, what do we find them to have been? We can take as a sample university the University of Paris, oldest of all the universities and mother of them all. Here we find well developed by the thirteenth century faculties of arts, medicine, law, and theology. Arts included the study of the Latin language—for educated persons then as now cultivated a special language in which to express their fine thoughts—and of "philosophy," which meant largely formal logic and physics with a rather insignificant bit of metaphysics and slightly more ethics. Medicine, law, and theology were the "higher faculties," with a certain training in the arts as prerequisite for their students, although it is interesting to note that only medicine required that the entire course in scholastic philosophy be completed, that is, that the student entering on medicine be a master of arts. Law and theology made relatively little of scholastic philosophy. Then as now not all universities had all four faculties. Theology was frequently missing.

With some adjustment made necesssary by the evolution of human knowledge, all this sounds rather familiar to us, but there is something further in the picture which seems truly strange. The universities are called universities not because this term at first meant a center of learning, much less because it meant a place where all learning—universal learning—was cultivated. For *universitas* in medieval Latin meant no such things at all. It meant a corporation, so that there could be universities of butchers and barbers just as well as the University of Masters and Scholars Living in Paris (*Universitas magistrorum et scholarium Parisius degentium*). These corporations were really guilds, and the medieval university was a group of teachers' guilds—or, at Bologna and Salamanca, an association of students hiring their own teachers and preparing themselves to enter the guilds to which the teachers belonged whom they hired! Reception of a degree was admission to the guild or union. One became a master of arts (later on in other universities a doctor of philosophy, for the two terms historically mean exactly the same thing), or a master or doctor of medicine, of law, or of theology, in a process parallel to that whereby one became a master butcher or a master carpenter. One had to pass through an apprenticeship, and a qualified apprentice was called a bachelor—bachelor butcher, bachelor carpenter, or bachelor of arts, medicine, law, or theology as the case might be. Each faculty formed a separate guild united under the larger corporation or *universitas*, and one had to be admitted to each guild or union separately.

The corollaries to this organization were that all the students in a university were technically apprentices learning to teach and that the universities themselves were, strictly speaking, nothing but normal schools. Moreover, they had the power of educational accrediting associations, for at first by mere prestige and later (1291-1292) by papal bull the graduates of the universities of Bologna and Paris were given the *ius ubique docendi*, the right to teach anywhere. Other universities had seen to it that they, too, had this official accreditation by papal bull. Indeed, they secured it sometimes earlier than Bologna and Paris— Toulouse, for example, in 1233—for their prestige was less than that of Bologna and Paris, and needed more bolstering toward the start.

It is true that many students went to the universities not to enter on a career of teaching, but to acquire sufficient learning to make an impression in the extrauniversity world, as courtiers or legal advisers. But, however frequent this practice was, the universities did not officially sanction it, and from at least the year 1366 to 1452 recipients of the master of arts degree at Paris had to take an oath that they would teach for two years, although a certain amount of evasion was countenanced, for the statute adds the familiar proviso *nisi rationabili causa excusatur*, "unless excused for a good reason." We know that there proved to be many good reasons, but the principle of enforced regency still stood. Moreover, bachelors in any of the faculties were expected regularly to help out with the teaching duties of the masters.

We smile at this academic inconsistency, or even duplicity, which made little provision for the reality of the situation and treated all university students as apprentice teachers. But are we any more consistent or honest in our own practices? We still call the closing exercises of the academic year a "commencement." Commencement of what? Of teaching, although none but a small minority of those "commencing" are commencing any teaching at all. For a doctoral degree we generally require a defense of a thesis, most often after all the real requirements have been met. This "defense" is historically the inaugural act whereby the person inducted into the guild or union as a full-fledged teacher exercised his prerogatives of teaching on his own authority for the first time, and proved his prowess by winning out against any attempts to unhorse him intellectually. Finally, when a student today finishes at medical school, we call him a doctor—that is, a teacher—of medicine, although he has rarely any intention of ever teaching medicine at all. This is not mere archaism, but a kind of duplicity. "Doctor" retains enough of the connotation of teacher—the man who really knows—to have an aura of high respectability about it, for teaching is more profoundly respected than we think. I suspect that most medical students would much rather receive an academic degree as doctors of medicine than a certificate vouching for them as practitioners of healing.

With these inconsistencies of our own, we can smile a little more sympathetically at the plight of the medieval university where, again in theory, each faculty was a guild of teachers engaged in teaching other prospective teachers to be teachers so that these could teach still further prospective teachers to be teachers in turn, and so on ad infinitum. The pattern is amusing, but one conclusion can be drawn from it unmistakably: the medieval educational apparatus was certainly in the hands of the educationists. More than that. These educationists were officially not interested in anyone except themselves and other prospective educationists. Can it be that we are this badly off today? Yet this teacher-centered institution, the medieval university, is by no means a sterile thing, but is rather the great wellhead of twentieth century education and intellectual life.

III

The dominance of the teacher's or educationist's outlook in the medieval and Renaissance university becomes even more evident when we examine the subject which is most typical of the medieval university curriculum, logic. Medieval scholastic logic is practically synonymous with the beginnings of universities. Where you have one of these phenomena, you have the other. However, only within the past ten or fifteen years, with the work of Moody, Boehner, Bochenski, Mullally, and others, have we begun to understand what medieval scholastic logic was. It was not simply Aristotelian logic, for it advanced in many ways far beyond Aristotle, following the work of Peter of Spain, Ockham, Buridan, and others. Neither was it a part of Thomistic theology or philosophy, for, although Peter of Spain was an almost exact contemporary of Thomas Aquinas, this great theologian seems to have been quite unaware of the tremendous developments in logic in his day, or at least uninterested in them. Those who call themselves neoscholastics or Thomists today, with very few exceptions, have shown no interest in medieval scholastic logic. It has been rediscovered by practitioners of modern so-called "mathematical" or "symbolic" logic, which is basically a highly quantified formal logic, and which has been developed at the hands of Boole, Frege, Whitehead, Russell, Carnap, Quine, Lukasiewicz, and their associates. For medieval scholastic logic is basically the same sort of instrument as modern symbolic logic, only without the symbols. It, too, is a highly quantified formal logic.

Here, however, it is not the nature of the logic which interests us so much as the value and aims which its medieval proponents imputed to it. We today are inclined to consider logic as the art of thinking, but this is a very late notion of logic, which hardly antedates the sixteenth century. Before this, in the central tradition of scholasticism and the universities (although sometimes not in St. Thomas Aquinas) logic was taken as synonymous with dialectic, and this logic or dialectic was defined in Cicero's terms as the art of discourse (*ars disserendi*). Until the past few hundred years, men did not commonly consider thinking itself as something which took place in a walled-in private mind but as something which took place in connection with discourse, in a kind of dialogue setting—a notion of thinking which the sociologists and psychologists are enabling us to recover and refine today. We think as we talk—to others or to ourselves.

Now, if logic is the art of discourse, under one of its aspects all discourse can be thought of as teaching. When I speak to you, I manifest something which, presumably, you do not know, and thus I "teach" you something. Perhaps it was inevitable in academic circles that this didactic aspect of discourse be emphasized. At any rate, it comes to be emphasized, consciously or unconsciously, from the Middle Ages down to the flowering of aesthetic theories of expression in the nineteenth century. Speaking for an earlier tradition and adumbrating the future climate of opinion, in *An Apologie for Poetry* (written *ca.* 1580, printed 1595) Sir Philip Sidney arbitrates the respective claims of poetry and history and philosophy by deciding which *teaches* most effectively.

If logic or dialectic is the art of discourse, and discourse is preeminently teaching, logic or dialectic should be basically the art of teaching. And such we find it to be, not only at the time of Sir Philip Sidney and into the seventeenth century, but also at the very beginning of the major developments of medieval logic in the thirteenth century. In the famous definition which opens Peter of Spain's thirteenth-century *Summulae logicales,* dialectic or logic is defined as "the art of arts and the science of sciences, providing the way to the principles of all curriculum subjects" (*ars artium et scientia scientiarum ad omnium methodorum principia viam habens*). This is even stronger in its didactic orientation than it appears at first blush, for "art" and "science" themselves suggest not what they suggest today but rather curriculum subjects. The definition thus reads almost as if one were to say that logic is "the curriculum subject of curriculum subjects, providing the way to the principles of all curriculum subjects." Hence, logic is here the equivalent of a course in education. It is the course in educational methods. For it was assumed that all courses should be taught "logically," although the ways in which "logic" was really applied to teaching, while more forthright than they are today, were quite various.

The implications of this view with regard to the hold which professional educationists may have had on education are not far to seek. As we have seen, at Paris, the mother of universities, and at most universities patterned on Paris, among the students of the higher faculties only the medical students were required to complete requirements for masters of arts before they could take up their more specialized work. But the students of law and of theology, even when they did not complete the master of arts work, did go through the logic course and were generally required to do so. Translated into the perspectives we have been working out here, this manifestly means that not only all masters of arts but all students on the higher faculties as well were required to take the full complement of education courses. However bad matters are today, they are not this bad. To be a doctor of medicine, one does not have to take courses in education, even though the title M.D. signifies literally that one is not a curer of diseases but a teacher of a certain store of knowledge.

IV

Lest this reconstruction seem too fanciful, let us recall some facts about the humanists' attack on the scholasticism of the universities in the fifteenth and sixteenth centuries. The humanists were in many ways first and foremost educational reformers. And the chief butt of their attack was not "scholasticism" in general, but scholastic logic and whatever areas of learning were directly affected by scholastic logic. Erasmus and More regard St. Thomas Aquinas, who today is considered the scholastic of scholastics, as hardly a scholastic at all, classing him rather with the Fathers of the Church. But the scholastic logicians, Jean Buridan, Duns Scotus, Walter Burleigh, Ralph Strode (Chaucer's "philosophical Strode"), and particularly Peter of Spain are looked on as despicable educators by Ioannes Caesarius, Juan Luis Vives, Erasmus, More, Ramus, and other sixteenth century humanists of varying complexions.

Because of the way in which logic was held as the art governing teaching procedure, this attack by the humanists is an attack not on a subject but on a teaching method, on an educational outlook and practice. The basis of their attack is the same basis used by most educational reformers: this formal logic, and hence the whole educational procedure which it purportedly governed, corresponded to nothing in reality. What is learned in a class in logic has nothing to do with actual life and actual mental activity. Such was the verdict of Peter Ramus, who set out to produce instead a "real" logic—in fact a kind of rhetoric-logic—corresponding to what he took for actuality.

The humanists' attack on scholasticism is thus an attempt to liberate education from the realier professional educationists, persons who stressed method to the neglect of content. But the humanists themselves were professional educators, and excellent promoters, with a new promotional procedure to rely on, namely, printing, in which an extraordinary number of humanists were directly and deeply involved. From the Manutii in Italy, to the Amerbachs in Basel, to Johann Sturm in the lower Rhineland and in Paris, to the family of Sir Thomas More in England, we find the humanist milieu active in the printing and publishing business.

These educational reformers had not only a new program backed by a new device but also a new educational outlook and practice, for humanism stood not only for a new curriculum, with a de-emphasis of logic and more emphasis on literary expression, but for a new method, too. The new method was, basically, the grammatical or linguistic method as revitalized by a typographical culture. Instead of devoting itself to logical structure as to a kind of mathematics, education would now devote itself to explicating literary texts and their language, and to producing new literature of a value comparable to that of ancient Greece and Rome. The study of language, with a strong emphasis on printed works, was to dominate all fields. We can see this in the manner in which new subjects, such as geography and history, now make their way into the schools. They come in not labeled frankly as geography and history but wrapped in heavy disguises, associating them with textual study and understanding. One learned history because one read Livy or Tacitus or Caesar, or because one needed to interpret their accounts of *res gestae* in terms of the larger background of modern and ancient history accumulating in man's mind. One learned geography in order to understand Virgil or Caesar, or to relate their knowledge of the earth's surface to the more advanced knowledge which the explorers were retailing to Europe.

The humanists were professional educationists less than were the scholastics of the university tradition in the sense that they were not necessarily members of the teachers' guilds or unions. They were often hired tutors in families of the nobility or *haute bourgeoisie*, retained not to educate other teachers like themselves but to prepare the youth of the family for extracurricular life. Thus many, or even most, great early humanists, such as Rudolph Agricola, Erasmus, Vives, and Sturm are not committed to any university, nor are their educational programs. Indeed, humanism in part disintegrated the medieval university, for it precipitated the separation of secondary schooling from the university program, in which secondary, and even some elementary, education had been more or less closely incorporated through the Middle Ages.

Humanism remedied a weakness in the lower levels of university instruction. The apprenticeship system of teaching which technically obtained in the medieval university had been particularly unsatisfactory in the arts course, where students were regularly teen-agers, since one finished the entire arts course, all of philosophy included, and received the highest (and only) degree, that of master of arts, commonly at about the age of eighteen.[2] This meant that pupils at present high-school or even elementary-school ages—for many university masters undertook to provide grammar-school education as part of their program—were likely to miss the close supervision and personal interest they required. As apprentices, they could learn or not learn as they pleased, unless they had the good fortune to find an especially interested master. This framework for education might work well on the higher professional faculties of medicine, law, and theology, but it obviously had its disadvantages at the high-school level. The humanists proposed instead a more pupil-centered system expressly preparing for "life" rather than for teaching, and the success of their system in the college of Johann Sturm at Strasbourg, in the Jesuit colleges founded all over the Continent, and in other similar colleges throughout Europe and, later colonial America, siphoned off students from the university or university-associated arts course, at least at the lower levels of the course. These Renaissance colleges were really agents of the family, charged with doing their best with the boys committed to them, rather than unions to whom youngsters were apprenticed for better or for worse.

The Renaissance humanist "college" is the forerunner in Europe of the secondary schools which prepare for higher education. In the United States, and to some extent in Canada, it is the forerunner also of our universities. Harvard College, the first college in the United States, was such a college, and its growth into a university has been matched all over the United States and in parts of Canada by the development of other similar institutions. For this reason, unlike European universities, which even at the undergraduate level have only highly specialized programs, American and Canadian universities are also organs of general or liberal education, in the tradition of the Renaissance colleges from which they are descended.

And yet, despite the fact that the humanists were not technically committed in their schools to preparing teachers as such in the way in which the medieval universities had been, the medieval view that institutions of higher education are basically normal schools had ways of making itself vaguely felt even among the humanists. Thus Harvard College was founded primarily to provide a literate and well trained ministry—which is much the same as to say to provide teachers. And among the theses which little boys at Harvard defended through the mid-seventeenth century—always, of course, in Latin—many are a defense not of what the pupil has presumably learned but of the pedagogical methods by which he has been taught. They are teacher-centered theses rather than pupil-centered. Samuel Eliot Morison's *Harvard College in the Seventeeth Century* provides these samples of such theses, which I translate from the Latin: "Languages are to be learned before the arts," "Languages are more readily learned by practice than by rule," "The art of physics is to be learned from things, not fabricated in the mind." The self-consciousness and the defensive attitudes of the teacher, who is never really quite sure than his curriculum and method are the best, are nowhere more evident than in these theorems about the curriculum which were stated and "defended" by early New England youngsters before their proud and nervous—and probably critical— parents and friends.

V

In these complex and interwoven patterns of educational history through the Middle Ages and the Renaissance we can discern two momenta not unlike momenta which are developed today, namely, a move toward specialization and a complementary move toward de-specialization. The educationists, then as now, are torn between the two movements. Logic had appealed to the medieval mind as a despecializing device. If everything intellectual was "logical," the thing to do before one specialized was certainly to master logic and thereby to master the whole intellectual ground at once and, presumably, all of life as well. But at the same time, specialization had also appealed to the medieval mind. The three higher university faculties of medicine, law, and theology are permanent reminders of this fact. Indeed, from its beginning the university has proved itself consistently a specializing organ rather than a despecializing organ, so that, generally speaking, only in North America, where universities are Renaissance humanist colleges or secondary schools transmuted into universities, do we find universities which ambition general education as any part at all of their program. Specialization had grown so far in the universities by the time of the Renaissance humanists that logic itself, the generalizing subject, was too intricate to be of any further practical use as a leveler or common denominator for intellectual life.

To the Renaissance humanist, linguistic or grammatical studies (including, of course, rhetoric) were to be the generalizing medium, the common denominator of intellectual activity. Ramus and his disciple Johann Thomas Freige (Freigius) proposed studying Virgil's *Georgics* as the proper approach to physics. But this arrangement, too, evolved toward specialization. For, generally and practically, linguistic or grammatical studies meant to Renaissance man Latin studies. Greek and Hebrew were supposedly included, but there was in actuality little real emphasis on Greek and almost none on Hebrew, so that Latin carried the day. Latin was indeed a common denominator, if not as matter for literary study, at least as the normal vehicle of communication among learned men of all nations and in all fields. But when the vernaculars rose, Latin, too, became a specialized subject, as, despite its favored position in certain secondary-school traditions, it is today.

Thus twice in succession we have a subject which promises to unite all the other subjects of the curriculum and captures the imagination of teachers, become too specialized to serve its originally envisioned purpose. Whether this specialization is a degeneration or a development depends on one's point of view. Which it may be is, for our present purpose, immaterial. What is of interest at present is the fact that when humanism attacked formal logic as too specialized a discipline, it was attacking a too specialized subject which had originally appealed because it was not specialized; the further fact that the linguistic program which the humanists substituted for formal logic became too specialized in turn; and the concluding fact that this uneasy seesaw between despecialization and specialization was intimately connected with the desire of professional educationists to arrive at an adequate educational method. From this point of view, medieval scholastic logicians and, later, Renaissance humanists were both professional educationists. The charge leveled in time against both groups, but specially the scholastics, was the familiar charge against educationists: they cultivated a perversely obfuscated jargon which no normally intelligent person could understand.

VI

I hope to have challenged the notion that there was a time when education was not in the hands of the educationists. Here it might be feasible to suggest a descriptive definition of an educationist. He is a man preoccupied with techniques of communication and with techniques of communicating these techniques. Through the history of learning and research there has been more preoccupation than we might suspect with techniques and theories of communication. We often fail to recognize this preoccupation because it is not labeled educational theory, but it is there nevertheless. From the very beginning the very heart of the university has been concerned with the arts of communication, the *artes sermocinales,* not only logic or dialectic, but grammar and rhetoric as well. And the university has been the most critical and influential educational institution from medieval to modern times. The humanists shifted the emphasis among these arts but remained interested primarily in communication.

If we think of the educationist as a man interested in communication techniques, schools of thought which at first blush seem diametrically opposed are seen to share many common preoccupations. Those who wish to ground general education on either of the two earlier bases we have discussed here, that is, on logic, as in the medieval pattern, or on grammatico-rhetorical language studies, as proposed by the humanists— and there are still persons who want one or the other of these—are often incensed against a kind of education propounded by many educationists today which stresses social skills and "getting along" with other persons. Without undertaking to defend such an education, I should like to call attention to the fact that it, too, is in its own way concerned with the classical problem of communication which has formed the central node of general or liberal education from ancient times to the present. If it stresses the social aspect of thought, we must face the fact that our modern achievement of reflective social consciousness affects our notion of intellectual activity, too.

It has become fashionable in many circles to denounce the watering down of the curriculum when more substantial courses are placed in competition with, or are even supplanted by, other courses developing in the student adaptability, social poise, and simply "charm" (a term which actually occurs as the title of courses given in certain college and university adult-education programs in the United States). Certainly our educational system in the United States is suffering from such watering down. I leave it to persons better informed than myself to say what the state of affairs is in Canada. However, a movement such as this is a historical fact, and as such deserves dispassionate historical examination even more than it may deserve denunciation. It is certain that today the social aspect of communication and of thought itself is more important, and is recognized as more important, than it was in past times. The hectic interest in courses of this sort is a symptom of a larger reorientation in man's relationship to other men.

Granted that the basis of liberal education is skill in intelligent communication, what should this mean in a society evolved as ours has evolved to the point where so much intelligence is being diffused—for better or for worse—through mass media such as the press, movies, radio, and television? Granted the prime importance of language as the most direct and lucid means of intelligent communication, used presumably with intelligence behind the scenes even by those who make movies and direct television programs, can we afford to consider language now as standing alone in the communications field? Verbal expression now seems inextricably intertwined with other newly specialized forms of expression. Should such a fact affect our approach to a liberal education? I do not believe that it is necessary to give courses in Intermediate Radio Listening or Advanced Television Viewing. Yet it may well be that until we can make students break through the press-movie-radio-television barrier in their own lives, they cannot react intelligently to language at all. Until they can replace the undiscriminating hypnotic response to these media in which they have been trained from infancy with a discriminating response, they remain impervious to any communication or thinking other than the crudest sort. My own experience has been that persons undiscriminating in their reaction to these mass media are undiscriminating in their thinking and speaking, and that a person unaware of the way in which advertisements and Hollywood movies work is incapable of responding to a good contemporary poem or to any first-rate literature. But discrimination here cannot be learned without attention to the sociology of communication. Could it be that older ways of taking language and the thinking processes in isolation from the total social complex are too narrowly specialized to be fully serviceable today?

What it means to be preoccupied with techniques of communication, to be, that is, an educationist, cannot be understood apart from a knowledge of history. This is the final point to which I hope the present paper leads. Most quarrels between educators would be better handled, if not actually resolved, if both sides showed a more detailed knowledge of their own historical *raison d'être*. The educationist needs a knowledge of history to be aware of the enviable and complex record of educationists in the past, which should be an inspiration and a challenge to him. It is no small matter that the universities, which have shaped so much in the modern world, were in their origins normal schools. The worst disservice an educationist can render to his cause is a rootless educational theory. Educational theory and a genuinely liberal education are in effect much the same thing.

This the antieducationist would do well to remember. What is needed, he should remind himself, is not fewer professional educationists and fewer professional education courses, but better educationists and better education courses. To think that modern education can be carried on under the direction of anyone but an educationist—a person preoccupied with techniques and theories of communication—is a pipe dream. The origins of our modern systems of educational point to an entirely different conclusion. The history of learning, of scholarship, of research, is the history of teachers teaching teachers and, in great part, of teachers teaching teachers how to teach.

NOTES

[1] The factual material used in this paper is available in or through Hastings Rashdall, *The Universities of Europe in the Middle Ages* (new edition edited by F. M. Powicke and A. B. Emden; Oxford: The Clarendon Press, 1936, 3 vols.); in two books by the present author, *Ramus, Method, and the Decay of Dialogue* and *Ramus and Talon Inventory* (Cambridge, Massachusetts: Harvard University Press, 1958). *See also* Samuel Eliot Morison, *The Founding of Harvard College* (Cambridge, Massachusetts: Harvard University Press, 1935) and *Harvard College in the Seventeenth Century* (2 vols., continuously paginated, Harvard University Press, 1936).

[2] The University of Paris was a slight exception to this practice, for there certain statutes provided that no one could actually act as master of arts until the age of twenty.

NINE

Grammar in the Twentieth Century

I

IF we believe the reporters on our educational system, there is no doubt that we live in a time when grammar has fallen on evil days. Certainly, in terms of earlier emphases, the neglect of grammar in our present educational tradition represents a major cultural attitude. Furthermore, the neglect cannot be accounted for as simply the unfortunate by-product of blowsy educational theory, for educational theory, blowsy or not, has a history with extremely complicated and profound roots, some of the most profound and perplexing in human existence. The conspiracy theory, which traces all our ills back to a clique of subversives, will work even less well in intellectual history than in social and economic and political history. Grammar, as a matter of fact, has not been put aside by hostile forces. It has suffered a falling off among its own followers. Of recent years persons who in another age might have become grammarians have manifested very little inclination to do so. Grammar itself has lost its appeal and its nerve.

This failure of appeal and nerve had its beginnings much earlier than our generation. Already in the latter half of the nineteenth century Robert Browning had published his poem, "A Grammarian's Funeral," a typical Browning tour de force, for a grammarian was already by common consent the most impossible of all subjects for poetry. He was a dull subject at best, and the fact that in this poem he was dead did not make him any more interesting. Grammarians were almost always moribund. Browning's grammarian, who

> . . . settled Hoti's business—let it be!—
>   Properly based *Oun*—
> Gave us the doctrine of the enclitic *De*,

was at the peak of his career

>   Dead from the waist down.
> . . . The multitude below
>   Live, for they can, there:
> This man decided not to Live but Know.

Moreover, it would be a mistake to think that the conditions reflected in Browning's poem apply only to the late nineteenth century. Its subtitle, "Shortly after the Revival of Learning in Europe," shows that the poem actually refers to conditions in the Renaissance, and these conditions were by definition a reproduction of still earlier conditions in classical antiquity, so that, if we can conclude from Browning and the humanists, the failure of nerve on the part of grammar traces to troubles which were present to grammar more or less from the beginning.

II

To understand in some measure what the loss of nerve on the part of grammar comes to, we can establish as historical points of reference two grammarians. The more distinguished, whom we shall come to only at the end of this essay, is the late Otto Jespersen, dean of recent English grammarians and creator of modern English grammar. The other, from whom we shall take our departure, while not so distinguished as Jespersen, is a typical representative of the general grammatical tradition as it existed before the past few generations. He is James Harris, a family connection of the Earls of Shaftesbury and a less distinguished spokesman for the Enlightenment, who at the very middle of the eighteenth century was writing on what he and his contemporaries called universal grammar.

Operating in the wake of scholasticism, Harris treats grammar as do most Western Europeans before Romanticism had achieved its full force. He is fascinated by the possibility of having "principles" with which everything in a particular area of knowledge can be connected—fascinated, that is, with the notion of structure, a notion, we might remark, closely associated with thinking in terms of spatial models. Harris's universal grammar was to be a structure containing the principles of all existent and possible grammars, and in the course of getting up what he conceived that this structure might be, we find him writing in 1751 as follows:

Even in Matters of Art and *human* Creation, if we except a few Artists and critical Observers, the rest look no higher than to the *Practice* and mere *Work,* knowing nothing of those *Principles,* on which the whole depends.

Thus in *Speech* for example—All men, even the lowest, can speak their Mother-Tongue. Yet how many of this multitude can neither write, nor even read? How many of those, who are thus far literate, know nothing of that Grammar which respects the Genius of their own Language? How few then must be those who know GRAMMAR UNIVERSAL; *that Grammar*, which without regarding the several idioms of particular languages, *only respects those Principles that are essential to them all?*[1]

Harris is informative for us not because he is profound—for he is not profound at all—but because he is a spokesman for a learned tradition. Dr. Johnson, who Boswell says considered Harris "a prig, and a bad prig," nevertheless respected him as a representative of such a tradition. So did others, for after both his and Johnson's death, the book from which our excerpt here is made, *Hermes, or a Philosophical Inquiry Concerning Universal Grammar,* was translated into French and published in 1796 by order of the French Directory as a kind of official expression of what the enlightened mind was supposed to think about language and grammar.

The passage follows Harris's explanation of how, in any and all philosophizing or scientizing, man must move up from "effects," which he encounters most immediately, to "causes," which he finds are the last things he comes upon, although they must necessarily in themselves precede their effects. In this present passage, Harris is indicating precisely this movement from "effects" up to "causes" or "principles." He is saying here, in effect, that oral speech is the effect of reading, reading the effect of writing, and writing the effect of grammar. Or in reverse, the principles of grammar "cause" writing, writing "causes" reading, and reading "causes" oral speech. This altogether shipshape account blinks entirely the simple fact that so far are reading and writing from "causing" speech that most men who have lived in the world have done all their speaking and the evolution of language has pursued nearly its entire course without reading or writing at all. Harris would certainly have owned this had he thought of it here. The interesting fact is that he did not even think of it. It seemed to him natural that grammar should be derivative more immediately from written than from spoken language.

Harris's presuppositions and outlook can be paralleled in a thousand places in the world around him, and not only in the eighteenth century world but all the way back through antiquity as far as we can go. The mentality to which they bear witness is memorialized in the very term "grammar" itself, which comes from the same stem as the Greek word *graphein,* to write, and thus insinuates always, despite the most industrious semantic policing, that to study grammar is to study written rather than spoken language. This mentality is part of a much more widespread supposition, seldom articulated but generally operative, which only recently has become unpopular: namely, that any scientizing of speech involves first silencing it and thus removing it from the world of sound and fixing it in the world of space.

Studying written speech is, of course, far simpler than studying spoken speech, and it is not strange that the early attempts to scientize speech, almost without exception until just a few years ago, veer toward the consideration of written or literary language exclusively, disregarding or slurring over the fact that this is language at second remove. Thus, for example, although Diogenes Laertius and Priscian make some distinction between the *figura* or shape of a letter and its *potestas* or pronunciation value, this distinction is exceptional, is not really held to even by those who make it,[2] and means very little indeed in the learned tradition as a whole. Indeed, Priscian's very proffering of this distinction shows that his approach to sound is through letters themselves: sound is taken not as existing in its own right but as a derivative of letters. It exists at second remove.

This degradation of sound is a regular by-product of an unreflective graphic culture, and has many parallels in such a culture. Thus from Cicero to Ramus and beyond into our own day, it has been common to think of "parts'" of words as letters—marks laid out in space—rather than as what we today call phones or phonemes. The terms and the concepts of "phone" and "phoneme" are very recent formations, new in linguistic equipment. "Letter" or *littera* is a very old piece of equipment, and a concept much easier to form. Similarly, "linguistics," formed by reference to the Latin *lingua,* tongue, with the explicit suggestion of sound, attests a new way of scientific thinking. "Grammar," built on the notion of writing, attests the old. To be sure, there was from ancient times a linguistic study called *rhētoricē* or *rhetorica* (root in *erō* or *ereō,* "I speak"), but wherever this achieved a status of its own independent of grammar, it had to do with a study comparable not to grammar in any sense or to modern linguistics, of which grammar is a part, but to public speaking and/or the modern study of literature.

III

Given the nature of oral speech and of writing, it is possible to discern convincing reasons why early grammar should have veered consistently toward the written rather than the spoken word. Nothing is more evanescent than sound, which has its being only while it is in process of perishing. *Verba volant, scripta manent.* If sound is metamorphosed or reduced to spatial equivalents by writing, the resulting product has, if not eternal duration, at least a repose which suggests imperishableness. Science favors fixity or repose. It has a nostalgia for the unchanging. Hence scientific-type knowledge involves concepts formed by reference to space rather than to time: it is interested in "structure" or "patterns" or "principles" ("first takings"—*primus-capio*) to which other items are "reduced" (brought back) or "referred" or "related" (carried back).

When sound itself is explained scientifically, it is processed in terms of this sort, after having been metamorphosed into spatial equivalents such as wave lengths, intensity indications, and the like. Science must consider fluidity by freezing it, in one way or another. It is thus understandable that the first scientific attack on language should have been made where language was already rigidified, that is on written speech. By the same token, we are not surprised that early grammar tends to be rather exclusively normative, interested not merely in observing and reporting but specifically in prescribing what people ought to do when they use language. They ought to use it according to the norm of those who *write* it, and to avoid the usage of those who merely talk it, for, in contrast to modern descriptive grammar, more humble in its approach to linguistic fact, early grammar shows practically no interest in living colloquial speech.[3]

In view of the close connection between the scientific and the scriptural outlook, it is not at all surprising that, so far as we know, the first scientific treatment of language, far from antedating the invention of writing, does not come until a long time after writing is established. There is also a curious feedback here, for if it is processing in spatial terms which makes language at first amenable or inviting to scientific analysis, scientific analysis itself, whether it is concerned with language or anything else, can hardly come into being before a graphic culture, for writing gives the needed fixity to the constructs required by scientific analysis. It is impossible to keep a definition entirely unaltered in a completely oral culture. It is impossible even in a manuscript or a typographical culture, but here at least something more like permanence can be maintained.

However, if at first it is written language which inspires linguistic and grammatical science, this science can ultimately be brought to bear on the spoken language itself in the way in which modern descriptive grammar and other branches of linguistics seek to do. But study of the spoken language is much more difficult than study of the written record. It involves taking not what is already fixed in space and working it up into other structural patterns, but taking what is fleeting in time and working it up into structural patterns. As has been seen, to do this inevitably involves fixing sound in some way or other—for example, with the oscillograph, which can reduce the flow of sound to patterns of waves in space which can be "frozen" into charts. This is, in many ways, a more serviceable metamorphosis than the metamorphosis effected by the alphabet or by character writing, for it obviates the innumerable misleading impressions regarding the nature of speech which writing of any sort, and particularly alphabetic writing, creates and perpetuates. With more ingeniously contrived and flexible spatial models, such as those which wave analysis or phonemic analysis provides, linguistic treatment of spoken languages can become more and more precise, more subtle, and more adequate.

Nevertheless, however refined, any reduction of sound to the fixity of space is still a degradation of sound. It seems that the need of science to make such reductions to fixed patterns means that it will never be able quite to catch up with the oral and aural linguistic reality. For there is a kind of incompatibility not only between sound and space, but more profoundly, between the process of communication itself and reduction to a static form. Communication is something which goes on, not something which simply perdures. Because of this it has a natural affinity for the fluid world of sound, where, if the flow does not continue, everything perishes. In such a world, communication, which takes place always between persons or depths, not objects or surfaces, has its normal material mode of existence. The space world may supply more fact of the object sort, more surface to observe, but it is poor in personalist resonance.

Space is simply not so communicative as sound. The closest spatial equivalent of voice is not posture, but gesture, and by comparison with voice even gesture is half dead: it can be stopped, as voice cannot, and leave a kind of permanent remainder in the medium in which it exists. Gesture can be resolved into a succession of spastic poses which do not go on but merely perdure. In so far as grammatical analysis, even of living, spoken language, must reduce language in terms such as "structure," it must reduce language in some sort, directly or indirectly, to such spastic poses. There must be "conjunctions" like couplings on railroad cars, "prepositions" or words "put before" other words, "interjections" or words "thrown between" other words, "adjectives" or words "thrown against" nouns, and so on. Even the verb, which is the word par excellence, the predicate or category—or, to take the root meaning of these two words, Latin-based and Greek-based respectively, "that-which-is-cried-out"—even this verb must be analyzed as "complementing" or "filling out" the subject. In this context "nouns" are degraded from the status of "names" or cries, to "things."

It is true that these old parts of speech are far from exhaustive or complete as tools of grammatical analysis. Evolved gradually by the early grammarians to deal with Greek speech and later adapted with moderate success to Latin, they do not, as we know, serve adequately even for Modern English or for Standard Average European generally. But the schemes which supplement or supplant these parts of speech, while often much more adequate and true to the genius of language, all seem inevitably to labor under the same difficulty of seeking to *envision* or to reduce in terms of spatial models what is essentially not visual at all, but auditory. If you are going to scientize language, this you must do.

Improved linguistic terminology is, if anything, even more diagrammatic than that of unreconstructed grammars. The term "context," so assertive today, meaning something like what-is-woven-together, just as much as the term "syntax" (a "setup" or "array"), is dependent for its formation on a patently spatial model. It is a picture term. Other neologisms are no better. Seeking to approach linguistic facts in as unprejudiced a manner as possible, J. R. Firth, followed by R. H. Robins and others, in analyzing a given language, does not look for "parts" of speech either in general or in particular, but for what he calls "formal scatters"[4] of any sort. These are to be described, and the terms of the linguistic analysis are to be derived directly from these descriptions. "Formal scatters" is a fascinating term, for it shows, first of all, an awareness of the disability from which all analysis and particularly linguistic analysis, suffers: the disabilities attendant on freezing things in terms such as "part" or "form" (etymologically associated with the notion of "outline"). Particularly in the initial stages terminology must not be too formal, too rigid, too inadaptable. We shall then not look for speech "forms," which we presumably should have set up in our minds in advance. Rather, we must look for "scatters," which are things which we encounter without preparation. But they must be *formal* scatters! The form has indeed been deemphasized, at least temporarily, but it has to be there after all. We may have determined not to analyze the language in question into "forms" or any other terms given beforehand, but we have determined to find its "structure," and therefore have assumed that it has *some* kind of structure—in other words, we have come to it convinced that even the sound pattern must be reduced or tamed or metamorphosed by being reinterpreted by analogy with things in space—where we have simply replaced form or "outline" with structure or "setup."

I do not wish to appear to be making fun of the notion of "formal scatters." It seems to me that this approach to language is a good one, better than those which I know it supplants. I only wish to point out the limitations of any analysis of language. There is something in the realm of sound which eludes the very idea of analysis itself. Ultimately —we cannot go into this here—it is the element which belongs to the world of persons, who obviously cannot be "broken down" by analysis. When we approach even spoken language scientifically, we reduce it in one way or another in terms of "structure," which means in terms of space. We take communication out of the world where it has its real existence and treat it in terms of analogies and models. In reducing sound to structure, we can handle it very accurately and discriminatingly. In terms of "structure" we can account for everything there is here—except for the mystery of sound itself. A whole volume of diagrams of sound waves makes no noise. There is indeed nothing that we can do about this situation except recognize it, and with it the poverty— which is not at all the same as inaccuracy—of any scientific treatment, not only of sound, but of anything.

IV

The modern approach to grammar, with its awareness of the fact that linguistic performance is primarily oral performance and only derivatively graphic—"grammatical" in the basic etymological sense—carriers with it an awareness, or the possibility of an awareness, of the limitations in the scientific approach to reality. This awareness of the limitations of science is very much a part of modern life, where it paradoxically accompanies a confidence in the possibilities of scientific achievement within limited fields. We live in an age which, if not entirely free of brashness in its scientific enthusiasms, has grown increasingly aware of the limitations of what had once been thought to be all-conquering scientific fact and theory. Classical or Newtonian physics has been discovered to be a certain kind of physics, supplemented or transcended by relativity and quantum physics. Euclidean geometry is accurate, but it is now known to be a special geometry for special situations which does not exhaust geometrical possibilities at all. Aristotelian logic is a marvelously accurate logic, but, as Lukasiewicz has painstakingly worked out, one designed for certain special situations and far from adequate for the analysis of all thought structure. What was once taken to be "universal grammar" has been discovered to be not universal at all, but a special grammar fairly adequate for the Greek language and quite incapable of accounting satisfactorily for performances in languages unrelated to Greek.

A sense of the limitations of grammar has thus developed in conjunction with a sense of the limitations of all science. But in the case of grammar this discovery of limitations has been associated with a new awareness of the primacy of the spoken over the written word. As is perhaps apparent from what has already been said, recognition of the fact that grammar has ultimately to deal with speech and with sound has not only been associated with a sense of the limitations of science but has strongly reinforced this sense. Sound is more important in language than anywhere else, and sound as sound exhibits curious resistance to scientific treatment. Attention to the vocal as vocal normally brings some kind of awareness of the limitations endemic to notions of "structure," that is, to nonvocal frames of reference.

Now any mature consideration of communication must include an awareness of the psychological meaning of sound as sound, and thus, to cut short what is already a long story, we must frankly admit that a mature consideration of communication must by the same token gnaw away at the foundation of grammar itself in so far as grammar is interested in what can be interpreted as structure and diagram. Indeed, in developing the general awareness of the particularity and limitations of science, the mature study of language plays a leading role, perhaps the leading role. Grammar has in a sense succumbed to the maturing of language study. While we recognize the need for studying languages in terms of fixed forms, and the necessity of teaching normative grammar at the primary and secondary school levels—and even at higher levels, unfortunately, as a therapeutic measure—we can no longer attach to these forms so much importance as earlier ages did. It is no longer possible in our day and age to have the unshakable confidence in the adequacy of schematic models of language—which are ultimately space models of language—that earlier ages had. Scientific awareness must be complemented here by other awarenesses, by poetic or existentialist or phenomenological awarenesses which give insights into linguistic phenomena while preserving at the same time the sense of profound mystery with which such phenomena are involved.

V

All this suggests that the misfortunes of grammar in our schools cannot be dealt with intelligently if we think of them as the result of wrongheadedness or stupidity or even perhaps moral fault on the part of those who supposedly "control" our education. The failure of nerve on the part of grammar, the hesitancy to enforce rules, may be and is a bad thing which one is supposed to be teaching normative grammar. But it is to a great extent understandable. It arises out of a tremendous complex of causes, which none of us completely fathom but which we can do something to understand. Like other large-scale cultural developments, the swing away from grammar—a swing which can certainly be overestimated, and often is, but which seems in many ways quite real— is part of a pattern too extensive and ramified for any one person or group of persons to "control." We are in some ways apparently at the end of the Gutenberg era, the age which climaxed the structural approach to language and perfected the printing press, reducing once resonant words to items on a mass production assembly line and bringing us to think of a book no longer as a record of utterances or cries emanating from a living person but as a structured object or thing.

We should be naïve, however, if we expected the structural approach to language to go. Far from it. The human mind does not forget or put aside its former achievements, but builds on them. Indeed, we might conjecture that there will be more and more attempts at describing and otherwise investigating language in terms of structure, more and more schemata of language, more and more elaboration of classifications— allomorphs, morphemes, articulatory phonetics, phonemics, "bundles and fascicles of isoglosses," "assortments of isoglosses,"[5] and so on. But here the very multiplication and proliferation of the structures which are used to interpret language will bear witness to the elusiveness of the linguistic situation as a whole when approached through scientific analysis.

Moreover, as the number of languages subjected to analysis increases, the structures serving for interpretation will have to be more and more enlarged. At this point, another cause of the present grammatical malaise can be indicated. It is nothing other than the growing global consciousness of mankind, the human race's growing self-consciousness and self-possession. It was easy to be devoted to Greek grammar when that part of the human race which was in Southern Europe was not aware where the rest of mankind was, or even that there was a rest of mankind. Now that we know, or can learn, a little of the linguistic of Hopi or Shona or Bassa, the enthusiasm for the older closed grammar systems must yield to more open or elastic schemata.

The present situation has not merely multiplied the items with which grammar and other divisions of linguistics must deal. The developing global consciousness of the human race has also placed a new accent on communication, which is to say on language as functioning, on language as living rather than as frozen in grammatical analyses, and thus ultimately again on that mysterious thing, sound. The old concept of universal grammar, involved with Harris's and others' naïve approach to language through writing, has consequently badly suffered. We had promised earlier to compare the eighteenth century universal grammarian, James Harris, with a modern grammarian, the late Otto Jespersen, and can turn to this comparison now. In Jespersen's famous work, *The Philosophy of Grammar*, first published in 1924, we find the notion of a universal grammar yielding to that of "living grammar"—a term which forms the title of Jespersen's first chapter. The essence of language, Jespersen begins by observing,

is human activity—activity on the part of one individual to make himself understood by another, and activity on the part of that other to understand what was in the mind of the first. These two individuals . . . should never be lost sight of if we want to understand the nature of language and of that part of language which is dealt with in grammar. But in former times this was often overlooked, and words and forms were often treated as if they were things or natural objects with an existence of their own—a conception which may have been to a great extent fostered through a too exclusive preoccupation with written or printed words, but which is fundamentally false. . . .

The spoken and the heard word is the primary form of language.

At this point Browning's dead grammarian comes to life. This is a declaration in favor of freedom and in favor of communication itself. By the same token it is a declaration in favor of the internationalism toward which all men and all communication must move. It promises not an easy universalism of communication, but one which is more universal than that of a statically conceived, so-called universal grammar. Is it entirely an accident that the most eminent modern English grammarian and the champion of vocal sound over mechanized silence should be not an Englishman or even an American but a Dane? Jespersen's devotion to a language outside and beyond his own registers the drive toward internationalism which linguistic studies today frequently foster.

Jespersen's view here is, moreover, representative of most modern grammarians', who, however they may differ in various theoretical details, commonly agree that grammar must study primarily voice, not writing. Jespersen's philosophy of grammar may not be perfect, and it is certainly not complete, but in so far as he and others today acknowledge the primacy in communication of the living world of sound, they are keeping language in a condition where it can continue to be serviceable to twentieth century man, and to man of the twenty-first and of the thirtieth centuries. Moving ahead out of the Gutenberg era, even as we perfect our primitive translating machines, we have also to face the fact that communication is ultimately rooted not in things but in persons. Like persons, it is alive with a mysterious interior life, so that what is most meaningful in it radically resists being "structured" at all.

NOTES

[1] James Harris, *Hermes, or A Philosophical Inquiry Concerning Universal Grammar,* 2nd ed. rev. (London, 1765), pp. 10-11. The first edition was dated 1751.

[2] R. H. Robins, *Ancient and Mediaeval Grammatical Theory in Europe* (London: British Book Centre, 1951), pp. 13-14.

[3] *Ibid.,* pp. 4, 38, etc.

[4] J. R. Firth, "The Technique of Semantics," in *Transactions of the Philological Society of Great Britain* (1935), p. 62; cf. Robins, pp. 91-99.

[5] See H. A. Gleason, Jr., *An Introduction to Descriptive Linguistics* (New York: Henry Holt & Co., Inc., 1955), p. 293.

❧ TEN ❧

The Vernacular Matrix of the New Criticism

I

IN our accounts of the status of contemporary criticism one dimension is generally left completely out of consideration. This is the changed relationship in the past few generations between the vernacular literatures and the learned world. Today the study of the literature of the English language is a commonplace activity, well established in England and even more firmly and widely in the United States, where it not only flourishes in the elementary and secondary schools, but also is to some degree compulsory even at the level of higher education for students who want a degree in almost any subject at all. But this state of affairs is quite new.

A hundred years ago the McGuffey readers were familiarizing elementary school pupils across the country with English literature and a great deal of American literature, but the better secondary schools for the most part would as yet have none of either. At the level of higher education, in the universities, it was not until nearly the turn of the century that one could hope to get a moderately comprehensive coverage of the "field" of English. Before this, in academic circles literature meant Latin and some Greek. Ezra Pound's poetry reveals the marginal position of his generation. He is the last of the classicists, and he moved from the ancient world into the modern by passing through intervening stages of interest in Old English and Middle English, which had established themselves as foci in the university curricula before later varieties of the vernacular because they were strange and hard to learn—like Latin and Greek. Only within the past eighty years or so have textbook surveys of English literature been designed, and only within a much briefer time have they become at all common. English language and literature is one of our newest university subjects. Its appearance in the curriculum is as much a mark of our age as technology is.

If we are to consider the significance of the New Criticism in any fullness, we must begin with an awareness that it comes into being against this academic background, by now grown unfamiliar or completely forgotten. Literary criticism is not entirely academic, but its dependence upon the academic community is greater than we sometimes acknowledge. This is true of all criticism, and perhaps more of the New Criticism than of any other. One does not have to agree with Professor Northrop Frye in *The Anatomy of Criticism* that all teaching concerned with literature is in reality the teaching of criticism, not of literature itself, in order to be aware of the effect of the academic world upon critical activity. If literature were no concern of the formal educational system, how much literary criticism would there be? And of that which existed, how much would be read? Certainly William Empson's *Seven Types of Ambiguity*, F. R. Leavis's *The Great Tradition*, I. A. Richards's *Practical Criticism*, and Wellek's and Warren's *Theory of Literature* would not be selling in paperbacks as they are doing today.

Until the past few generations the existence of any English-language literary tradition, great or small, was not formally acknowledged in academic circles. In the West, the most distinguished writings not only in the vernacular but about the vernacular had virtually no effect upon the academic program until almost our own century. Dante's *De vulgari eloquio* did influence some extra-academic thinking about literature, but it has no discernible results in educational circles. Renaissance works modeled on it, such as Du Bellay's *Défense et illustration de la langue française* have no effective academic impact. Richard Mulcaster's *Elementarie,* so often touted for its enthusiasm about the English language, is frankly a treatise about preschool training, concerned chiefly with youngsters hardly seven years old and devoted in great part to methods of teaching how to write the alphabet. Mulcaster knew very well that when his pupils started in a regular grammar school they would be learning Latin, and learning it from textbooks written in Latin, and to this he registers no protest. Sidney's *Apologie for Poetrie* in places waxes enthusiastic about English, but it is so unacademic as to propose that English has no grammar and needs none. The *Apologie* is thought out along lines which Sidney learned from classical authors, and merits attention not for being original, as it is often made out to be, but for being merely exceptional in that it is a rare English treatise on poetry among scores of Latin treatments, many of them far more learned.

When critical attention shifted from the past to the present it shifted in two stages, at the end of which the New Criticism had formed itself. The first phase was the shift from interest in classical Latin and Greek to interest in the vernacular. The second, which followed immediately, was the shift within the field of English itself from interest in the antique to interest in the contemporary.

The New Criticism arises at the moment when the focus of literary study and theory shifts from the past to present performance. To date, we have seen no large-scale application of the New Criticism to ancient literature, although Robert Coheen, Richmond Lattimore, and Herbert Musurillo have recently made good starts, and, despite some few passing attempts in the late lamented *Scrutiny,* very little application of it even to medieval literature. To the Renaissance, which presents to us a modern face for a variety of reasons, and to subsequent ages more patently modern the New Criticism has chiefly addressed itself, but with its highest concentration of attention on contemporary or near-contemporary productions. Now that the first lean years are past and the college and university faculties of the United States are populated with those raised from their teens on the New Criticism, we learn from *College English* that the university student moving in some of the livest instructional circles is being introduced to literature through *Finnegans Wake*, Faulkner, Salinger, and—*The Catcher in the Rye* being already outmoded—Kerouac.

In times before our own, academic contact with one's literary coevals was not so easy. In fact, it was impossible. The literary-academic interchange was complicated by the classical-vernacular relationship. This relationship, moreover, was far from a straightforward thing. The classical languages and the vernaculars were not in official contact with one another, and yet they were by no means completely divorced. The academic world officially attended only to the classical languages and literatures. The extra-academic literary world did its own writing in the vernacular for the most part as the sixteenth century wore on into the seventeenth, until by the eighteenth century Latin literary productions often became little more than tours de force. But the extra-academic world attended explicitly to the classical languages and literatures, too. Since Latin, with some sprinkling of Greek, was the only literature in which formal training was possible, and since criticism always has strong academic roots, criticism of the vernacular was habitually screened through Latin and Greek frames of thought.

We seldom attend to the weirdness of this situation. Here we encounter no straightforward question such as the recent one: Do we or do we not retain Latin in the curriculum? Latin (with a bit of Greek) *was* the curriculum, at least in its lower reaches. The academic world thought and spoke Latin and Greek while teaching boys who more and more were using only English after school hours—or even during school hours, for by the eighteenth century the practice of teaching Latin in Latin from Latin textbooks, normal in the sixteenth and much of the seventeenth century from the beginning of grammar school on, was definitely giving way. Although this tension between the classical and vernacular had certain advantages, it could be quite distracting. In the eighteenth century we notice in criticism signs of a permanent, if benign and sometimes productive, schizophrenia, of which the ancients-versus-moderns furor was a syndrome.

The aim of the early humanists was to read and to write classical Latin and Greek—not merely to write an occasional letter or oration in one or the other language, but to write virtually all one's literary production in one or the other (Latin, in point of fact, for Greek never became current). Erasmus did this to the extent of ten huge folio volumes, and so did hundreds of others. Those who were educated in the humanist tradition, which, being extant even in the nineteenth century, survived far longer than the humanists themselves, were assumed to be operating with the same aims. In accordance with these aims, the humanist program of formal education produced not only a Neo-Latin literature of far greater massiveness than most persons suspect today, but it also produced, despite its aims, far more creative vernacular writers than genuinely creative Neo-Latinists. Indeed, without intending to do so, it produced all over Western Europe a wealth of vernacular writers such as earlier ages had never known.

The masters of the vernaculars seem never to have adverted to the fact that they had no formal training in the languages of which they were masters. The Shakespeares and Montaignes and Lope de Vegas simply failed to think of their vernaculars as having anything to do with formal education, even ideally. Shakespeare certainly never thought of anyone's teaching Shakespeare in a school. In schools even for small boys, one taught Latin, and to a lesser extent, Greek.

This Latin orientation of formal literary training gave to all literature a curiously public and formal, although not necessarily an unemotional cast. This was because Latin was no longer a vernacular language. The vernacular enters into areas of life where other languages cannot enter—the family, intimate personal relationships, and, most of all, the depths of the individual consciousness initially opened and permanently occupied by the terms and the concomitant concepts through which the individual first becomes conscious of his own existence as he learns to think and talk. Latin could be somewhat intimate in the letters of an Erasmus or More, but it was never a family language. Humanists actually advocated—and practiced—the expulsion of young boys from their families at around the age of seven so that they would be free of corrupting vernacular influences, particularly from womenfolk, including the child's own mother. For even the humanists' wives did not coo to their children in Ciceronian Latin—or in any Latin at all. No one ever entered into his first awareness of himself and the world around him through its ministrations. Latin was foreign to absolutely all of those who after classical times for well over a thousand years read and spoke and wrote it so well, but as a learned tongue.

The result of this dominance of a nonvernacular language on criticism is marked. Literature tends to be judged as somewhat doggedly public, free from intimacy, exterior. Yet there is, of course, another side to the picture. Literature cannot exist without some expression of human intimacy. Habituation to nonvernacular modes of expression tended to strengthen and make more virile the intimate notes in communication when these did appear, inevitably, in vernacular productions. There is a dignity about the relationship of Shakespeare's Romeo and Juliet, or about Cordelia's or Hermione's tenderness which we find great difficulty in establishing through vernacular media today. English could and did profit from the coexistence of a nonvernacular Latin tradition. Everyone knows how it assimilated the well tooled Latin sophistication—how, for example, Tudor and Stuart drama profited from Seneca.

But the peculiar relationship of the two languages, vernacular and Latin, is evident from the fact that borrowing was a one-way street. English could assimilate Latin poise, but Latin could not assimilate the intimacy of the vernacular tongue. Complete languages commonly have a women's vocabulary and a man's, but Latin had no currency among women, or even in the company of women, with some few exceptions such as Margaret More or Queen Elizabeth. Swift's *Journal to Stella* is unthinkable in Neo-Latin, not only in its vocabulary but in its very tone. When we say that Latin was an international language, we must remember that most human experience is not international and that large areas of human life eluded Latin precisely because of its over-specialized "universal" and scientific status. The price of "universality" was severe circumscription. Erasmus's works would be richer, and doubt-less less coarse, if he had been able to think of women as part of his audience.

II

The nature of critical activity was sure to be affected by the curious status of the two languages, competing and supporting each other at the same time. Criticism under these linguistic conditions could not be what it had been in ancient Rome or Greece, any more than it could be what criticism is today.

Nevertheless, in certain crucial ways the critical tradition of the humanist and posthumanist age up until the time of Coleridge is closer to ancient classical writing about literature than it is to the criticism of the post-Coleridgean age up to our own time. Before Coleridge, to speak generally, the rhetorical, or more explicitly the oratorical tradi-tion inherited from ancient Greece and Rome dominates with a force which we today find it hard to believe. In this tradition, the central literary or expressive activity of man is taken to be the oration or public address, and all other forms of discourse tend to be prescribed for, analyzed, and judged more or less by analogy with the oratorical form. The way in which even today we designate the general art governing effective expression as "rhetoric" memorializes the situation: *rhētōr* is the Greek word for an orator, and *rhētorikē* is originally the art govern-ing his skills.

The tyranny of oratory over other forms of expression can be seen from the fifteenth into the seventeenth century when letter-writing manuals treat the letter as one form of the oration, discussions of poetry commonly assume that the poet's aims are essentially no different from those of the orator (generally to instruct, and to move and please in so far as these aims serve the end of "teaching"), and many scientific or semiscientific tracts such as Rudolph Agricola's *Dialectical Invention* conclude each section with a "peroration" labeled as such.

The rhetorical tradition is so strong as to make it questionable whether literary criticism in the modern sense of the word—evaluation of literary performance on its own terms, gathered from the interior economy of the work itself—ever really existed on any appreciable scale from ancient times through at least the seventeenth century. If we mean by literary criticism nothing more definite than discussion, more or less formalized, concerning literary works and evaluation of their various effects on some ground or other, we can of course say that literary criticism goes back to the ancients, and doubtless beyond. The old rhetorical tradition did concern itself with literary effects in a most detailed fashion. And yet, although it is a tradition devoted to the meticulous study of literature, the difference between the study of literature which the older tradition had favored and what is meant by literary criticism in the English-speaking world today is staggering, and this in at least three obvious ways.

First, the older tradition, as manifest by its oratorical focus and related phenomena, retained massive commitments to the previous oral-aural culture of still earlier preliterate society. These commitments favored thinking of human expression as recited rather than as written down, as "epos"—to use Northrup Frye's recent terminology—rather than as "fiction." Under these conditions it is questionable whether in the ancient world we are concerned with literature at all. Can a preliterate culture or a culture still governed by preliterate foci have a literature? Or should what in such cultures corresponds more or less to literature today really be thought of in quite different terms? The ancient Greek and Roman educational system employed manuscripts to a limited extent, but it was oriented toward producing the vocal man, speakers rather than writers or analysts. Its end product was the orator. This was true not only in Rome but, as H.-I. Marrou has brilliantly shown, in Greece as well, where "wisdom-lovers" such as Socrates, Plato, and Aristotle operated well outside the normal educational perimeter, which was rhetorical or sophistic, and where Socrates paid dearly for doing just this.

Secondly, the rhetorical approach to literature differed from present-day Western approaches in its minimizing of the purely aesthetic. The professed primary aim of expression was to teach (*docere*), to move or persuade (*movere*) and to delight (*delectare*), but quite generally the last two aims were subordinated in all discourse (poetry included) to the first, the pragmatic one of teaching or instructing. Moreover, the rhetorical approach made one's attitude toward literature not only didactic but also dismayingly practical. The art of rhetoric was a way to "get ahead" in society, an avowed means of making friends and influencing people. Even when rhetoric was oriented toward show (as in the Isocratean or Gorgian tradition) rather than toward persuasion regarding some serious practical matter, it still remained a training for the public-speaking platform rather than for the stage or for the writing desk. Rhetoric prepared one primarily to address an audience not in character, as an actor might, nor from a distance in time and/or space, as a writer might. The *rhētor* or *orator* faced a flesh-and-blood audience more *engagé* than the audience in a theater or than readers who meet an author only in the silence of a book. The orator's audience was open to direct persuasion, and the orator's person interacted with the living audience before him, so that persuasion to action was a feasible and inviting aim even when this aim might not be avowed or expliciitly adverted to.

Since the study of literature was dominated by the study of rhetoric, or even identified completely with this latter study, literature itself was assimilated to action more than it is today. Letter-writing, philosophy, history, and poetry alike were felt as existing in a rhetorical framework, and by this fact were thought of as having somehow a directly pragmatic value such as critics and authors alike would hardly allow to any of these types of writing now. In *An Apologie for Poetrie* Sir Philip Sidney is in the main line of the classical tradition when he considers poetry as a form of rhetoric and as having teaching for its principal aim. Sidney's concept of teaching is of course considerably refined. He can hardly be said to favor an annoying or assertive didacticism. Yet the fact remains that for him the aim of all poetry must be somehow to teach—gently, sweetly,. indirectly, even deviously, but none the less resolutely and with a dismayingly single eye.

Thirdly, the older approach to literature was more prescriptive and normative than ours is today, and by more or less the same token more elementary. This was true particularly of the academic approach, but it was also in great part true of the extracurricular approach as well, for this could not help registering in one way or another the academic climate. Collections of earlier "critical essays" from the ancient, Renaissance, or eighteenth century world are quite different from collections of literary criticism today. They consist for the most part of literary recipe books, some philosophical discussion, and various occasional pieces, such as prefaces, which register attitudes, presuppositions, and theories. In sophistication and profundity this criticism from ages before ours is hardly up to the best literature of the age in which it appears. Literature was appreciated and reacted to profoundly and sensitively, but the ability to be articulate about either the work or the reaction lagged far behind the ability to write literature and to respond to it. Dryden's criticism, for all its suaveness, cannot compete for breadth of knowledge and understanding with the best criticism today. Pope's *Essay on Criticism* approaches literature in a platitudinous, if consummately clever, legislative mood which today a person of Pope's intelligence would not allow himself to manifest even at the age of twenty-three. By the time of Samuel Johnson, it is true, through periodical series such as *The Idler,* some nonacademic criticism was approaching the significant criticism of today, but it still remained relatively unsophisticated and uncomplicated by present-day standards—a treatment restricted to two or three dimensions as against treatments which habitually use more. In the pre-Coleridgean world there is nothing which even remotely compares to a book such as Wimsatt's and Brooks's *Literary Criticism: A Short History* or Kenneth Burke's *Counter-Statement* or Hugh Kenner's *Gnomon,* to take three quite diverse present-day productions.

The points made by earlier critics tended to be directed to a relatively uninformed audience, which one tacitly assumed wanted to be instructed, and the points tended to be larger—which might mean that they were more profound and sweepingly philosophical under some aspects, but also that they were much grosser in others.

The habit of looking back over one's shoulder to antiquity, acquired by reason of the Latin and Greek cast of the formal educational tradition, tended to keep one's view in focus with that of Plato, Cicero, Horace, Quintilian, and others who really exhibit little interest in what we should today call appreciation of literature but concern themselves either with prescribing how boys should be taught to be effective orators or citizens, or with reflection on tricks of the literary trade, or with philosophizing about literary effects in ways which are profound but by no means adequate to the total literary situation as we now know it. Aristotle's *Poetics* and the treatise *On the Sublime* perhaps by Longinus, from which a mature literary criticism could be developed, were commonly neglected, and when they were not, their beginnings were hardly matured in the general academic tradition. Even Dionysius of Halicarnassus, who in many ways approximated more than any other ancient or even any pre-Coleridgean writer what we should call literary criticism today, is in the last analysis interested in prescribing better recipes for rhetorical effectiveness, as S. F. Bonner points out in *The Literary Treatises of Dionysius of Halicarnassus*. Dionysius' sensitivity is out of the ordinary, but his interests remain basically pedagogical.

III

The lag in criticism is attributable to a number of causes. Criticism is a complex activity, exploiting insights furnished by a great many fields of knowledge. By comparison with criticism today, earlier criticism is sure to appear impoverished because the fields of psychology, sociology, anthropology, history—literary and other—linguistics, and comparative literature were rudimentary or nonexistent. There was a feedback here, too, for the importance of literature in understanding the structure of the human psyche and of society itself could not be explicitly known until these sciences were developed. Moreover, until recent times literacy was not so widespread and leisure was rare. It is perhaps noteworthy that the country with the shortest working week, the United States, has produced the maximum interest in literary criticism.

Nevertheless, among the principal causes at work in keeping criticism where it was, was the curriculum structure in its relation to the teaching of Latin. This structure has a long history. In the Middle Ages, the aim of Latin teaching had been to give a boy a working knowledge of Latin so that he could read, write, and speak it in pursuing his studies, whatever they were. For all formal education was in Latin: "philosophy" (which included logic and, in germinal form, psychology, physics, astronomy, and the rest of what we today would call "science"), medicine, law, and theology. The study of the Latin language was therefore an elementary school subject. Indeed, it was *the* elementary school subject.

The humanists later charged that in the medieval curriculum little attention was paid to literature. And, although some medieval teachers must be exonerated, the charge was generally valid. As soon as he could manage Latin fairly well, a medieval schoolboy was put to logic, physics, and other "philosophy," perfecting his Latin as he worked with these things, or muddling through somehow. Doubtless most boys wrought havoc with the language.

Humanists set out to better this situation. Indeed, they sometimes envisioned a study of Latin (with some Greek and Hebrew) so intensive that it seems nothing but literature was to be studied by anyone at all. Erasmus is very vague about the question as to when those who followed his program would ever get around to logic, physics, and the rest. And Peter Ramus tried substituting for physics a commentary on Virgil's *Georgics*. But this type of program did not establish itself. Try as they might to devise a curriculum in which the study of Latin (and Greek and Hebrew) literature topped the other studies, the humanists finally had to succumb before the pressures which had produced the medieval pattern. The study of Latin literature, or "rhetoric," although somewhat amplified beyond what it had been in the Middle Ages, remained a relative elementary part of the curriculum. It never recovered the eminence which it had enjoyed in classical times, when "rhetoric," or the training of the orator, was virtually synonymous with the whole of formal education, as Cicero and Quintilian make clear.

The humanists were caught in a series of contradictions of which they seem to have been blissfully unaware. Proclaiming the classical rhetorical doctrine, which made the aim of education the training of the public speaker, they were as a matter of fact not training Latin orators at all. Latin was going or gone in courtroom procedure, and in a public assembly political or forensic orations in Latin were in all but exceptional cases entirely out of place. Occasional ceremonial orations in the sixteenth and seventeenth centuries might be in Latin—as, once in a rare while, one might even be in Greek. In *The Unfortunate Traveler* (1594) Thomas Nashe in high spirits imagines such a ceremonial oration "presented" at Wittenberg to the Duke of Saxony by "a bursten-belly inkhorn orator called Vanderhulke" who speaks his "broccing double-beer oration" in Nashe's ebullient mock-heroic style. Nashe's refusal to take Latin oratory seriously is symptomatic. Most of the serious, practical public speaking done by the millions of men who as boys had studied Latin in school from the fifteenth through the nineteenth centuries was certainly in their vernaculars.

Moreover, existing as it did in a typographical rather than an oratorical culture, the humanist enterprise trained for writing with an emphasis unthinkable in ancient times. As it shifted from oratorical to typographical channels, the course of academic Latin can be plotted in terms of the popularity of the oration, the epic, and the mock epic. In seventeenth century textbooks the sixteenth century interest in the oration is obviously losing some ground to interest in belles-lettres of the sort which are read, not recited. Attention to the poets grows. Latin verse could be measured and described in visual terms of "long" and "short" syllables even when one was a thoroughly unskilled reader. And in ancient Latin poetry, what better than Virgil's epic could be taught in the classroom? Horace was too sophisticated for grammar-school students, Catullus and most of Ovid too risqué. (In the sixteenth century, Sir Thomas Elyot, recognizing the importance of Ovid's mythology but obviously worried about his morals, had suggested that the master summarize Ovid's stories for the boys.) Similar reasons urged against Greek poets other than Homer, so that in Greek, too, the epic was the literary form to teach. Honor, loyalty, military prowess, "courage," as Sir Thomas Elyot had put it, and other similar ideals assimilable by boys in their early teens could be discovered in the epics—although sometimes the discovery took discreet searching, for, as Pope was later to announce in "A Receipt to Make an Epic Poem," it was never quite settled "whether or no it be necessary for the hero of a poem to be an honest man."

The result of this academic concentration of attention was that the epic, already launched as an important literary form with the other classical forms enjoying humanist sponsorship, received an emphasis such as it had never before known in the history of Western civilization. *Paradise Lost* is only one of the many consequences, if the most valuable one. Many of the hundreds upon hundreds of other seventeenth century epics were in Latin—as *Paradise Lost* would have been had John Milton not lost his conviction that he could rise above second rank as a Latin stylist.

By the next century, the eighteenth, the epic theme had been worn thin and trite, and the Latin language associated with it was losing caste. Under other circumstances the epic might have dropped out of public attention, as Gothic novels have today. But, unlike Gothic novels today, the epic continued to be taught in eighteenth century and nineteenth century schools as the very core of the literature treated—Latin literature, of course. Unable for the moment to wring anything more from the genre directly, and yet filled with its idiom through their school days, poets could only turn to the mock epic to unburden their imaginations. One can parody only what is thoroughly familiar. The result is the hundreds upon hundreds of "-iads" which flood through the eighteenth century and the early nineteenth century: *The Dunciad, The Beeriad, The Parsionad, The Fanciad, The Gymnasiad, The Battiad, The Old Woman's Dunciad, The Nowiad, The Prussiad, The Murphiad, The Ballooniad, The Mousiad,* and all the rest. Among the causes of the satiric spirit of the eighteenth century the condition of the curriculum must surely be counted, although it seldom or never is. For the same forces which produced the mock epic out of the Latin classroom would inevitably help produce a generally satiric climate. All boys studied Latin, and virtually no other language (except the satellite Greek). What would a boy make of a world into which he was introduced by being forced to study a language which, it was becoming more and more likely, he would never speak or write, and only that language? One can hear the Voltairean cackle from the schoolroom benches. Moreover, throughout much eighteenth century satire the Latin substructure generating the satiric reaction is patent in explicit references within satiric works. The relation of the Latin curriculum to the general satirical climate certainly deserves some fuller study.

By pointing out these strange tensions in the humanist program I do not mean to say that the program failed to produce competent Neo-Latinists in numbers well through the eighteenth century. But the numbers of those who were capable of original composition in Latin was incredibly small by comparison with the total number of boys and young men who studied Latin in grammar school or university. We may complain today about the literary incompetence of those who have studied English or other vernaculars. But this incompetence would be breath-taking virtuosity compared to the incompetence in Latin of most boys who in the past studied the ancient tongue.

Exact figures are unavailable, but one might project some—if only to spur someone on to a detailed study on the basis of which they could be challenged—relying on a fairly long-standing acquaintanceship with the Neo-Latin milieu. I should be surprised if, of the boys who were taught Latin in the British Isles during the sixteenth century more than 10 per cent ever read any extended writing in Latin during adult life.

The extreme popularity of translations into English from the Latin at this early date is sympomatic of the state of affairs. And the number of adult readers of Latin steadily dropped. By the ninteenth century, I should conjecture it was not more than ½ of 1 per cent of those who had had some Latin education. For mid-seventeenth-century England we have a contemporary statement: in 1655 John Wharton, pushing the cause of the vernacular in his *New English Grammar,* conjectures that only one boy in a hundred has any need for Latin after he leaves secondary school.

One might argue that these estimates reflect the fact that a great many beginners in Latin never got beyond the most elementary stage, failing to terminate their studies. This is true. But such a fact has tremendous implications for the Latin-speaking and Latin-writing community. What sort of literary criticism can be generated in an academic community where the language which is the center of attention exists for most of those in contact with it at a stage at which it never really serves as an effective medium of communication even when it is made a compulsory medium enforced by the use of the birch?

But to have finished the Latin course, even after the humanists' campaign to make the study of literature something more advanced and sophisticated, was hardly to have moved beyond the elementary stage. Even after the Renaissance, boys commonly terminated all contact with Latin Literature—orators, historians, and poets—at about the age of fourteen. Such was the case, as Father George E. Ganss shows in *Saint Ignatius' Idea of a Jesuit University,* even in the Jesuit tradition, where so much was made of literary training. Since the ordinary boy's linguistic capabilities are necessarily rudimentary at this age, real competence in Latin was perfected, when it was perfected at all, as one dealt with the logic, physics, and other "philosophical" matters after one had terminated all classroom study of literature as such. This was not the way the humanists had wanted it, but it was the way it continued to be.

Some few scholars might individually pursue philological studies on their own initiative, but until the nineteenth century there were virtually no regular courses in any literature available anywhere beyond the secondary school level, or even beyond the lower reaches of the secondary school level. With some few exceptions (as in the Italian "academies") professors even of classical literature from Renaissance times on to the ninteenth century had normally only youngsters as their pupils.

Advanced work, when it developed, became possible first in "philology" and much later in literature itself. The development of graduate programs in literature is a phenomenon of the last few generations.

Comments met with throughout the Neo-Latin period make it evident that under the conditions which prevailed earlier even the knowledge of Latin which could be expected of a fourteen-year-old was not always met with in a pupil fourteen years old or even older. Writing his *Notes on the Reform of the University of Paris (Prooemium reformandae Parisiensis academiae)* in 1562, Peter Ramus protests that of the one thousand or more students who he says go daily to hear the lectures of the regius professors (those later grouped together as the Collège de France), barely two hundred have a knowledge of (Latin) grammar, rhetoric, and logic sufficient to follow the lectures. And matters at Paris were better than they had been elsewhere. Shortly before this time, after floundering about the philosophy classrooms of Spanish universities, Inigo de Loyola had ultimately settled in Paris to do serious work on the Latin which would finally enable him to understand what the professors of philosophy were saying. Paris impressed him sufficiently for him to prescribe later that the schools of the Society of Jesus which he had founded were to follow the *modus Parisiensis*.

In England, matters were not more inspiring. William T. Costello's recent book, *The Scholastic Curriculum at Early Seventeenth-Century Cambridge,* makes it clear that despite the fact that the age of entering students at Cambridge was far higher than it had been a hundred years before, Latin skills still had to be taught through the first university year, which was devoted to rhetoric. And a recent doctoral dissertation at St. Louis University by William Henry Kenney, concerned with John Locke's educational background, presents evidence that one of the subjects which most occupied the attention of Oxford dons in Locke's youth was the incompetence in Latin manifested by students even when they were finishing at the University. During the period studied by Mark H. Curtis in *Oxford and Cambridge in Transition 1558-1642,* the gradual substitution of extrastatutory instruction, conducted privately and hence not necessarily in Latin, for attendance at statutory university lectures (in Latin, of course) undoubtedly registers and abets growing neglect of Latin.

From the sixteenth century through the nineteenth Latin tended to be strung out higher and higher in the curriculum. This was not because students knew it better and thus were demanding more advanced courses but for quite the opposite reason. They were not learning it so well in the lower classes, and instruction in Latin had to continue on into the higher. Latin was on the decline. The reasons for this were many—the growth of nationalism; the increasing importance of the tradesmen, artisans, and small merchants, who were schooled in arithmetic and the vernacular but not "lettered" in Latin; the linguistic complexities attaching to the development of colonies; and many other interrelated developments.

But with all these reasons a more basic one was operating: the fact that the increase of human knowledge was such that one could no longer afford the luxury of a curriculum demanding that everybody who went to school devote to a foreign tongue as much time as Latin had traditionally demanded. Earlier educational programs, well through the seventeenth century, called for the study of Latin, and nothing else, for some six to ten or more years from the time when the boy first entered school to the time when, at what would correspond to our later years of high school, he began the study of "philosophy." Philosophy was already a massive subject in the sixteenth century, including as it did all of human knowledge purveyed in the formal school curriculum short of language study and the higher specialized subjects of medicine, law, and theology. The rudiments of what we now know as psychology, astronomy, meteorology, general physics, astrophysics, zoology, botany, mathematics, and music were all understood as part of "philosophy" and, in principle if not in fact, were covered in the philosophy course.

This was bad enough, but when present-day fields of study began to assume somewhat autonomous shapes, and items such as geography, history, political science, economics, and the rest, not to mention a scatter of modern foreign languages and literatures and the vernacular as well, intruded themselves as large-scale separate disciplines, the problem of instructing in all these things after one had put all of one's elementary and secondary schooling into mastering Latin proved too much. More and more, Latin was pushed aside—which meant that it was strung out as one of many subjects later and later in the curriculum until, in recent times, we have men older than medieval university masters of arts and doctors of philosophy (often around eighteen years of age) taking up for the first time in their university days the Latin which in Shakespeare's time was a subject—or rather *the* subject—for all seven-year-old schoolboys. Unfortunately, because the evolution of

Latin in the curriculum has been so poorly understood, the university students are in some places still studying the language by the same methods which were devised originally for elementary school teaching and which have leaked up under pressure into the higher reaches of the curriculum.

As Latin was crowded up and out of many curricula, the situation for the Latin teacher was self-aggravating. Teachers not well prepared in Latin because of the academic deterioration of the language were finding it harder and harder to be stimulated to excellence through extracurricular activity in the ancient tongue. The number of books in Latin steadily diminished from the seventeenth century through the nineteenth. Where the appeal of Latin had once been so general that no one needed to give reasons for studying it—it was the door to all learning—now one had to find reasons, often highly specialized and sometimes even specious ones. So long as the academic study of literature was tied to a language in these straits, criticism could hardly be expected to develop a high sophistication or suppleness. Language study became "philology."

IV

The basic reason for the straits in which Latin was finding itself was the fact—seldom if ever adverted to by the humanists—that it was a language wholly and entirely dependent upon the academic world for its very existence. It had become thus dependent when, through the seventh to the ninth century of the Christian era, spoken Latin had evolved away from ancient usage enough to make it meaningful to speak of Romance tongues, French or Catalan or others, which were no longer ancient Latin. At this point—impossible to determine precisely, of course—when the vernaculars became identifiable as Romance languages, Latin had lost its hold everywhere except in more or less formal education, becoming what we may call Learned Latin.

Later apologists for Latin, particularly in the Neo-Latin age (from A.D. 1400 on), blithely equate the academic language as used in their times with the language of ancient Rome without adverting to the vast changes in its employment as a means of communication—for example, the patent fact that in their times the language was used only by males and the fact that the language had no childish or nursery forms, which are the forms through which every complete language initiates its normal speakers into the language itself and into contact with the reality about him in the all-important days of infancy. Writers such as Sir Thomas Elyot in *The Book Named the Governor* (1541) or Roger Ascham in *The Schoolmaster* (first published posthumously, 1570), at the very moment when they are prescribing that a boy begin to speak Latin when he is around seven years old, are legislating also that he be kept at all costs from using anything but fully adult Latin forms even at this tender age. Elyot wants him sent away from home and from the company of women to prevent the development of any nursery or other less-than-adult forms of speech.

Present-day linguistics provides a way of describing the foregoing state of affairs by means of the term "creolization." This is a process whereby a language serving as a lingua franca for a community of adults of diverse linguistic stock is filled out with childish and nursery forms when the community raises children in the language. Learned Latin is like a lingua franca in serving groups of varied linguistic stocks, but it is a lingua franca in which the self-appointed custodians of the language regularly take a steadfast stand against creolization of any sort. The humanists were determined that their Learned Latin would not become a complete language—although they, of course, did not put it this way. As children of the manuscript culture of the Middle Ages, now, by their new attachment to typography, doubly devoted to the word-in-space rather than to the spoken word, they failed even to notice that their manuscript-plus-typography commitment to Latin was utterly the reverse of the vocalist Cicero whom they professed to admire.

The Latin of the academic world after the rise of the vernaculars from about the seventh century on, which we have styled Learned Latin, still needs description in modern linguistic terms. It resembled an artificial language in that it was maintained in existence by a set of rules preserved among initiates by explicit agreement and in writing. (Any language governed by a formally developed grammar is of course to some extent an artificial language.) Despite the popular impression, Learned Latin was not a "dead" language in the sense that a language is "dead" when it forms no new terms. Neo-Latin is glutted with new terms, as Professor Paul W. Blackford and his associates compiling the Neo-Latin lexicon now in progress well know. New terms are still being coined in Neo-Latin today, where it persists as an ecclesiastical lingua franca or in some few learned circles, mostly among classicists themselves. But all neologisms in the language are governed by written usages. There is no such thing as a formation developed through vocalization habits, nor has there been for hundreds of years. Even when it is used vocally, the language is controlled by writing and latterly by printing. It could perhaps be described as an artificially preserved language, chirographically (and in part typographically) controlled.

Such a language naturally tends to detain instruction at an elementary level. Instruction in any foreign language has to begin at a level more elementary than formal instruction in one's own language learned at home. A child entering school even with very little intellectual promise at all knows large numbers of words in his native tongue, together with all the phonemes and a tremendous number of the morphemes out of which meaningful utterance is built, as well as the basic grammatical and morphophonemic systems which his language employs. He does not know them perfectly, but his knowledge of them has in many ways an inerrancy which qualifies it as highly advanced—more advanced than the knowledge had by most persons who learn the langauge after childhood will ever be. But in the areas of a foreign language none of these things are known.

Moreover, in the case of a language artificially removed from all but certain areas of life, the normal areas for developing real skill through casual use are closed. In the sixteenth and seventeenth centuries valiant attempts were made to meet this difficulty by physical isolation of the pupil from all but Latin speakers, as has been seen, and by the provision that pupils should use Latin at school, even when they were playing, as well as by the publishing of textbooks with sample Latin dialogues between pupil and master, between pupil and pupil, and between various assortments of other characters.

These dialogues were to provide the constructions and words for ordinary conversation—the words for table, games, broom, floor, ceiling, and the like which one needs for daily living but which one encounters seldom in Cicero, Horace, or Virgil. The enterprise and ingenuity displayed in some of these dialogues is admirable. Little boys complain about their teachers, ask questions about everything on earth and in heaven, quarrel among themselves, sulk, fight and make up, and all in Latin. But such brave pedagogical efforts could have only moderate success. This is not the way one first learns one's native tongue—by finding in a textbook the words one wants to use, matching one's expression with a book. We learn to speak in the first instance by matching our expressions with our infantile insights and needs, and that in the social context of the family, where our errors themselves are prized as achievements. At the time when we are first being introduced to the reality around us and encouraged to form those initial concepts which will permanently orient our thinking, language is a vocal experience, far removed from any written, visual control. In the case of Latin, for well over a millenium now, no one has been able to speak it who has not been able to write it as well.

We may think that today the base of elementary instruction which we must supply in English is far out of proportion to what it should be. We should be able to work through English usage more rapidly so as to devote more time in the total educational process to the assimilation and appreciation of literature. This may be true. Nevertheless, the bases of elementary instruction which had to be supplied for Latin were far greater than what we supply for English. We may be dismayed that pupils make so many errors in their English expression. If the entire formal instruction in the schools were in Latin, they would not even be in a position to make any errors until we had begun to work with them.

There is no doubt that the Latin-centered curriculum helped produce competent writers. But the fact is that we have no accurate knowledge of the processes whereby it helped do so. We do know that, because everything was in a foreign language, the student had to be forced into a contact with language itself which was much more intense than is usual today. The mere structure of the ordinary curriculum in the sixteenth century, for example, is ample evidence of the intensity of the linguistic experience: some six to ten years studying virtually nothing but Latin (with some attention to its ancillary Greek) all year long! Students' notebooks and annotated textbooks yield corroborative evidence as to how doggedly the student was forced to immerse himself in words. Many of the textbooks show Latin orations and poems with marginal annotations identifying for page after page every trope or figure which could be rooted out of the text: anachresis, catachresis, zeugma, polysyndeton, onomatopoeia, prosopopoeia, and so on indefinitely. This procedure, followed even in grammar schools, was invaluable in tooling up the rhetorical machinery of a Shakespeare. What it did for the less talented is more open to question.

But whatever it did, it is hardly what we mean today by literary criticism. It sounds much more like the most deadly *Wissenschaft*. And, as a matter of record, one can find sixteenth century commentaries on classical texts representing classroom lectures which, bored with their own dullness, total up the number of times various figures of speech are used in one or another oration of Cicero's. Peter Ramus gives the following "summary of rhetorical analysis" as the result of his literary exploration of Cicero's *Third Catilinarian* (I translate from Ramus's own Latin, leaving, however, individual Latin terms where the English equivalent would today be just as mysterious and less accurate):

In tropes, the elocution is good and rich. Metonymy occurs sixty times, synechdoche about the same number of times, irony not once, metaphor eighty times. . . . Of the figures of sentence . . . *optatio* is not used, *prolepsis* occurs three times; prosopopoeia twice, but concealed as digression and *dialogismus; praeteritio* is used once, other figures of sentence not at all.

This sort of thing was typical of Ramists, but it was not peculiar to them. Literary formalism included not only this type of "analysis" but also the use of recipes for praising and blaming persons, places, and things. These formulae set a structure: one could vituperate a person by working from first his country, then his remote ancestors, his proximate ancestors, his relatives and friends, his clothing, physique from head to foot, and so on, vituperating each of these items successively and in detail through consideration of their causes, effects, adjuncts, opposites, and thus through all the various "places" or *loci communes* which provided "arguments." This formalism is frightening and seemingly deadly, but it could keep a grammar school boy busy for a long time. In the hands of a skilled writer such formalism was even liberating, for it could free his imagination from preoccupation with structure and allow it to vent its full fury on detail. Much of Shakespeare's most effective writing is strung on a framework of these recipes, learned originally to compose in Latin for grammar school assignments. Shakespeare relied on such formulae for that facility which brought Ben Jonson to say of him that he was too facile and had to have a drag put on him, "*Sufflaminandus est,* as Augustus said of Haterius. His wit was in his own power." But Jonson, too, used the formulae.

Few students were as prolix or linguistically gifted as Shakespeare and Jonson, and the long-term effect of an educational system thus centered on an artificially preserved chirographic and typographic language was inevitable. Of the effort given to teaching Latin, almost all went into rudimentary instruction at a level far below that of rudimentary instruction in the vernacular today. Few of the academic community with Latin skills used these skills at a level where anything approximating literary criticism could be set in motion. There was no sizeable community in which a dialogue among critics could develop.

V

Formal instruction in language and literature persisted in a predominantly rudimentary state longer than we commonly imagine. English crept into the university lecture halls through the eighteenth century when it gradually became generally tolerable for professors to lecture in their native tongue. But the infiltration process did not forthwith go so far as to bring professors of literature to regard their native language as a subject of instruction. In academic circles at the time of the American Revolutionary War, "literature" unqualified still meant Latin and Greek literature, only equipped now, most likely by a kind of tacit consent, with explanations in English.

Classrooms and lecture halls are numerous and professors are even more numerous and are reticent about their own behavior as well, so that we shall certainly never know exactly all the breaches, large and small, through which English leaked into the curriculum either as a vehicle or as a subject of instruction. Nevertheless some of the breaches about which we do know are worth examining for the light they shed on the situation of English literature and criticism. Some of the pioneer efforts in favor of the teaching of English literature were made not in England itself but in Scotland and Ireland.

In Scotland, according to the report of Norman Kemp Smith in *The Philosophy of David Hume*, Francis Hutcheson (1695-1746) began to teach philosophy in the vernacular sometime after 1729. By the mid-eighteenth century at the instigation of Henry Home, later Lord Kames, and others a succession of public lectures was initiated at Edinburgh on the subject of belles-lettres. Home, a judge who in 1762 was to publish his own famous three-volume work entitled *Elements of Criticism*, managed to secure the services of Adam Smith, who began his lectures in the winter of 1748 and continued these lectures until in 1751 he became

Professor of Logic in the University of Glasgow and moved on to his better known economic phase.

Smith was succeeded by Robert Watson, who became Professor of Logic and Rhetoric at St. Andrews in 1758 and who was succeeded in the belles-lettres lectureship at Edinburgh by Hugh Blair. Blair's lectures were delivered in the University, but as Robert Morell Schmitz explains in his highly informative book *Hugh Blair,* only after June, 1760, when Blair became Professor of Rhetoric, did they have any standing in the University curriculum. They were published in an Edinburgh and London edition of 1783, with an American edition the following year, as *Lectures on Rhetoric and Belles Lettres.* One feels that all this ostentation about "belles-lettres" instead of literature was the Scot's way of reminding the Englishman that even when interested in English, the right-minded Scot kept his French commitments flying. In all likelihood, Professor Schmitz conjectures, the published lectures were in virtually the same form as that in which Blair had presented them orally each year at the University of Edinburgh since 1760. The lectures are important in their peripheral relationship to the university curriculum and to English literature, as well as in the widespread influence they exerted on critical theory.

Blair approaches literature generically rather than English literature specifically. This was quite in accord with common eighteenth century practice, which inclined toward viewing languages and literatures in a universalist way, from the point of view of a hypothetical generic language of which individual languages were taken to be simply specific variants. There is little awareness of an English tradition as such. Instead we find lectures considering the subjects of taste, criticism, genius, sublimity, beauty, and other "pleasures of taste," the rise and progress of language and of writing, structure of language generally and then of English as a particular instance, style, perspicuity and precision, metaphor, and so on, down through public speaking (called eloquence) and the various genres of writing. The middle group of lectures appears to be a residue left by the two-part Ramist rhetoric of several generations earlier: eighteen lectures treating figurative language, style, and eloquence (here in the sense of oratorical composition) correspond roughly to the first part of rhetoric which Ramists called style (*elocutio*), and the one lecture on delivery which follows at a little distance corresponds to the Ramist second part of rhetoric, called by the same name, delivery (in Latin, *pronunciatio*). In terms of space allotted to it, this was always minuscule by comparison with the more massive first part.

Throughout the *Lectures* reference is made to literature, but this is looked upon as material to clarify or "illustrate" Blair's own discourse. The literature referred to is indifferently Latin and Greek or English, with occasional references to that of other languages. In discussing the eloquence of popular assemblies Blair features Demosthenes; for pulpit eloquence, where a Christian had to furnish the subject matter, he takes up Bishop Atterbury. Epic poetry is illustrated with Homer, Virgil, and Lucan from the Latin, Tasso from the Italian, Camoëns from the Portuguese, Fénelon and Voltaire from the French, Milton from English. Drama is treated mostly in terms of Greek, Roman, French, and English plays, with considerable attention to the unities of time and place and a generally unenthusiastic response to the British playwrights, most notably to Shakespeare, whose faults, Blair conjectures, are probably at least as great as his merits. In only six lectures out of forty-seven—that on Bishop Atterbury's sermon, four on the style of the *Spectator*, and one on Swift's style—is Blair concerned directly and chiefly with English literature. And at that, Swift was an Irishman.

Blair's relative indifference to English is the more noteworthy because to some extent part of the plot set afoot by Home in promoting the Edinburgh lectures was that the lecturers should treat English-language authors. Home and others had set up the Edinburgh lectures originally, as Schmitz shows, in an effort to Briticize Scotland, conceiving that the proper way to do this was not to import an Englishman, sure to be suspect north of the Border, but to make use of a sufficiently Briticized native who could rub the edge off the Northern burr with greater diplomatic finesse. Adam Smith had been a Scot with an Oxford education, and Blair not only had attended Smith's lectures on rhetoric but had avowed the continuity of his own lectures with Smith's. In a sense, Blair's lectures thus can be taken to represent a maximum treatment which could be given to English literature at the time.

This maximum attention to English literature in the *Lectures* destined to be among the most used critical works for over a hundred years turns out to be peripheral to academic treatment of English as such on several scores. First, it takes its origin from a movement not to provide formal education for youth but to "improve" the citizenry generally.

Even after Blair had moved his lectures into the University there was an attempt to open them once more to the nonacademic public. Blair was offered an increase of one hundred pounds in his stipend if he would consent to this arrangement, but rejected the proposal on the grounds that open lectures would be "not only less profitable (except financially) to myself, but ruinous to education." This remark illustrates sufficiently the nonacademic character of the quondam audience bidding for readmission. Secondly, Blair's *Lectures* are peripheral in that not English, but the classical languages, remain Blair's central preoccupation. Moreover, the lectures are peripheral in that they appear in a Scottish setting, where English itself was a peripheral language. It is by no means an accident that where Scots dialect was the real language of the people it was easier to think of formal lectures concerned with English than it was to think of such lectures in England itself. A degree of unfamiliarity was needed to establish academic interest. One hundred years later, that interesting Vermont lawyer and scholar George P. Marsh in the fifth of his remarkable *Lectures on the English Language* (1859; fourth edition, 1865) gave the then still accepted verdict:

The systematic study of the mother-tongue, like that of all branches of knowledge which we acquire, to a sufficient extent for ordinary practical purposes, without study, is naturally very generally neglected. It is but lately that the English language has formed a part of the regular course of instruction at any of our higher seminaries, nor has it been made the subject of as zealous and thorough philological investigation by professed scholars, as the German, the French, or some other living languages.

The currency of Blair's *Lectures on Rhetoric and Belles Lettres* was phenomenal. Schmitz lists 25 editions in the British Isles (20 in London, 2 in Edinburgh, 3 in Dublin) plus 3 Continental editions in English and 10 editions of translations, 37 American editions (in the one year 1817 alone, 3 New York editions), 53 abridgements in Great Britain and America, 6 editions of questions for the *Lectures* (all in the United States), and 8 different textbooks (number of editions not given) using Blair's *Lectures* in part. The bulk of these were before 1850, but mid-century is by no means a sharp cut-off date. Blair is representative of a state of affairs persisting pretty generally till the last quarter of the nineteenth century and by no means entirely vanished at the century's end. Here the literary focus of the academic world and of academic criticism remains basically and in principle Latin. English is still felt to be more or less under the tutelage of the older tongue—we must not forget that only in the past decade of our own lifetime has an English grammar based on the straightforward description of English without resort to Latin analogues begun to come into use.

This tutelage was being contested perhaps a bit more in Ireland of the mid-nineteenth century than in the Scotland of Blair's day. John Henry Newman had set up in the 1850's a chair of English at his University in Dublin when there were no such chairs elsewhere in the British Isles except in Scotland and at King's College in London. He brought to Dublin as Professor of English Thomas Arnold, younger brother of Matthew. But in Newman's program, as detailed in Father Fergal McGrath's *Newman's University: Idea and Reality,* English literature turns up only after the first two years at the University are completed and then only as one of six subdivisions of literature in the program, competing on an equal footing as an elective with Latin, Greek, Celtic, Hebrew, and any two modern foreign languages. Moreover, Newman fears that if financial difficulties force curtailment of the University program, Arnold's chair of English is likely to be among the first to be sacrificed, simply for want of pupils.

Newman's 1856 comment on Arnold's pioneer history of English literature is a fascinating document in a variety of ways. It shows the amorphous state of English literary studies here at their beginnings. Newman hesitates about Arnold's proposed omission of Clarendon and Milton, yet owns that neither belongs to any school, puzzles about leaving out the novelists yet queries anyone's ability "to get boys seriously to read them," and so on. We are a long way from our present-day courses in the Novel in Contemporary America.

But, with all this stress on Latin and humility about English, the status of Latin is obviously no longer what it was two hundred years earlier, when learned books were still written in Latin by the thousands. As has been shown by Richard Foster Jones in *The Triumph of the English Language,* by Stephen Potter in *The Muse in Chains,* and for a more specialized area by Howard Mumford Jones in *The Theory of American Literature,* English was becoming an established fact, even academically, by the end of the nineteenth century. Massive reading of Latin works was a thing of the past.

The early treatments of English tend to be textual, formalistic, highly systematic, and "logical," like the Latin teaching which they supersede. The frames of reference in Blair's *Lectures,* like those in medieval and Renaissance rhetoric, are by today's critical standards often incontestably elementary. Preoccupied as they are with preserving schemata, the *Lectures* cannot follow with great suppleness the uncharted maneuvers one is sure to meet with in original work. The heritage of Latin teaching can be recognized here. For the elementary schoolboy with limited Latin skills abstractions were handled more easily than concrete complexities. The twelve-year-old who is incapable of expressing himself regarding the niceties of writer-speaker relationships (commonplace now in college and university literature courses), regarding the attitudes of the writer toward his material, his use of various "masks," or his polysemous and archetypal symbolism, can be counted on perhaps to distill out of a literary work a "theme" or an "argument" which showed the purportedly "logical" structure of the work, or to fit the work into a predesigned schema.

Blair's abstract and schematized approach is representative well into the beginning of the present century, when students were still taught about literature more than they were brought to read it. A great number of persons over fifty today were taught English literature in terms of biographies of authors, genres, classifications, and schemata of all sorts sketched on blackboards, while the works to whose authors and titles they were being introduced remained largely unread in the keeping of librarians who, rather more than today's librarians, liked their books to remain on the shelves.

One reason for this situation proves the existence of the situation: good texts of English and histories of English literature were hard to come by. Manuals, outlines, and histories of English literature generally preceded the anthologies. And only with the Great Books programs do we meet with a large-scale breakthrough to a "new" method, in which texts, and not books about texts, are the center of attention.

A surfeit of manuals, outlines, and histories and a paucity of texts manifest the tendency to treat literature as a *fait accompli* which was a major tendency encouraged by the classical heritage. The hostility of the New Criticism, as represented by Dr. F. R. Leavis, to this tendency so marked a generation ago is vocal and well known. In the academic atmosphere prevailing at the turn of the present century literature was not something around oneself, but something to which one betook oneself. The pursuit of the literary rather uniformly presented itself as a kind of triple withdrawal—into Latin, into the study, and into the world of one's own youth. Housman might be the key symbol here: a classicist, and a disenchanted one at that, a recluse, and a eulogizer, albeit in English, of Shropshire adolescence. Since literature in this tradition existed as a kind of preformed corpus handed on from one generation to the youth of the next, to return to one's youth was to sense literature in its fullness. The predominant academic note was nostalgia. To be interested in literature in a serious, academic way was thus by definition to be regressive. As late as George Lyman Kittredge and Sir Arthur Quiller-Couch, to whom later generations indeed owe so much despite it all, this feeling for literature still persists: the impression is delicately conveyed that it is basically a matter of quiet evenings by the fire, with a flagon of ale and a hot poker.

If literature was a corpus, by 1917 or so Mr. T. S. Eliot, encouraged by Mr. Ezra Pound, was determined to make it sprout. The importance of Eliot's "Tradition and the Individual Talent" is now an established fact, and its affinity with Bergsonian and other thinking which has helped twentieth-century man keep abreast of actuality is plain to see. But the relevance of this essay to the situation of English literature in the academic world has been less well attended to. The world to which Eliot presents "Tradition and the Individual Talent" is a world which is academically just emerging from the study of Latin into the study of English. Tradition is here a particularly sensitive issue. Eliot belongs to the first generation of students, as we have seen, who could get thoroughgoing instruction in English literature at Harvard, where Francis James Child, who had become Harvard's first professor of English in 1876, had died only a few years before Eliot entered the University and where George P. Baker was during Eliot's own student years developing interest in venturesome dramatic productions in English. Pound, who was educated elsewhere—at the University of Pennsylvania and Hamilton College—remains much more in the overtly Latin and Greek tradition, the last classically trained mind, it has been said.

The New Criticism, whatever it is, is certainly represented on the one hand by Eliot and Pound, university graduates and quondam faculty members, and on the other by F. R. Leavis, who has remained in the academic community. None of these three have ever stopped talking to the academic community. Indeed, of late, it has seemed that it is chiefly the academic community to whom they are talking. This is particularly true with regard to the United States, where the literature of the English-speaking world, including the most contemporary literature, is taught both to more students and with far greater intensity than vernacular literature is taught in any other Western country, because of the curious American tradition which considers liberal education in the sense of general education to be a part, not merely of secondary school's business, but of the universities' business as well.

At the end of the belated Latin language crisis in the academic community the New Criticism has been born. It is because it came into the world speaking an academically new language that its postnatal cries have attracted so much attention. The New Criticism—again, whatever it is—was born of the vernacular matrix newly formed within the universities of the English-speaking world.

This New Criticism may be defined in various ways, but it is easy to make clear what we mean by it simply by saying that it is the criticism which is practiced diversely by certain persons in our day, such as, for example, besides Eliot and Pound and Leavis, by I. A. Richards, Cleanth Brooks, Allen Tate, William K. Wimsatt, Jr., Marshall McLuhan, Northrop Frye, Hugh Kenner, and hundreds of others, almost all of them more or less permanently denizens of the academic world. Even if we try to define the New Criticism more precisely, for example with Northrop Frye, who in *The Anatomy of Criticism* distinguishes "fantastical learning, or myth criticism, contentious learning, or historical criticism, and delicate learning or the 'new' criticism," I should still say of this New Criticism what seems to me to be the conclusion of the assortment of facts and reflections which has been presented here. It is the criticism you get when an academic community supplies an audience for vernacular literature large enough and mature enough and intellectually sophisticated enough to make possible intelligent, and often subtly contrived, talk about literary performance. The New Criticism is, in other words, simply a type of criticism which matures as the study of literature matures with the emergence of the vernacular full blown on the academic scene. It is not always correct or inspiring. Sometimes it is wrongheaded and mediocre. But, even if you disagree with the New Criticism, there is no point in looking back to a conjectural Old Criticism which previously performed the offices of the New. There was no Old Criticism. There were no academic vernacular offices for it to perform.

ELEVEN

Latin and the Social Fabric

I

WITH agitation over the teaching of Latin having its effect even at Oxford and Cambridge, the Latin question has again become a matter of some public concern. One of the strangest aspects of the current discussion, however, is the relative lack of knowledge, even in supposedly informed circles, about the teaching of Latin over the last few centuries and the vast changes in the role the language has played in Western culture.

There is to date no adequate descriptive treatment of Latin from the sixth century of the Christian era to our own times done from the point of view of modern linguistics or from the related point of view of sociology, but such a description is badly needed. For an adequate description several features would have to be kept in mind. First, from the end of antiquity Latin was a language which, while widely used, was foreign to absolutely everyone who used it. In this it resembled an artificial language. It had a set of rules which, strictly speaking, actual usage was not supposed to modify—as usage modifies natural languages —but to which usage was to be forced to conform. Using Latin was like playing a game whose rules could never be changed.

There was some tendency to neglect the rules, of course, and even some tendency to develop Latin pidgins—mixed languages or jargons combining Latin and other languages. But after the Romance vernaculars were formed through the seventh to the ninth century, these tendencies were on the whole slight. More important, after the formation of the Romance vernaculars, the Latin language was never creolized. Indeed, severe repressive measures were often taken against incipient creolization. Creolization is the process which goes on when a language native to no one of a group of persons is taken as the lingua franca of the group and used by the group to raise children, to whom the language is then native. Creolization has occurred in various pidgins of the Caribbean areas. It rapidly fills out a language with childish and nursery forms—those children use when learning the language and those adults use in speaking to children learning the language. (Childish forms and nursery forms are not always the same.)

Some of the central aims of Renaissance humanists can be stated in modern linguistic terms by saying that they wanted to guard against the development of any pidgin tendencies in Latin and against any creolization. Latin was not to be allowed to feel the influence of any vernacular which users of Latin knew. This meant that the measure for Latin usage had to be taken from a period when, whatever the external influences at play on the language—and there were always external influences—these influences were not the modern European vernaculars. Thus the classical age became the norm. Adherence to classical usage guarded against the development of pidgins, such as "kitchen Latin."

Creolization was another matter. From the time when vernaculars had developed, Latin had ceased entirely to be a family language. The tendency to creolization therefore could hardly have been a great threat. But the Renaissance humanists seem to have felt some threat, as Sir Thomas Elyot shows in *The Boke Named the Governour*. As long as women were around—and they seemed to be here to stay—the danger existed that children in their play would be allowed to develop not only a creole Latin but—*O tempora! O mores!*—a baby-talk Latin, or, more likely, that they would not speak Latin at all, since it was not to be expected that any but the most exceptional woman would know enough Latin even for nursery talk. Hence exile from the company of woman at the age of seven was decreed.

It is certain that such isolation of the young boy was by no means universal, even in families with humanist proclivities. But the fact that it was sometimes enforced or even that it could be put forward as a serious proposal helps make clear the social implications of Latin for the times. Erasmus had complained that educators commonly regarded boys as merely small men, and that some allowance should be made for their youth. But Erasmus did not have in mind making much. Boys were to be forced from near infancy to speak a language which was only for adults. Such demands account for a certain amount of Renaissance precociousness and for the extraordinary sensitivity to language which we find in a Shakespeare, Ben Jonson, or John Donne. But for every boy who was made by the system, there were undoubtedly scores who were completely frustrated or crushed by it, or who were simply so resistant to it that it had no great effect on them. Anthony Trollope, who left Harrow at the age of nineteen in 1834, makes it clear in his *Autobiography* that he was unsuccessfully educated in essentially the same tradition, for from the age of seven to nineteen "no attempt had been made to teach us anything but Latin and Greek." The system ran against a stone wall in his case: "Those were twelve years of tuition in which I do not remember that I ever knew a lesson. Whatever knowledge I now have, I have acquired since I left school." Certainly most boys in the sixteenth and seventeenth century—not to mention the eighteenth and nineteenth—who studied Latin (and a little Greek) and nothing else for some seven to twelve years, seldom if ever read a single Latin book after they had finished. But this was not true of all. In the sixteenth and seventeenth and even eighteenth centuries a certain number did read —and write—such books. The educational system was really designed for them.

II

Latin is still popularly described as a "dead" language, and this description is generally taken to apply to it from the time when ancient Latin was replaced by the vernaculars which grew out of it. The description is seriously misleading, for it suggests that in the Latin of this later period there were no changes being made. There were a great many changes in vocabulary through the Middle Ages. New concepts were formed with the help of Latin words and the vocabulary adjusted accordingly. New words and meanings in this period are numbered in the thousands. And the same conditions obtain even after the advent of the Renaissance humanists with their ambition to return to the classical vocabulary and mode of expression. Students of Neo-Latin know that the humanists themselves multiplied words and meanings again by the thousands. Although some humanists did pretend otherwise, it is as a matter of fact quite impossible for a language to be used without growing.

I should like to propose a better way of describing Latin after it became exclusively a learned language. When it was replaced in family use by the vernaculars, Latin became first a chirographic language and later, to some extent, a typographic language. That is to say, it became a language in which all oral expression was (at least theoretically) controlled by written expression, and later, to some extent, by typographic expression. New words could be and were invented in great number. But they were subject entirely to written control in form and use. A new Latin word invented by a Frenchman whose spoken Latin was virtually incomprehensible to a Yorkshireman was nevertheless entirely comprehensible in manuscript or print to the Yorkshireman who knew Latin, because the whole economy of the new word was governed not at all by the way a Frenchman might pronounce and hear Latin, but by the rules for handling Latin in terms of the written alphabet. Through the seventeenth century and even well through the eighteenth Latin was spoken fluently by thousands of persons, but what one speaker might say aloud was not always comprehensible to other speakers used to different articulatory habits. A modern linguist would say that a Spaniard and an Englishman used different morphophonemic systems in speaking Latin. But each carried in his mind a representation of what the Latin looked like spelt out. He could match the strange sounds fairly well with a spelling and transfer meaning accordingly. What was distinctive of Latin was not that it was "dead" but that there was no one who could speak it who could not also write it. It was never learned independently of the written word. For this reason it can be conveniently designated as Learned Latin.

Control of Latin expression by the written word varied from age to age and from place to place. Since seemingly any use of normative grammar involves an attempt to make oral usage subservient to written practice to a greater or lesser degree, some control of oral expression by written existed even in classical times. But the great age of Latin grammarians—the age of Donatus, Priscian, Diomedes, Dositheus, Sergius, Victorinus, and Cassiodorus—falls not in the age of Cicero and Quintilian but at the end of the classical period, where reliance on written normative grammar became more of a necessity as spoken Latin moved into Vulgar Latin and thence into the modern Romance vernaculars. Normative grammar had to replace the spoken norm to preserve the older tongue as Learned Latin.

The manuscript culture developed by the Middle Ages made formal learning far more dependent upon written records, however well or badly handled, than it had been in the rhetorical cultures of ancient Greece and Rome. Medieval Latin was fluid only in minor details. Few medieval writers invented new terms with the prolixity of Cicero. Humanists, however, envisioned a much stricter control than the medieval tradition had ambitioned or achieved, a control in fact so strict that it is doubtful whether it could have been realized or even imagined without the services of the new art of typography.

The coincidence between the development of humanist interest in ancient texts and the development of printing through the early and mid-fifteenth century is striking. Typography provided not only means of rapid diffusion of writing but also means of closer control of a text than had ever been possible before. Early printers were often humanist scholars themselves—Johann Sturm, the Manutii, the Amerbachs, Episcopius, and countless others—or worked intimately with humanists. It would appear not only that the new art of printing sparked the humanists' ambitions to establish accurate texts from the ancient world and to bring contemporary usage into line with the true written records, but also that the humanists' ambitions spurred printers to greater efforts. Very likely the complex of forces which produced the development of printing and the complex which produced the humanist mind had much in common.

The gap between a language chirographically and typographically controlled and a language vocally controlled can be seen in instructional performance during the sixteenth and seventeenth centuries. Here we find not intellectual parvenus and desperadoes, but leading educational and intellectual lights such as Peter Ramus or Robert Cardinal Bellarmine actually teaching languages (in Ramus's case Greek, in Bellarmine's Hebrew) before they even knew all the grammar. Ramus saw the first half of his Greek grammar through the press before he himself knew the second half. This kind of performance, it is true, was necessitated by the shortage of teachers for these two tongues. And yet it would have been unthinkable on the part of a tutor hired by one of Ramus's or Bellarmine's contemporaries to teach French. Vernaculars were not academic languages, and they were generally picked up by foreigners more or less directly. In the sixteenth century few grammars of European vernaculars were available. Greek and Hebrew were academic languages, like Latin artificially preserved and chirographically and typographically controlled. They could be sectioned in space—the pages of a book—and learned piecemeal, for one did not really have to *say* anything in them until one was well through a purely mechanical process. The experience of Latin as an academic language made Ramus's and Bellarmine's approach to other academic languages not only feasible but to a certain degree respectable.

III

The monopoly which Latin exercised in formal education combined with the structure of society in the West up until the past few generations to give the language its strangest characteristic. It was a sexually specialized language, used almost exclusively for communication between male and male.

Until the nineteenth century—and for higher education until the very late nineteenth century—formal education or education in school classrooms was restricted almost entirely to boys. Girls and women were by no means all illiterate, but what they learned they nearly always learned at home. And since the language at home was the vernacular of the region, or some other vernacular imported through tutors because of family connections or interests, the girls did not learn Latin. There were some exceptions in households such as Sir Thomas More's, particularly if the boys themselves were taught Latin at home instead of being sent to school. But these exceptions were insignificant; and the few scattered instances of girls actually attending school are even more insignificant. Of the rare cases which Foster Watson did find and report in his book, *The Old Grammar Schools,* several make it explicitly clear that a little girl was allowed in a school which undertook to teach the alphabet and its elementary use through practice with English words, but that she was dropped as soon as the boys moved on to Latin. In other words, she was admitted for a sort of preschool work, since many "grammar" schools demanded that a pupil know the alphabet *before* admission.

This pattern is closely connected with the position of women in society and with the fact that until recently the learned professions, where Latin was used, were closed to them. No one, least of all the women themselves, wanted to educate for frustration.

Vernacular literature was not regarded as genuinely learned, and here women did have a place. Occasionally they wrote it. But much more often they read it—or its authors like to think they did. Through the Middle Ages and the Renaissance, it was largely a women's audience which kept vernacular romances alive. In the nineteenth and twentieth centuries, the entrance of girls and women into institutions of formal education has as an almost exact coefficient the diminishing of the hold of Latin in these places and the rise of instruction in the vernacular, although what is cause and what effect in these complexes of change is not easy to say. Certainly there were more things at work than woman's demand for a better education and the tradition of teaching Latin only to boys. But the close correlation between these two items has significance.

Even though the restriction of Latin to males was due to no particularly conscious design, the persistence over hundreds of years of such a sexually restrictive communication system in segments of Western society necessarily involved fascinating sociological phenomena. In a recent article in *Studies in Philology* (1959), "Latin Language Study as a Renaissance Puberty Rite," I have presented considerable documentation, but by no means all that is available, in an attempt to show how this particularly male world of Latin-and-formal-schooling found itself enmeshed in some of the social forces which are responsible in primitive societies for what anthropologists know as puberty rites.

Puberty rites have been studied in great detail by Arnold van Gennep, A. E. Jensen, Hutton Webster, and many others. From studies by such persons we know that people of simpler cultures have well developed ceremonials for inducting adolescent youths into full participation in tribal life, which makes special demands over and beyond those made by family and clan and known to the child from infancy.

The rites which are used for the induction into tribal life have certain more or less well defined characteristics. A boy is made to feel strongly that he is in what anthropologists call a "marginal environment," that he is on unfamiliar ground. Sometimes the rites begin when the young boy is forcibly torn from the company of the women of his home by the men who are to initiate him and who invade the home. Certain excesses forbidden him before the initiation rites started may be not tolerated but commanded. Various forms of license—theft, arson, violence, or at least things which have some air of outlawry about them —are at times expected, to emphasize the sense of breaking with earlier habits of life. The boy is made to do many things that are hard, and to do them with an acute awareness that they are hard. Special taboos are enforced and an atmosphere of continual excitement is established. In the article on "Initiation" in *The Encyclopedia of the Social Sciences,*

Nathan Miller speaks of the "ingenious torments, sleeplessness, and nerve-racking frights" through which "the candidate becomes keenly sensitive to the power of his preceptors and indelible, life-long impressions are made."

Men now well past middle age may be tempted to impute this description, with a wry smile, to their own experiences when they first began Latin in secondary school. This is particularly so if they were in an all-boys' institution. The secondary school normally brings boys through puberty, and the all-boys' secondary school of a few generations ago was likely to provide what anthropologists could well recognize as a "marginal environment," calculated to produce "nerve-racking frights" and "life-long impressions."

Not all men of a few generations ago looked back on secondary school as a traumatic experience, but some distinguished men certainly did. The tortures of his days at Harrow lived with the indomitable Anthony Trollope to the end. "I feel convinced in my mind," he writes in his *Autobiography,* "that I was flogged oftener than any other human being alive. It was just possible to obtain five scourgings in one day; and I was often able to boast that I had obtained them all. . . . How well I remember the agonies of my young heart." Trollope's reminiscences can be duplicated much more recently, as in the case of the late George Orwell, who once speculated as to whether it was even possible to teach Latin at all without corporal punishment.

Trollope, like Orwell, is the professional writer whose stories of his own experience are the more telling because he knows that they match the experiences of many of his readers and thus hold them the more. Interestingly enough, in his *Autobiography* he expressed no great resentment at the fact that he was flogged. What he resents is that the floggings did not achieve the end which he feels they should have achieved: they never produced in him the sense that he "belonged." He remained "a wretched farmer's boy, reeking from a dunghill," isolated in school where he had to sit "next to the sons of peers." Likely enough, without fully rationalizing the situation, he had put himself in the way of the maximum five beatings a day in a desperate effort to wring the most out of the initiatory situation, to convince himself and the hostile eyes around him that he was really "with it"—yes, more than anyone else was. But bootlessly.

The sons of peers were thrashed, too, and they somehow realized the increment of camaraderie which the thrashings normally produced, and which masters and boys—not often reflectively or explicitly, but subconsciously and really—have always been aware helps justify the beatings which so often mark the pubertal age. But for Anthony it did not work out that way. The fact that what Anthony resents is not the beatings but the failure of the beatings to incorporate him into the strange, extrafamiliar society around him (he was stuck *within* his family as a reeking farmer's son) hints that the situation he found himself in was definitely a puberty-rite situation of sorts.

The violence detailed by Trollope, which still persists in a mitigated form in English public schools although it has disappeared for the most part in the United States and on much of the Continent, was a feature of pedagogical procedure virtually everywhere when Latin was still the totality or core of the curriculum. In medieval illustrations and sixteenth-century woodcuts alike, the "attribute" identifying a schoolmaster is regularly a handful of switches. Beating was explicitly associated with teaching the boy aspirants to monastic life in Aelfric's *Colloquy* around the end of the tenth century and persisted in sixteenth century Jesuit schools, where the *corrector* was, however, never to be one of the teachers but either another student or a person specially hired for the purpose.

The association of this violence with formal education links the Latin-centered school and primitive puberty rites all the more when we remember that puberty rites themselves are essentially didactic, and constitute or climax the "broad liberal education" which a primitive society provides for its males. Anthropologists describe them as a cultural vehicle linking one generation of a society to the next and transmitting a cultural complex. In them the young initiate is given an understanding of the religious, magical, and quasi-scientific lore of the tribe. What brutality they exhibit occurs fundamentally in a context of high seriousness.

Moreover, like secondary schools featuring beatings, puberty rites involve sexual segregation because they incorporate youth into the tribal life, where the two sexes have strikingly different roles. There are boys' rites, and there are comparable but different girls' rites. Needless to say, in keeping with men's role assigned by society, the rites for males are more violent, though not necessarily more trying.

What has been said so far draws a rough parallel between puberty rites and practices in schools which, as a matter of fact, did teach Latin. But how far does the parallel exist not because the schools we have treated of were concerned specifically with Latin but because they were schools for boys? Does Latin itself have any special connection with the puberty rite situation?

It does when one regards it in its full social context. As has been seen, first of all, Latin had become not merely a subject which happened to be taught to males, but a genuine male prerogative. Latin was insulated from the *mundus muliebris* not only because virtually no women spoke or read it but especially because it was prevented from developing infantile and nursery forms, and thus from real association with childrearing. Those who learned it, from the beginning were treated as little men—as having moved out of the family away from feminine influence into the tribe, no matter how tender their age.

Secondly, Latin was not merely one subject among many or even among several. When it was in the ascendency (with its acolyte Greek) Latin effected *the* transit from ignorance to tribal or communal wisdom. From Erasmus' time and earlier, well through the dispute about the ancients and moderns in the seventeenth and eighteenth centuries, youngsters were given to understand that the treasures of all understanding were stored in the ancient tongues—in effect, in Latin, since Greek and Hebrew were never to become at all genuinely current. The boy learning Latin was on the threshold of the wisdom on which his society was supposed to be founded. He went on from Latin to the study of "philosophy," but by that time he was a bit past puberty and was an initiate. It was during the time they studied Latin that boys were commonly given their floggings.

Thirdly, Latin literature was frequently viewed as a subject fit of itself to toughen a young boy, to develop his manliness and "courage." This is evident in sixteenth century writers such as Sir Thomas Elyot and Sir Philip Sidney, and through the seventeenth century Latin-supported cult of the epic and of the warlike epic hero. Working with Latin authors from the age of seven to his thirteenth year to familiarize himself with the tongue, "the childes courage," we are told by Elyot, "inflamed by the frequent redynge of noble poetes, dayly more and more desireth to have experience in those things that they so vehemently do commende in them they write of." It is significant that Latin literature, in practice so largely epic-centered, is associated with moral toughness at the very time when the vernacular literatures, and particularly the vernacular drama, were being charged by Stubbes, Gosson, and others with fostering unmanliness and effeminacy.

One had to be highly selective with Latin (and Greek) literature to give the impression that it promoted manliness, but Elyot, Roger Ascham, and the other writers on education were ruthlessly so. No Catullus or Propertius. Largely Virgil (and Homer) and Horace, with a cautious bit of the playwrights and some expurgated Ovid and Martial. In this highly chastened mold, Latin literature showed nothing like its full form, but it served admirably—or so it was maintained—to toughen the character of the young boy.

This argument in favor of Latin is no longer urged. Something like it came into currency in the nineteenth century, when Latin was on its way out of many curricula and many other new curricula were growing into prominence which had never known Latin at all. Here one begins to hear that Latin, even when one does not go beyond elementary grammar, "toughens the mind," or "trains the mind." When Latin was really being used, this explanation of its value seems to have been unknown. The language then was learned because one was expected to read, and even write, books in it and to talk in it. But the nineteenth century argument, still urged today, perhaps could be traced back in some way to the earlier notion that Latin literature strengthened the boy's character. By the nineteenth century, there was less and less Latin literature being read, and what was earlier imputed to the literature had now to be imputed by default to the grammar itself.

IV

When Latin is seen in the historical perspectives so inadequately sketched here, it becomes evident that the question of teaching Latin today has very little to do with Latin teaching at the time when Latin was the core subject of the curriculum, because Latin was the means of communication through which all the subjects of the curriculum were taught. The social structure has changed, and with it the means of communication. One could not possibly teach atomic physics or most of the subjects in today's curricula in Latin.

One might argue that it would have been possible to teach such subjects in Latin if Latin had continued to develop after the new impetus it had been given by the humanists. But this new impetus proved in the long run an ineffective one. Even in the sixteenth century, as is now certain, most boys who studied Latin and nothing but Latin in school seldom read a book in Latin after they had finished their formal education. Scholars and persons corresponding to what we today would call scientists of course did read and write Latin books, and in quantity. But Latin was withdrawn from the ordinary life of society by the very fact that it was Learned Latin, a chirographic and typographic language at root. By their insistence on imitation of the ancients, the humanists made Latin more exclusively than ever chirographic and typographic. The ordinary person who wanted to know more about the classics went to Philemon Holland and other Renaissance translators. Those who exploited the classics for their own writing made use of the mass of dictionaries, commonplace books, lists of quotations, and other reference tools which, as we are now aware, burgeoned, with the translations, from the sixteenth century on. The Shakespeare which modern scholarship reveals turns out to be more and more a thumber of literary handbooks. It has been no secret for a long time that this is what Ben Jonson was, although he also knew the classics directly better than most.

The changes in Latin teaching over the past few centuries have been brought about chiefly in two ways. First, Latin, which (with a smattering of Greek) was originally the entire lower curriculum, has been crowded into a corner as other subjects—history, geography, arithmetic (no longer considered the business chiefly of tradesmen), English itself, and other subjects—were found necessary because of the widening horizons of man's knowledge. Secondly, partly as a consequence of ill success in teaching it in brisk competition with other subjects, Latin has tended to be taught later and later in the curriculum to older and older pupils, often, unfortunately, with no adaptation of earlier teaching methods.

In the history of the epic poem a significant large-scale development already treated above in "The Vernacular Matrix of the New Criticism" throws interesting light upon what was happening. By the seventeenth century, the humanist insistence on studying the Latin authors and on writing as a literary exercise produced a spate of epic poems such as the world has never seen before or since. Great numbers of the epics are forgotten because they were in Latin. By the eighteenth century, however, matters have changed. The age of the mock epic has arrived, and through the eighteenth and early nineteenth century these are produced in quantities again such as the world has never known before or since. But the mock epics are nearly all in the vernaculars. A period of success while Latin was in a relatively uncontested position in the curriculum is followed by a period in which Latin is under more or less concealed, or perhaps subconscious, attack. Not the language itself so much as its typical institution known from classroom practice, the epic poem, becomes the butt of humor.

This shift in attitude toward the epic advertises the real state of affairs. Although Latin was still being used in almost all lecture halls in Europe well through the eighteenth century—if the masters were doing what the academic statutes said they should do—the status of Latin was actually quite different in George Washington's youth from what it had been in Shakespeare's. When George Washington was a boy there were opening on all sides frontiers in human knowledge which Miranda in her vision of a brave new world had not remotely glimpsed.

By the mid-nineteenth century, although English literature as such was still virtually unknown as a subject of formal instruction, English was well established as the language of the classroom, and in most European countries the respective vernaculars were similarly used. English as such was given most explicit and direct attention in curricula preparing for the business world. Relicts of this association of the vernacular with business can be seen in secondary school catalogues of only a generation ago, where the "commercial course" (without Latin or with little Latin) is distinguished from the "classical course." Academic attention to English moved up from the elementary level to the higher levels slowly. T. S. Eliot and Ezra Pound belong to the first generation of Americans able to do real study in the literature of the English language at the university—and even so, Mr. Eliot did his doctoral dissertation for his uncompleted degree at Harvard in philosophy.

V

These historical perspectives should make it clear that to assume that the reasons why Latin actually is present in various curricula today are reasons which can be urged for its retention is entirely unwarranted. Latin is obviously going to continue to be taught somewhere somehow in our educational system. Our culture needs a living knowledge of Latin to maintain its self-possession by maintaining its hold on its past. But the reasons which can be given today for the teaching of Latin are virtually all different from those which have served former ages, when Latin had different functions in society from those which it can have today. The concept of a liberal education has to be thought through over and over again by each succeeding era. Today linguistics has turned from an analysis of language based on the study of the written word to a direct analysis of spoken language. This development is both a symptom of a radically new state of affairs and a certain cause of further change. New linguistic techniques—necessarily in a highly modified form—are now being applied to the teaching of Latin. But this development is itself enigmatic, since no one looks to see Latin become a genuine means of oral communication on any large-scale basis again.

Whatever it becomes, or whatever becomes of it, we shall do no harm to our cause—whether we are pro-Latinists or anti-Latinists—to be aware of the historical pattern which has brought the issues to where they at present are. What I have rehearsed here does not purport to answer the Latin question. But I hope it helps us to see what the Latin question is, or is not.

💮 TWELVE 💮

Wired for Sound

TEACHING, COMMUNICATIONS, AND TECHNOLOGICAL CULTURE

I

FROM the time of ancient Greece, communication processes have always been at the center of Western education. Early academic study focused on grammar, which gave birth to rhetoric. Rhetoric formed a matrix for dialectic and logic, and all these conjointly help shape physics and medicine, and ultimately modern science. Through the Middle Ages, the Renaissance, and into the nineteenth centry, education began with grammar, rhetoric, and dialectic or logic, the *artes sermocinales* or communication arts.

Teachers are still especially interested in communication, not merely because they are incidentally involved with the process but because their work itself is communication par excellence. At the point where teaching is going on, the knowledge which men have accumulated and communicated to one another out of the past thousands or hundreds of thousands of years is being communicated again to inexperienced youth, to give this youth that experience reaching far back beyond one's own years which sociologists call culture. But as teachers channel this knowledge to succeeding ages, they do so by talking it over, rethinking it and recommunicating it among themselves. In the person of the teacher, who is the depository and communicator of knowledge, mankind constantly reviews what it knows, revaluates its knowledge, revises it, detects its deficiencies, and sets up the framework for new discoveries.

The teacher's work involves him in a constant interior dialogue with the past, the present, and the future. Since the only source of knowledge is the experience we have had up to the present time, or in other words past experience, he has to communicate with the past, to raid it for what it has to tell him. With his students, he puts out feelers into the future to orient his knowledge effectively. And he has to bring his knowledge of past and future into focus within the present system of communication, the one in which he has actually to do his teaching.

Hence it is not strange that teachers are sensitive more than other men to changes in communication processes. And teachers in the field of language and literature are most sensitive of all. In these fields a great deal of restlessness is observable today. The furor about why Johnny can or cannot read, the agitation concerning foreign language programs, the tendency of structural linguistics to replace older grammar, and the general overhauling of language-teaching and literature-teaching processes which has been taking place for the past thirty years or more are symptoms that something is stirring. What is it?

II

Probably a great many things are stirring; but it is certain that many of them can be summed up by saying that we are leaving the Gutenberg era behind us. As we move further into a technological civilization, we meet with abundant signs that the relationship between the teacher and the printed word and hence those between the teacher and a large area of communication, which includes practically all of what we generally mean by "literature," are no longer what they used to be. These relationships were set up in the Renaissance when a typographical civilization appeared, climaxing the intense development of a manuscript culture which had marked the preceding Middle Ages. The present swing is to oral forms in communication, with radio, television (oral in its commitments as compared to typography), public address and intercom systems, or voice recordings (to replace or supplement shorthand, longhand, typing, or print). As a result of this swing, older relationships are undergoing a profound, if not often perceptible, realignment.

Early teaching was aural and oral in cast. Socrates taught by means of person-to-person dialogue. Although Plato in great part choked off this dialogue when he and his followers captured, stiffened, and mounted it on the written page, he nevertheless thought of himself as preserving dialogue itself by putting its form on record. And although Aristotle seems to have moved further away from the dialogue form than Plato, a careful and astute reading of his works by Werner Jaeger, Joseph Owens, and others has shown how strongly the dialogic approach persists in them. Cicero's whole framework of culture was oral in a way in which the text-oriented Renaissance Ciceronianism could never be. To bring Greek culture to Rome, Cicero did not simply read books but went to Athens to listen to the oral exposition of philosophy there and thus to learn what to transmit viva voce to his compatriots. Sallust and Quintilian both attest that Cicero "reduced" his orations to writing after delivery. Vocalization remained primary. St. Augustine remains similarly oriented. He was disillusioned less by Manichean writings than he was at the oral presentation of Manichean teaching by Faustus, who, after exciting the highest hopes, explained so little and so unconvincingly. When Augustine heard the fateful words, *Tolle et lege*—we know from what he has to say elsewhere about reading habits in his day—he took up the Scriptures and read to himself *aloud*.

By contrast with the ancient world, the Middle Ages produced a more purely manuscript culture. But their teaching methods retained massive oral-aural commitments. Socrates' dialogue, to be sure, was reduced to the university master's monologue, eventually styled a "lecture" or "reading," since it was typically a commentary on a written work and itself regarded as something committed or to be committed to writing. Yet the practice of testing intellectual prowess by oral methods alone, such as disputations, was retained. Written assignments or written examinations after grammar school remained unknown and apparently unthought of. A thesis was not something one wrote but something one asserted and defended orally as one's inaugural act upon induction into the teaching profession. Medieval culture is thus a transitional culture, oral-aural at root but scriptural in bent.

The printed page completed the pedagogical shift away from the oral. It silenced the medieval disputation and, as Marshall McLuhan so well put it in the volume *Mass Culture*, "created the solitary student," and the school textbook as well. From the beginnings of printing the greatest source of revenue for book publishers has been the classroom and its purlieus. Early publishers liked to ally themselves with humanist educators. The massive plaque on Erasmus' tomb in the Münster at Basel is erected by three grateful publishers whom he helped make affluent: Amerbachius, Frobenius, and Episcopius. At a time when not more than a few pages of any book could be kept standing in type at any one time, the Wechel firm of Paris and Frankfort-on-the-Main published at least one hundred and seventy-two editions of one or another work, almost all for classroom or academic use, by Peter Ramus and his literary lieutenant Omer Talon (Talaeus). Erasmus, Ramus, and Talon are only three among thousands of textbook authors whose works are published and read more than those of almost any "literary" writer.

The connection between printing and teaching was from the beginning as subtle and profound as it was financially successful. The notion of "storing" unassembled letters (and consequently dismantled words and books) in "fonts" of prefabricated type, which lies at the heart of the typographical developments of the fifteenth century, exhibits a close psychological connection with the doctrine of the *loci communes* ("commonplaces" or simply "places") taught in rhetoric and dialectic or logic classes in fifteenth century schoolrooms. One "drew arguments" from the places as one drew type from a font. As the printed book took over, and with it faster and faster silent reading habits, the commitment to eloquence and oral expression lingering as a heritage from the Renaissance devotion to classical antiquity became, more and more, lip service. The "elocution contests" of a generation or two ago were the dying gasps of the old tradition. It seemed that the printed book had won the day.

It still seems so in the sense that it is unlikely that printing (or its recent manifold variants such as mimeographing or planographing) will ever be done away with in teaching or elsewhere generally. It is incontestably convenient to have the spoken word frozen in space, and frozen in exactly the same space for everyone among one's auditors. The teacher is not likely to forego the luxury of being able to say, "Everyone now turn to page 83, line 4 from the top, and look at the third word from the left." This luxury is too hard-won. For such a directive was entirely impossible before the invention of printing, when, if the students had manuscript books, every book would have every word in a different place from every other book. Except in certain academic horror stories, no one really seems convinced that the modern world is going to regress into a pretypographical or a preliterate culture. What is happening is more complicated than this. If students are losing their hold on reading and on grammar, this is in great part because, in their relationship to the other items involved in communication, reading and grammar are not what they used to be. They are still there, and will be, but the constellation in which they exist is shifting its formation.

III

One of the principal causes of the shift in status of reading and grammar is the increased importance of oral-aural communication in our technological society. It is paradoxical that a society given so much to the use of diagrams and to the maneuvering of objects in space (from giant aircraft to atoms) should at the same time develop means of communication which specialize not in sight but in sound. Yet the signs of a shift are everywhere. Grammar, which was originally the study of written language (*gramma* in Greek means a letter of the alphabet) and which, as normative grammar, has rules based less upon what speaking people do when they talk than upon what literate people do when they write, is yielding to linguistics, which, while it includes grammar, is rooted in the study of oral performance. The trend toward discussion groups has been under way for a long time. It manifests itself not only in the classroom under such guises as "Deweyism," but also in business, where meetings of all sorts have multiplied beyond calculation in the course of the recent managerial revolution. The same elaborate business organizations which solve many of their problems by computing machines have found that back of the Univac there must be large-scale and deliberate confrontation of person with person. Interest in group dynamics serves as a counterbalance to electronic computers. Often the most efficient way to attack a problem has been found to be the "brainstorming" session, where members of a group stimulated by the rest of the group as an audience, suggest orally whatever solution to a practical problem may stray through their heads, no matter how zany the solution may at first blush appear.

Libraries themselves have undergone significant reorientations. The oldstyle Renaissance public or semipublic library, with its books chained to keep the users from carrying them away, yielded some years ago to the lending library. Both these institutions were spectacularly quiet. The new library makes allowance for noise, and utilizes noise. It includes seminar rooms and all-purpose rooms for larger meetings. Acoustic insulation, of course, has made these possible. But, by whatever means the effect has been achieved, libraries have recently become places where people can get together to talk. Our attitude toward books, our concept of what they are, is sure to be affected by such a change, especially as more libraries are being run on an open-stack plan. Librarians, including librarians of early lending libraries, until recently appear to have existed chiefly to keep books in the library, from which they would issue them with ill-concealed reluctance, placated only by thought of the savage reprisals which would result if the books were not returned by the detested borrower almost immediately. Today's librarians all want books to go out, and feel frustrated if they do not. The result is that more and more books are now read in a world alive with sound, to musical backgrounds provided by radios and hi-fi sets.

The oral-aural emphases of today run counter to certain typical phenomena of the Gutenberg era as diverse as the invention of printing and the exploration and observation of the surface of the globe. These activities reached their peak together, and both focused attention in space and thus vaunted sight. The microscope and telescope, developed as epiphenomena of printing and exploration, did the same. But a new age is upon us, and its shift from sight-emphasis to increased sound-emphasis spans this entire area from the diffusion of the word to the exploration of one's surroundings. In the realm of words dictaphones replace shorthand writing, and audio charge systems replace written library records. Exploration no longer depends on moving the human body through space. It is conducted by radar and radiotelescopes (more informative in many ways than visual-type telescopes), and by Sputniks, which are launched into space as little speaking voices. In these devices sight, of course, plays a role, but no longer so exclusive a role as before. Press reports on the first nearly successful moon rocket noted that at its apogee it could not be seen even with the most powerful lens telescope on earth, but that it could be "heard."

In their whole trend, modern developments in communications, while they have not slighted the visual, have given more play to the oral-aural, which a purely typographical culture had reduced to a record minimum in human life. The sequence of development running from silent print through audiovisual telegraph to the completely aural radio is an obvious instance of increasing aural dominance. Even television belongs partially in this visual-to-aural series, being only equivocally a regression to visualism. For the visual element in television is severely limited. The amount of detail feasible on a television screen is far less than that visible on a movie screen and not remotely comparable to that tolerable and easily discernible in photographs. Details on television have to be filled in aurally, by explicit vocal explanation or by suggestion through music and sound effects. Silent television is hardly an engaging prospect.

IV

Heightening the oral-aural element in a culture does much more than merely de-emphasize vision. It subtly heightens the personalist element in a culture. For the plenary development of sound, the human voice, is a manifestation of the person. Even more than it is a manifestation of an understanding of objects, speech is a calling of one person to another, of an interior to an interior. Sight presents always surfaces, presents even depth as a lamination of surfaces, whereas sound presents always interiors, for sound is impossible without some resonance. The post-Baconian preoccupation with sight and "observation" produced the world of the Enlightenment, a world of objects and things without convincing personal presences, giving us the strangely silent universe which Newtonian physics and Deism both supposed. Printing was the harbinger of this Newtonian world, for printing is spectacularly allied with surface or "object" treatment of reality. Picasso's collages use bits of printed posters or newspapers to establish a sense of flat surface because print is sensed as indissolubly allied with surface. Scraps of printing in the collages serve precisely the function of returning the eye from the perspective depths in other parts of the assemblage to the plane surface of the painting—it is unconvincing to imagine print on anything other than something relatively flat and smooth.

Strangely enough, although it is in part a visualist development, television has moved away from this effect of print. It has been a personalizing, not an objectifying, medium. The discussion panel, with its interchange of personalities, is properly a television phenomenon. Such personal interchange was difficult to manage on radio, for there individual persons could only with difficulty be kept distinct. Hence the use of voice was not brought to its fullest fruition. By the same token television is a more feasible means of education than radio. This is not because it can use visual aid devices (figures written on a blackboard on television cannot be seen by any viewer unless the camera is turned on them—they lack the permanent availability of figures on a classroom blackboard). It is because television better implements personal rapport between instructor and student.

But television is not the only manifestation of the growing interest in the human person which accompanies the resurgence of voice in our culture. Another manifestation is the self-conscious personalism of our times. The twentieth century, from one point of view the most mechanized of all the ages of mankind, is from another point of view the most personalized. No other age has generated a whole philosophy of personalism such as one finds in the works of Martin Buber, Gabriel

Marcel, and others. At a much less reflective, more superficial, and never-theless significant level, no civilization before our technological civiliza-tion has given such attention to problems of personnel and personality in matters even of industrial performance. The "I" and the "thou" have never been the objects of more explicit treatment than now. In the future, alongside the digital and analogue computers and other mathe-maticizing developments such as Western culture has specialized in more and more over the past few hundred years, the human person will receive more and more attention, not in every quarter but in significant milieus and ways.

One may object that earlier civilizations were, and other contemporary civilizations are, more personal in certain aspects of their structure than ours. Modern Arab culture, styled by Marcel Jousse "verbomotor" (*verbomoteur*), is still almost exclusively personal in orientation (as a preliterate culture must be), acting in terms of personal loyalties and without much "objective" insight into issues. Such cultures can be, as Albert Camus well knew, absorbingly interesting from a human and literary point of view. This is because of their personalist orientation. But from another point of view, and an utterly basic one, such cultures leave much to be desired in this same personalist orientation. Their respect for the elementary personal right to life can be quite minimal.

V

The influence which the present cultural shift toward the oral-aural is having on language and literature study and teaching is probably most important where it is least crass and striking. To think of adapting courses to present trends by exploiting as gadgets the spectacularly evident new media—radio, television, tape recordings, intercom—is to a certain extent to miss the point. These new media are not just new gadgets to be employed for what we are already doing with other less efficient gadgets. They are part of a shift which is inexorably affecting our very notion of what communication itself is. The question is not how to adapt television or tape recording to present courses in educa-tional institutions or present courses to television and tape, for the present shift is sapping the very notion of a "course" itself. A "course" (Latin, *cursus*) means a running through. The concept of a "course" in a subject, derivative from the process of teaching by "running through" a text, is a relict of manuscript and typographical culture. Moving in a more oral-aural setting, Socrates never gave a "course" in anything, and indeed had no notion of what such a thing as a "course" might be.

This is not to say that "courses" in language and literature or in anything else are on their way out. Evolution does not proceed by jettisoning earlier developments completely in working toward new ones. It tends rather to preserve earlier developments, even though these may have to be given new guises. Courses in language and literature are evidently going to be with us for a long time, perhaps for good. Nevertheless, their psychological significance is undergoing subtle and complex, but inexorable, change.

One way to express the nature of this change is to say that the old focus of literary studies on rhetoric is being replaced by a focus on dialogue. In ancient times, and through the Middle Ages, the cause of literature was the cause of rhetoric—which is to say the cause of the art of oratory. Poetry and all "ornate" expression was commonly referred to an eloquence which was associated basically with the oration or public speech before a group of persons. In contrast, the dialectic which split off from rhetoric and modulated into logic, first in Aristotle but more definitely through the Middle Ages, has pulled away from literature and helped generate modern science. The Renaissance sought to return from dialectic to literature by re-emphasis of eloquence and rhetoric, but the Renaissance effort foundered in the combined currents of an always ebullient scholasticism and of the modern scientism so closely related to scholasticism. Rhetoric and the areas of communication which it represented failed to develop any mature theoretical structure viable in the post-Newtonian world where neat theories seemed to account for everything else.

For some time now the Newtonian universe has been broken down, and the result has been a recrudescence of interest in language and literature. But the interest no longer centers on rhetoric, the art of persuasion, which in our day is much more the province of the advertising man and marketing specialist than of the *littérateur*. The more effective ally of literature has turned out to be the sense of dialogue which marks important philosophical developments of our age (and which is notably missing or *ersatz* in advertising). Literature is no longer standing so much alone as it did when "mere" rhetoric was arrayed against dialectic. It is painstakingly picked over by psychologists, physicians, sociologists, anthropologists, theologians, and others. Certain typically modern philosophies of the "existentialist" sort have been described as literary philosophies, conscious of and using literary form, as exploited by Camus, Marcel, Sartre, and others. We have become explicitly aware in our time of the intimate linkage between the process of communication and human thought itself. Many of the illusions of the Enlightenment concerning private thought and psychological privacy generally have been dissipated since the discovery of evolution, of depth psychology, and of the processes involved in the history of human thinking. We are intimately aware, as Gaston Fessard and others have put it, that science itself is only arrested dialogue. Voice is not an accretion, but a necessary adjunct or even a necessary dimension of human thinking. (It should be added that the "dialogue" meant here is neither medieval dialectic nor Hegelian dialectic, although it is related somewhat to both. Dialogue refers here to actual vocal exchange between person and person.)

It is through awareness of the paramount role of voice in human activity that students of English or of any other language today must seek to understand the reactivation of the oral-aural element in human culture. Voice is coming into its own as never before. But the ways in which it is doing so, and the elements in our culture which favor voice as well as those which militate against it, are complex in the extreme. We can arm ourselves and our students only by vigilant awareness of what is going on about us. In particular, teachers and students of language and literature must cultivate sensitivity to the more profound significance of the media of popular culture—which is not the same thing as either uncritical acceptance of popular culture or entrenched hostility to all its manifestations. Any kind of genuine sensitivity to literature of any age or culture has become thoroughly impossible unless a person has grown seriously, not phrenetically—reflective about contemporary communications media. Men today—and, above all, high school, college, and university students—live englobed in a universe of sound emanating from radio and hi-fi sets which surpasses anything any earlier human culture has known, both in the total decibel output at any given moment and in incessancy. Reflection on the condition of the new media and the changes they are effecting in human life will probably produce no pat formulae either to describe the totality of the present situation or to prescribe highly simplified lines of action. But it should enable us to live.

WILDERNESS

AND

BARBARIAN

🎋 THIRTEEN 🎋

Personalism and the Wilderness

I

THE United States has a magazine called *The Personalist* and American university campuses are peopled annually with more and more students having some knowledge of personalism as a philosophical movement related (sometimes by alliance and sometimes by opposition) to various forms of philosophy known loosely as "existential." Yet the relevance of a personalist philosophy to the American ethos or the conditions for making such a philosophy viable in the American climate are by no means clear. Material on which to ground a judgment concerning these matters is difficult to come by. One cannot simply ask whether Americans like a personalist philosophy. It is necessary to have some evidence as to what they would do with it, how the American ethos could set itself in active relationship to such philosophy, what facets of the American character such a philosophy would engage, and what the end result on the American character would be.

Material which certainly makes it possible to treat such questions is now present in a new book, *The Inward Morning: A Philosophical Exploration in Journal Form,* by Henry G. Bugbee, Jr., with an introduction by Gabriel Marcel. This book is not "about" philosophy or even "about" reality. It is a plunge into reality, is itself something to be explained, rather than a proffered explanation. It is a phenomenon which the author has deliberately provided for his readers, and a precious one. For it is an utterly typical American phenomenon, the product not only of the American mind but also of the American mind reacting with Europe in a way which is so typical of the American mind itself and which has been such a regular occurrence in American letters, accountable for much of the achievement of Henry James, Ezra Pound, T. S. Eliot, and so many others.

Gabriel Marcel is here the principal point of contact between the New World and the Old. Professor Bugbee comes to Marcel as a kind of chastened Thoreau. As Bugbee's morning dawns, through an unmistakable mist of Transcendentalism, finer and more penetrating, one feels, than Emerson's own, we become acquainted with a sensibility as fastidious as Santayana's, but more radically cisatlantic, as Attic as Robert Frost's, and as intent as Herman Melville's. The phenomenon which this book is consists in a thought and idiom as unabashedly American as that of William Carlos Williams, who seems to have some direct influence on Bugbee, or that of Wallace Stevens, who may be an influence or may be merely a related phenomenon.

Marcel's Introduction to Bugbee's journal-form exploration is remarkably perceptive, as appreciative of the chasms between Bugbee's thinking and Marcel's own as it is sensitive to the profound similarities between the two forms of thought. Marcel is fully aware that he has learned from Bugbee, and as fully aware that his appreciation of Bugbee remains basically French, that there are aspects of Bugbee's performance meaningful to Americans which remain somewhat occluded to him.

But despite the divergent national perspectives evident in Bugbee's sensibility and Marcel's understanding, we have here a discernible breakthrough in communication. In an atmosphere charged with Bugbee's personal, dialogic spirit, the shrill and lonely philosophy of the Western wilderness achieves not dignity, which it already had in its own way, but continuity with the rest of the experience of man such it has not hitherto enjoyed. This continuity has been established not only because it has become possible for the American to face into the realities of his own past (symbolized by Europe, purportedly disavowed) with more equanimity and a steadier vision than heretofore, but also because in the Continental philosophical developments loosely designated as personalist and existential, currents have been set up which parallel or intersect developments in American thought, so that this thought can now urge itself on Continental philosophers, as that of Charles Sanders Peirce has already urged itself on Marcel.

A favorite theme of existentialism and personalism has been the isolation of the individual human being. The American heritage from the beginning has been full of this theme, if not as an object of philosophic reflection, certainly as an experienced reality enforced by withdrawal from a highly socialized Europe to the loneliness of the frontier. The greeting which falls half-humorously from American lips today as a relict of the wilderness civilization out of which we have emerged is still "Howdy, stranger," a greeting which one feels might well serve as the countersign for admission to the Café de Flore, Les Deux Magots, or other existentialist rendezvous. It more than suggests the title of Albert Camus' "existential" novel, *The Stranger* (*L'étranger*).

Isolation is the key situation in Bugbee's exploration. Indeed, since it is not consciously exploited as a theme but simply appears as a presupposition in Bugbee's point of view, isolation is in reality more present to Bugbee than to any European counterpart. His being is steeped in it, just as was Thoreau's. But this isolation has all of the ambiguity of Thoreau's, too. Thoreau withdrew into himself (or into his *Journals*, which was the same thing), only in order surreptitiously to communicate his isolation to others, for if there is anything certain about Thoreau's *Journals* it is that he toiled over them as he did in order to have them published—the two-year "isolation" at Walden turned out to be no less than a public address to the entire world.

Professor Bugbee has none of Thoreau's cantankerousness, but with Thoreau he does feel the wilderness, both as a physical reality and as a mold and mode of existence. "As one is redeemed, reality is manifestly given to him as a wilderness, and he rediscovers it as such; it has been so all along." M. Marcel understands in great part the capital importance of Bugbee's notion of wilderness as a means of qualifying or mollifying the wasteland of the human heart, as is clear from his Introduction. There could be nothing more American than this conviction that it is the wilderness, and the wilderness alone, which is productive. Society is a wilderness shared. In this America, even cities are not truly urban as Europe's are (interiors of dwellings juxtaposed, with high walls between) but are individual homesteads (outside plots without walls, punctuated by houses) grown close together, neighboring wildernesses.

It is to this theme of reality as a wilderness that I want to move.

This, so far as I can tell, is the theme which unifies my own life. It enfolds and simplifies, comprehends and completes. Whenever I awaken, I awaken into it. It carries with it the gift of life.

Bugbee's struggle with the wilderness is evidently not to be the same as Marcel's assault on the wasteland. The European proceeds with an effort to establish a sense of person and community, fired by insights into the vast differences between persons and mere things. The American is strongly attracted by this personalist grounding of Marcel's thought, but he is not seduced from his proper vocation. He will not abandon his hold on things: "How apt are those Chinese scrolls which show men in harmony with all nature, men and things emerging *together* and not as over against one another." To a certain extent, the wilderness is even to be broached technologically. Bugbee conceives of dealing with it not by peopling it to give it personal resonance but by exploiting it for what it can yield to him and his associates. His frame of reference is that of the post-Baconian object-world: not man against man so much as man against objects. He is given to Stoicism, as is shown by his love of Epictetus, and of the question "which is like a refrain in Epictetus, What is and is not in our power?" The "what" here is, of course, what objects, what things.

However, this frame of reference built up of things does not positively and really exclude persons. Like Bacon, whose philosophy was inconceivable except within a society where a high degree of organization and personal understanding had been achieved, Bugbee takes persons for granted. Nevertheless, his thinking does not yield recipes or even experiences which are in any notable way poignant. Friendship for Bugbee, like personal enmity for a Stoic, may be a concern, but it is not a primary one. One feels that Bugbee's interest in friendship and in men is muted. Each man is challenged not by other men but by the wilderness—which at this point can be seen as a contemporary epiphany of what the Romantic and post-Romantic ages have called "nature."

Professor Bugbee is entirely aware of this somewhat apersonal drive in his exploration. His doctoral dissertation, he reports, finally completed after World War II with a dispatch which astonished even its author, was the result of "almost uninterrupted active meditation" during his service in the United States Navy as well as most particularly of the impressions which were made on him in the wilderness of the Canadian Rockies just before the war. But the inspiration and meditation remained lacking in personal resonances: they drew from "nature." Without giving evidence of any shattering distress, he nevertheless quite naturally thinks of himself in terms of the friendless Ahab: "Herman Melville must be sailing somewhere hereabout, as when he wrote in Chapter XXIII of *Moby Dick,* 'In landlessness alone resides the highest truth, shoreless, indefinite as God.'" Melville stands for the fact that "things exist in their own right; it is a lesson that escapes us except as they hold us in awe." And this respect for things is tied up irretrievably with "what I miss most in the thought of Marcel—the wilderness theme."

Yet, intense as it is, Bugbee's awareness of the want of personal dimension in what he explores does not enable him adequately to overcome his impersonalism. Not only does God remain indefinite, but, despite Marcel's perceptive and lucid pages on the difference between belief *in* (a person) and belief *that* (a statement is true), when Bugbee discusses belief and opts for faith in as more fundamental than faith that, it turns out that faith in is a faith not (as would be normal) in a person, but faith in an "it," namely action:

Our ultimate stake in action consists in the immediate clarification of its ground. But the ground of action only seems susceptible of clarification that is immediate, and its immediate clarification presupposes that opening of ourselves to it which is faith *in* it rather than belief about it.

The fact that there is an explicit declaration of the author's in favor of sympathy and of "standing by" other men does not destroy the abstractionist, man-against-"it" stands as the foundation of this entire exploration. Bugbee remains American, like the typical American novelists who, as Richard Chase has pointed out, must build their own world for themselves rather than set their action inside a vibrant social framework.

Whatever the rules which define its range, there is no doubt about the intensity of Bugbee's spiritual quest. The intensity is evident in the occasional narrative accounts set into the journal with titles such as "Building a Dam," "Rowing," or "Swamping." These proceed with the deliberate low pressure of a Thoreau or Robert Frost and reach their climax with the still more deliberate deflation which marks their close. The effect is like that achieved by telling a story in a barely audible whisper: the audience is made aware that whatever comes through will just barely come through and is thereby tensed and sensitized so that the most elusive wisp of meaning (which may be the only meaning there is) is seized upon with fierce and knowing delight.

But the intensity of feeling is a matter of more than this designedly low-pressure discourse. It is due also to the fact that the philosophical issues which Bugbee tries to flush out of the wilderness are undefined in terms of the going philosophical dialogue in the West. This is the reason for the little narrative inserts: they convey the concerns of Bugbee's exploration in the nonabstract forms in which these concerns must be conveyed for the good reason that there is as yet no abstract formulation in which to catch them. Needless to say, these apparently artless but really sophisticated little narrative vignettes are a far cry from the crude stuff of naked experience (which in a way they pretend to be, as coming directly from the "wilderness"). They are highly developed art forms.

Bugbee's quest, which we have already observed is self-centered, terminates in the last two paragraphs of the book on the peculiarly American note of "I." Some years ago William Carlos Williams ended a poem read at a Harvard commencement address with the curious assertion:

> I am a poet! I
> am. I am. I am a poet, I reaffirmed, ashamed.

Such an assertion is typically American. With many other similar performances since Walt Whitman's "Song of Myself," it lends credibility to Marius Bewley's statement in *The Complex Fate* that "the most reliable signs by which to identify an American poem today" are "security and faith in its own experience (whatever the experience may be), a reliance on will and assertion, and a feeling that it is pretty important." Seen from the other side, these elements add up to a desire to prove one's security to oneself in the only way which is possible, by asserting oneself before the entire world, or before all the world who can be prevailed upon to listen. With this in mind, we are fascinated by the closing words of Bugbee's exploration, where the word "I" recurrently obtrudes:

> I have noticed of late I have felt much freer to study than I did during the summer months. . . .
> I am not content with what I have worked out; but I have worked out enough, perhaps, to be content to consider more carefully as I move along, and to welcome all manner of thinking other than my own.

The accent is not on communion, a sharing of the self whereby the problems one feels are those of the community rather than one's own isolated problems. The problems here remain concentrated in the "I"— the "I" which is the problem in the wilderness. But the concentration is less strident than Thoreau's and certainly more genial than Emerson's. It is an open sort of concentration, as Henry Adams's concentration on himself in the *Education* is open to more of human experience than might have been the case with the earlier American mind.

II

By contrast with Bugbee's work Marcel's own *Journal métaphysique* is far more a communal exercise. Marcel's quest is carried on overtly in philosophical terms readily available out of the heritage of two millennia of philosophical discourse. One recalls his own protest that he does not wish to be known as an "existentialist" but merely as one who is continuing the conversation which Socrates was carrying on.

Of course, in a vein like Bugbee's, Marcel protests that "only insofar as we are isolated can we communicate." And yet between Marcel's and Bugbee's isolation there is a subtle difference which is supremely important. Marcel's *Journal* is a withdrawal into the self—that self which has been one of the great discoveries of Western philosophy (if a problematic and sometimes apparently frustrating discovery). Bugbee's withdrawal is not a withdrawal into the self so directly as it is withdrawal into the wilderness, which represents not a philosophical achievement but a simple thing which Western man, when he disembarked in North America (not elsewhere in the Western Hemisphere), encountered in the external world and became aware of in his soul.

A diary framed in the self suggests other persons against which the self is set. A diary framed in the wilderness is by this token unpeopled. One might wish, under these circumstances, to credit Marcel with the higher achievement. For, after all, are not persons more than things? They are, but I am not at all sure that Marcel's treatment is entirely to be preferred to Bugbee's, nor is M. Marcel sure of this himself, as his Introduction to *The Inward Morning* so perceptively and generously indicates. The fact is that there are serious limitations to most personalist philosophies which are too exclusively personalist.

One trouble with personalism, and with the various forms of thought called "existentialist," is an inadequate awareness, or even a total blinking of the fact that the human person appears in the universe only after an incredibly long period of impersonal evolution. Claude Tresmontant and François-Albert Viallet have pointed out this lack in their books on the thought of Père Pierre Teilhard de Chardin, S.J., in noting that Père Teilhard's thought does not lack this awareness, despite its personalist center. As the material world grows in organization, this growth involves a real preparation for the advent of persons. A universe of atoms and inorganic molecules susceptible to no organization more complex than that of a crystal matures after several billion years to the point where it can support the huge and incredibly complex protein molecules. Unlike crystals, which have little "interiority" in the sense that they can be grown to indefinite sizes without any changes in their properties, the protein molecule cannot be enlarged or elaborated without becoming something other than what it is. This relatively great interiority is followed by the still great interiorization of plants and animals before the advent of the ultimate interior which is the human person. Things themselves, therefore, are deserving of reverence.

Bugbee does not consider the human person against the massive background of cosmic history, as Teilhard does. But he does make room for treatment of individual history within a framework of cosmic history by the eminence which he insists must be allowed to things as well as persons. As against Marcel's critique of Sartre, which rightly takes Sartre to task for fixing the evidence so as to produce a caricature of the human person, without real love or sense of community, Bugbee's treatment of Sartre moves from a similar critique back again to his theme of the wilderness and its focus on things (but not necessarily divorced from persons):

I wonder what turn Sartre's thought would take if his understanding of honesty were to deepen. Would he still emphasize role-playing and self-consciousness as definitive of the condition of man as an active being? Would his café waiters remain mimics and imitation men? Would he find "bad faith" writ so large across the face of humanity? He has laid bare the waste-land in which we find ourselves insofar as we lack good faith—faith, that is. And this can be also a step upon the threshold that opens out into the wilder-ness that is the reality of faith.

Both Marcel's investigations and Bugbee's explorations need to be kept going. It is in the tension between them that we can live. The tension between *investigation* (always within society) and *exploration* (of a wilderness, but with the backing of society) corresponds roughly to the tension between Europe and America and ultimately to the tension between person and thing. The correspondence here is not an exact equation, by any means. There are, after all, persons in America, and there are wildernesses in Europe. A wolf was killed recently while attacking a woman in Sicily. Moreover, there are apparent contradictions in these correspondences. As Denis de Rougemont has so well pointed out in *Man's Western Quest,* when man faces to the west, he is in quest of the human person and its realization. Beginning with the early ecumenical councils of the Church, the rôle of person—first in God, latterly in man—is the underlying issue and preoccupation. It would seem that America, most westerly of all lands, affecting its inhabitants and their thinking with its own symbolic meaning (as all lands do), would be more devoted to the person than Europe is, would be the front of the personalist movement. But perhaps it is, even with Bugbee's recognition of the importance of things. For a philosophical appreciation of the person has been arrived at, historically speaking, only through a rigorous analytic approach to things.

FOURTEEN

St. Ignatius' Prison-Cage and the Existentialist Situation

I

THE writings of St. Ignatius Loyola are filled with passages more puzzling than a pedantic approach to the spiritual life likes to own. The Basque ex-soldier is a man whom one does not get to know all at once. Not because he was calculating, or inscrutable in any melodramatic way, but simply because of his genuine depth. He acted habitually from profound motives, and it is no discredit to him to say that he was not always capable of rationalizing in so many words the springs of one or another of his actions. He says this of himself often enough in his own *Autobiography* or *Testament*.

The *Spiritual Exercises* themselves are full of minor puzzles. Their general purpose is clear enough and explicitly stated: "That a man may conquer himself and order his life without being himself determined by any inordinate affection." And the general progression within the *Exercises* corresponds closely enough to the succession of purgative, illuminative, and unitive ways to be immediately intelligible in terms of the normal psychological progression which this succession registers. But within this framework, why this or that detail of the *Spiritual Exercises* should have appealed to their writer as particularly effective is not always so clear, as our great masses of commentary make only too evident.

To some of his techniques St. Ignatius seems to attach a special force which escapes us. I do not mean here the kind of thing one encounters, for example, in the talk about knights and kings, and the problems arising when such Renaissance imagery loses force in an age when knights are, for all practical purposes, extinct, and when kings, at best, are but symbolic relics of a once functional office. Here, despite the fact that these terms have become less "numinous" than they were, we can still sense what a knight meant to the sixteenth century knight, Inigo de

Loyola. There is a difficulty in our reaction pattern, but, given elementary historical information, no intellectual puzzle here.

It is quite otherwise with the peculiar "First Prelude" which occurs over and over again in the First Week of the *Exercises,* the picture of the soul in the body as in a prison, and of the whole, soul-and-prison, thrown out among brute beasts. This construct of St. Ignatius' has presented difficulties from the very beginning, and difficulties so puzzling that they are mostly not even touched on by commentators, and, if they are touched on, are not really faced but only blurred and set aside.

The basic text of St. Ignatius in question runs as follows:

In meditation on something invisible, as here on sins, the composition will be to see, with the eyes of the imagination, and to consider my soul to be closed up in this corruptible body as in a prison, and the whole composite as in exile among brute animals. I say the whole composite, soul and body.

This is a translation of the original Spanish of the *texto autógrafo* used by St. Ignatius himself, which reads:

En la invisible, como es aquí de los pecados, la composición será ver con la vista imaginativa y considerar mi ánima ser encarcerada en este cuerpo corruptible, y todo el compósito en este valle, como desterrado, entre brutos animales. Digo todo el composito de ánima y cuerpo.[1]

In the often reprinted 1548 "Vulgate" version prepared in proper Renaissance classical Latin by the Jesuit Latinist, Père André des Freux (Frusius), and approved by the Pope's censors together with the less "elegant" Latin text now known as the "Versio Prima," we find the following:

Sin autem speculationi subest res incorporea, ut est consideratio peccatorum nunc oblata, poterit loci constructio talis esse, ut si per imaginationem cernamus animam nostram in corpore isto corruptibili, velut in carcere constrictam; hominem quoque ipsum, in hac miseriae valle, inter animalia bruta exulantem.[2]

Although this "Vulgate" version was approved by St. Ignatius and the divergence from the original is here slight enough, it is plain that St. Ignatius' imagery had presented difficulties in Père des Freux. St. Ignatius' original is "la composición será ver" *(the composition will be to see),* and this is attenuated in Père des Freux's hands to "poterit loci constructio talis esse, ut si . . . cernamus" *(the composition of place could be such as though we were to see*). Frusius' difficulty is obvious: St. Ignatius seemed to be making too much of the image, and to be suggesting too strongly that it should be used for all meditations on things invisible.

St. Ignatius let his subject's alteration stand. He did not regard his text of the *Exercises* as partaking of the infallibility or inalterability of the Scriptures, and his whole attitude toward everything short of God, including certainly the *Exercises* themselves, is elastic and adaptable. But the fact remains that in the extant text which seems best to represent his thought and which he has annotated in his own hand, the Spanish *texto autógrafo*, with which the Latin "Versio Prima" slavishly agrees, he says that "the composition *will* be to see . . ." and, unless we interpolate some sort of emendation or *subintelligo* for which he provides no warrant, he proposes this "composition of place" for any and all "meditation on something invisible." Actually, this carries the composition forward only through the first four exercises of the First Week, for the fifth exercise is on hell—something visible, at least after the resurrection—and thereafter one is in the Second Week and the Incarnation, the regions of invisibility left behind. Still, the fact remains of the curious emotional strength attaching to this prison-and-brute-animal picture in St. Ignatius' mind, not to mention his curious association of it, above all other imagery, with the "invisible."

II

The immediate source of St. Ignatius' imagery need not trouble us here, although it is evident that what he invites the exercitant to picture has a long history in human thought, particularly in Western thought, Christian and non-Christian. The imagery suggests passages from the Old and the New Testament, as, for example, Wisd. 9:15: "For the corruptible body is a load upon the soul, and the earthly habitation presseth down the mind that museth upon many things," or Gal. 5:17: "For the flesh lusteth against the spirit, and the spirit against the flesh." Echoing such passages, countless other passages can be gathered from Christian secular and spiritual literature, and in particular from the Carthusian writers of whom St. Ignatius was so fond.

But sources in this case operate viciously. Instead of reassuring commentators of the validity of St. Ignatius' imagery so as to bring them to put themselves more thoroughly into it, these sources at best only deflect the commentators' attention back from what St. Ignatius says to analogies from elsewhere which say something like what he says without really saying the same thing at all. The general procedure among commentators has thus been one of blurring, comparable to, but rather more advanced than, that of Frusius in his Vulgate version.

Without going into all the interpreters, we can take three well known modern ones, one in French, one in German, and one in English—Longhaye, Meschler, and Gabriel. Longhaye sees the prelude as expressing two things: (1) the sorry plight of the soul in the body (in prison, loaded with chains, etc.) and (2) the sorry plight of man in his resemblance to brute beasts. The second of these two things reduces immediately to the first, for man is at the level of brute beasts because his soul is imprisoned in a body: "Je les domine par l'esprit; mais je me trouve à leur niveau par mes appétits corporels."[3]

Meschler does not consider the prison situation and the brute-animal situation as separate at all, but lumps them together and simply regards the first prelude as a whole as expressing "forcibly the sinner's vileness and degradation almost to the level of brute animals."[4] Gabriel considers the two situations separately.[5] The body has become a prison because, since the Fall, it has overpowered the soul. The brute-animal situation seems to have two phases: man is first pictured by Gabriel as in exile among "a rude and savage people," and then as among "filthy animals" because living as though "devoid of reason and judgment." These interpretations are not exhaustive, but they are typical of all the explanations or commentaries which I have ever been able to find— except for the large number which quickly skip the passage and move on to less puzzling phenomena.

The first thing to note about these explanations is that, beyond a doubt, they are doctrinally orthodox. Their general manipulation of the prison and brute-beast symbolism is well within the *analogia fidei* and can be paralleled by countless examples from spiritual writers. It is also well within what we might style the *analogia Ignatiana*, for in the second Addition at the end of the First Week we find this advice:

similarly in the second Exercise [on rising I should recall the subject-matter of meditation to mind], making myself out to be a great sinner in chains, that is to say, that I move about as though encumbered with chains on my way to appear before the most high Eternal Judge, picturing to myself as an example the way in which chained prisoners condemned to death appear before their temporal judge.[6]

This is something like the prelude we are considering, but it is not quite the same thing—although the explanations and commentaries would tend to make it so, through their tendency to dissolve the prelude in the usual commonplaces of Christian symbolism. This fact suggests a second point about the explanations: as related to the economy of St. Ignatius' own thought here, they are decidedly banal. It is often all right to be banal, and at times even necessary. But it is not all right here, for the precise difficulty to be faced is why this imagery was not banal to St. Ignatius' way of thinking, but rather extraordinarily forceful, so that he repeats it over and over again and allows it such prominence in his whole imaginative approach to the invisible world.

The third and most important thing to note about the explanations is that they do not face into the difficulties of the text. To say the least, the text itself invites us to a very clumsy and unmanageable picture. The soul is barred up, in a prison, which is the body. This prison, by every word for it in the Spanish and Latin texts, is a decidedly fixed thing. Yet it here becomes portable—and for that reason I shall refer to it from time to time as a prison-cage—as we are invited to picture the whole composite of soul-and-body in *exile* among brute beasts. St. Ignatius is not only explicit on this point but insistent: "I say the whole man, soul and body," soul and prison-cage. He is likewise explicit that the prison situation and the brute-animal situation are to be pictured together: "to consider my soul to be closed up in this corruptible body as in a prison, *and* the whole composite as in exile among brute animals." How can a prison be satisfactorily imagined as in exile?

The difficulty does not end here. To make an exile among brute beasts effectively undesirable, it would seem that the contact between the person in exile and the brute beasts should be at some kind of maximum. The person should be thrown up against the brute beasts, so to speak, in the raw. If his soul cannot directly engage them, as it of course cannot, at least it should not be positively sheltered from them. But in our prelude this is precisely the fact. Exiled among brute beasts, the soul should certainly find its prison-cage a decided asset. When you are surrounded by wild animals, the very next best thing to having them in cages is to be in one yourself. And thus the second part of the prelude seems to cancel out all the effectiveness of the first. Moreover, the difficulty here seems to be quite peculiar to the Ignatian text, with no clear counterpart in any of his sources which have now been so exhaustively studied.[7]

The recognition of the difficulty here does not make its way to the surface of even so classical a commentary as Roothaan's. But retreat masters are sensitive to it, at least subconsciously, as Père des Freux once was. If the writer's experience of retreat masters is any indication of their prevailing practice, they quite commonly substitute for this prelude of St. Ignatius' some other prelude of their own devising.

III

Several offhand solutions for the difficulty could be proposed. The prison and brute-animal imagery are to be used separately—either as alternatives or in succession. The text rules out this explanation, as has been seen. St. Ignatius is clearly proposing their use together. Secondly, one might suggest that the imagery used by the author of the *Spiritual Exercises* is confused in detail and to be taken only in a general sense as echoing the general Christian tradition—and indeed a pre-Christian and para-Christian tradition—which enforces the lesson of the degradation and sinfulness of man in a flood of debasing images of all sorts. In such an explanation the prison and the brute-animal imagery lack any precise function, at least as working in consort. Against this explanation, there is Ignatius' marked tendency not to be haphazard in the *Spiritual Exercises,* as well as the notable precision and insistence of his directions here. Finally, one might suppose that the images were hopelessly confused through some short-circuiting in Ignatius' own mind. This could be, for St. Ignatius is not infallibly "logical" in the use of images; but even if it is so, the fact would not dispense from further explanation but would rather demand it, for psychologists know too well that there is just as much reason for a particular confusion as for anything else in the conscious life. This final answer would thus leave us only with a further question: Why this confusion?

At the present time, it would seem, it is less necessary than ever to suppose that St. Ignatius' imagery here ran wild through some in-scrutable personal short-circuits. For we are perhaps in a better position than ever before to understand St. Ignatius' prison-cage and to profit from it, because of the great progress made in the past few decades in the elucidation of the archetypal symbolism on which human conscious activity builds. Any explanation along these lines must, of course, remain at this stage tentative and incomplete, for Catholic theology as a whole has hardly even begun to assimilate the study of symbolism which has grown up with both anthropology and psychological analysis and which is tending more and more to fuse these two sciences.[8] The images in question have evidently for St. Ignatius high but elusive symbolic valence, and it is just such images which recent analysis is most successful in explaining, by bringing to light the reason for the forcefulness of a symbol which was earlier operative without being consciously understood.

The kind of explanation which can be ambitioned here may be suggested, by way of preliminary clarification, in terms of the water symbolism in baptism. Regarding the explicit signification of the baptismal rite, we know from St. Paul that baptism of water in the name of the Father, the Son, and the Holy Spirit signifies not only the remission of sins (which it also effects, and which the baptism of John the Baptist had signified), but also death, burial, and resurrection in Christ.[9] Washing with water has for us an obvious relevance to the taking away of sins, which we know as uncleannesses, but as referred to the death, burial, and resurrection in Christ, the symbolism has commonly been invested by modern theology with a purely juridical force. Unless we lay hold of the roots of symbolism within the human psyche, we end by asserting in effect that things are this way because God has for no ascertainable reason set them up this way. This makes the death-burial-resurrection symbolism a kind of *appliqué* which we are encouraged to force onto the rite for reasons unknown to us, but which never seems to come alive, as one might well imagine the Divine Institutor of symbolism had wished it would. We are a far cry here from a scriptural or patristic age which was intensely aware that not only words but things themselves can signify, for we are victims of the tendency, which set in during the Middle Ages but was perfected only later, to reduce all the symbolism with which the Scriptures and Fathers abound to a kind of pious but ineffectual and rather irrelevant patter.

Psychological analysis, whatever its other difficulties, has not only helped reinstate the scriptural and patristic point of view but has made possible certain types of explanation which were unavailable to earlier

ages, although not out of harmony with earlier ways of thinking. This
is true particularly of such work as that done by Carl Jung or Victor
Frankl with archetypal symbols. Research in dream and other analysis
has revealed the fact that water, to the subconscious mind, is a symbol
of death, or conversely of life, for in the material universe these two
are inextricably intertwined, the generation of one thing being inevitably the corruption of another. This symbolism attaching to water
is not arbitrary nor accidental. That is to say, it always arises when
the human sensibility is brought into contact with the world around
it. Such symbolism is evidently at its profoundest depths related to
the fact that life, in its earliest forms, whether in phylogenetic evolution or in the history of a single individual, arises in some sort of fluid
medium—a fact which, by its universality, suggests that the close connection of fluid with life (and death) is itself not arbitrary, not the
result of a kind of eenie-meenie-minie-mo procedure on the part of
Almighty God, but intimately related to the nature of life and to
existence itself. The complex of relationships here is, of course, not
grasped all at once, for no one understands it in its full richness, but
it is ubiquitous enough to impress itself in a thousand ways on the
human subconscious, so that the human sensibility lays hold of an
elementary connection between water and life long before, and independently of, any scientific understanding of the real development of
the individual organism, not to mention the evolution of species. Thus
it is that its own particular symbolic value attaches to water in the
dream-life not only of office workers in skyscrapers but of the most
retarded of primitives. Water *means* death (or life). This is a result of
the economy of the composite world of human-sensibility-vis-à-vis-
reality, and due to the inherent proclivity of some things in this economy
to symbolize other things. The Christian sacramental symbolism is
embedded in and sanctifies this whole economy, and recent gains in
our understanding of the economy show the often unsuspected psychological depths at which Christ was operating in instituting His sacraments.

IV

St. Ignatius' prison-cage is not part of the sacramental symbolism
of the Church, but it seems to be a part of the world of symbolism into
which the sacraments were inserted. In this world it is not an incidental

item, a bit of imaginative décor, but something basic to the whole symbolic economy, so that St. Ignatius' inclination to throw great weight on this symbol becomes eminently understandable. Ultimately, the connection of the *Spiritual Exercises* with the world of symbolism is due to their concern with the self, which is a major preoccupation of the mind's unconscious and conscious symbolic activity. To glimpse some of the connections here, we need only draw on certain notions current more or less everywhere along the contemporary intellectual front, notions which are here taken as being, in general, well enough known in their larger aspects to make unnecessary any detailed documentation—which would run on endlessly anyhow, and which can be had by those who wish it in the various reports on contemporary developments in psychological research, anthropological studies, and phenomenological and personalist or "existentialist" analysis.[10]

In St. Ignatius' image of a prison-cage, the notion of separation or estrangement is evidently paramount. This is due to a concern with self, which means, conversely, a concern with the nonself or the other, and with the line of separation between myself and other selves. In terms of this separation, the body functions not in the way it functions in the rather more mechanistic body-soul or matter-form point of view, for it functions not as the seat of sense organs, the starting point for concepts connecting man with his surroundings, but rather in terms of man's interior, personal, and incommunicable self-consciousness, the individual's own private experience of his own individual existence which he can never impart to anyone else nor share directly with anyone else (save God). In terms of this self, the body is less a connecting than an alienating mechanism, for our consciousness is our "interior," and, while contact with the external world is a necessary condition of self-awareness, it is necessary not because it supplies the stuff of self-awareness—which it does not do at all, since the self is precisely what does *not* come *into* my consciousness from the outside—but because it gives us something, the "other" as a kind of background against which self-awareness can be constituted.

My interior is for me, but for no one else (save God), bright, luminous, vivid, by contrast with the dull, dead stuff of the world outside consciousness, and my body is the transit between the two realms of the interior and the exterior. The ambivalent character of St. Ignatius' prison-cage is due to the mediating role of the body here. In one way it functions as a prison, a limit, not only differentiating the interior from the exterior but actually constraining the interior, for, as Heidegger has well explained, the human self *ex*-ists. It does not merely *in*-sist but rather seeks to spread out, to bring the dead, dull, outside world within the circle of its own luminosity. But the body, the very organ through which the self becomes aware of the exterior, stands in the way, for it itself, despite its intimate connection with the self, is in a sense exterior, so that everything which comes *into* the soul through its mediation is invested with exteriority. There are other human selves, but, since the bodily senses mediate my contact with them, my knowlege of them remains radically an exterior knowledge. Even a husband cannot experience the consciousness of his wife as she does herself, nor a wife that of her husband. The one does not really know what it feels like to be the other.

As body, St. Ignatius' prison-cage symbolizes this tantalizing situation. It is a part of the self and it is not a part of the self. It is a prison and yet it can be thrown with the self into exile. Moreover, it can positively protect the self—from brute beasts. And why from brute beasts? Rainer Maria Rilke, very much in the Kierkegaard tradition, speaks occasionally of the dull, blank emptiness which stares out from the animal's eye. The animal is a living being, and as such suggestive of the human self, but he has no interiority, no self-consciousness, no self-possession. Because of this he symbolizes the situation we find ourselves in—or at least half of this situation. We have no direct access to the self-consciousness of others, although we know indirectly that such self-consciousness exists. In a world filled with real personalities we are, in a radical way, totally isolated, incapable of communicating our self-consciousness or of intimately registering that of others. The brute animal, totally devoid of self-consciousness, thus impressively symbolizes our isolation.

St. Ignatius slips quite naturally into this symbolism because he feels the isolation by reason of his religious preoccupations. Concern with God is in one way or another tied up with concern about this isolation of the ego. For God alone shares the interior of my self-consciousness, knows intimately what it feels like to be *me*. "Homo videt in faciem, Deus autem in corde" —"Man looks into the face, but God sees within the heart." Moreover, on the strength of the Pauline text, "Cognoscam sicut et cognitus sum" ("I shall know even as I am known"—I Cor.

13:12), we can believe that in the beatific vision we shall known God with a similar interior directness, as we have never been able to know other men. Compared to God's contacts with my soul, which will flower in the beatific vision, my relations with my fellow men are curiously empty, like relations with brute beasts where there is no "you" to respond to my own "I." At this depth the relevance of the brute animals to the prison-cage becomes somewhat discernible: the animals suggest the effective depersonalization of everything outside the tiny interior point of personal awareness which we call consciousness of self.

The animals, of course, mean other things too. They are the passions, as we know from psychological analysis as well as from the normal symbolism of mystical or paramystical experience. They are the passions not as known by rational study, situated inside the human composite, but the passions as experienced in the existentialist situation—something strangely other, for, while they are present as a kind of living threat, and thus as somewhat assimilable to myself, they are at the same time outside the circle of luminosity which is my conscious interior. Because they come from my "lower" nature, surging up from the dark depths of the senses and the unconscious, they are strangers to my self-consciousness, and hence are "other," felt as outside me, estranged from me by my body (in which, of course, they reside), and even capable, in extreme cases, of occasioning the weird interior alienation known as a "split" personality.

The same theme of self-versus-other which gives force to the prison-cage imagery thus gives force to the animal imagery too. The animal, writes Ortega y Gasset,

has always to be attentive to what goes on outside, to the things around it. Because, even if the dangers and incitements of these things were to diminish, the animal would perforce continue to be governed by them, by the outward, by what is *other* than itself; because it cannot go *within* itself, since it has no *self*, no *chez soi*, where it can withdraw and rest.[11]

The world outside the self is potential self, in that the self is continuously seeking to *ex*-ist toward it, to assimilate it, but it will not assimilate, it will cooperate only negatively, giving force to the self by contrast. This world, marked off by the body, is inhabited by brute animals as symbols of pure otherness, almost-selves which are nevertheless not selves at all. They are the *un*-contained. They are those beyond the pale, outside the prison-wall. Their presence shows why this prison is both stronghold and cage, partaking of the ambivalent situation of the human consciousness, where the notion of estrangement from others and that of self-containment are complementary. The interplay of the two notions of self-perfection and self-limitation thus produces the inevitable awkwardness in St. Ignatius' picture, in which that which causes the soul embarrassment (the prison-cage) at the same time affords protection from the brute animals who would swallow man up in pure otherness.

V

The notion of containment which here assimilates itself to that of estrangement determines an important characteristic of the division between the self and the other. The division must be pictured not merely as a terminus but as something which surrounds the self on all sides. This gives rise to the familiar mandala or mandala-type design which recurs constantly as symbol of the self in all sorts of art forms and apparently in all human cultures, paleolithic, medieval European, Pueblo Indian, down to our own day. The mandala or "magic circle," which has received so much recent attention as a result largely of the work of Jung,[12] who spent some fourteen years working over the symbols before venturing to interpret them, is a design commonly featuring some combination of circle and square (the predilection for fours and antipathy to threes is marked), with, commonly, a figure of high religious significance at its center—medieval European mandalas often build out from a figure of Christ (but in terms of the *four* evangelists, etc., not of the Trinity). The mandala constructs often appear as the perpetuation of a specific artistic or religio-artistic tradition. Here the most elaborate and beautiful figures are those of the Tibetan Buddhists and of the Orient in general, where mandalas are utilized as instruments for contemplation in the Tantric Yoga and reflected in the crafts, such as rug design. But mandala figures occur also outside any formalized tradition, turning up spontaneously, for example, when individuals of the most diverse cultural origins are encouraged to picture in a design the relation of their selves to the external world, or to form designs symbolizing the ideal integration of their lives or personalities, and so on. Psychological literature is now full of reproductions of this sort of mandala-figure elicited under more or less clinical conditions.[13]

The psychological implications of the mandalas are extremely rich and complicated, and only certain special applications of the figures can be touched on here. The circle which mandalas commonly feature as a basis of their structure is often a clock, bowl, ball, round table, or the like, and the square a four-walled room, public square, prison cell, college quad, four chairs around a table, and like arrangements. The presence of this kind of imagery in thought concerned with the perfection of self can be detected everywhere, once one is alerted to it: the Greek four-square man, the related Greek notion of encyclopedia which complements the four-square imagery with a "circle" of education, modern "Four-Square Gospelers," the four cardinal virtues (with the hinge imagery suggesting circular movement again), St. Teresa of Avila's "mansions" and "interior castle" (images repeated time without number among spiritual writers), and thus on indefinitely. Imagery of a similar type is, of course, utilized also by Christ Himself, who knew of what psychological stuff man was made, as when He says: "In my Father's *house* there are many *mansions*" (for the interior orientation of both house and mansions, cf. "The kingdom of God is within you"), or when He speaks of the "house" which is swept and garnished, from which the devils are expelled and to which they return. A more elaborate exploitation of the house imagery is found in Hebrews 1-5, where the house which Christ inhabits so much more confidently than Moses had— "which house are we" (3:6)—focuses the ensuing discussion concerning both the seventh-day rest of faith and Christ's priesthood itself. Passages such as this in the Scriptures may well have directly inspired some medieval Christ-mandalas.

The specialization of this symbolism in circles and four-sided figures (obviously related to the bilateral symmetry of the human body, and thus bearing a heavy material charge), and its tendency to avoid triangles (which, by contrast, carry a kind of spiritual charge),[14] is not a law imputed to mandalas by some sort of extrapolation of an overheated Pythagorean imagination, but a simple fact observable in the figures which actually occur. The reasons for such facts go deep into the structure of the personal consciousness and cannot, of course, be elaborated here. They have been and are being elaborated in dismaying detail in works such as those earlier referred to, for those interested in studying them. Neither the four-sidedness nor the circularity appears overtly in St. Ignatius' prison-cage, which is a primitive or residual mandala figure as compared with the elaborate mandalas worked out in the Orient. This fact is perhaps connected with St. Ignatius' way of easing intense concentration on the self alone by merging it with a concentration on Christ, who is a person and hence other, but at the same time, as God, inhabits the interior castle of my soul as effectively as I do myself.

But, despite its rudimentary character, St. Ignatius' prison is, beyond any reasonable doubt, related to the mandala-type constructs in its way of picturing the self in a kind of enclosure, isolated from an exteriority around it. St. Ignatius' prison is an embarrassing phenomenon because the walls of the self are ambiguous in implication: they are the walls of a prison, but a prison which is also a kind of house and protection, and a prison which, because it helps constitute the self, is also portable as the self is portable, and thus, in a way, seems not to be a prison at all, but something which I have tried to catch in the expression "prison-cage." Thus the "confusion" in St. Ignatius' picture has a *real* reason for existing: his image simply picks up, like a television set, a pattern which exists independently of it. Here we are up against a certain quality in St. Ignatius' thought which makes it particularly susceptible to a phenomenological or descriptive approach and which arises less out of any particular philosophy—attempts to "systematize" St. Ignatius philosophically are singuarly unconvincing—than out of an intensely personal, real, "existential" awareness of the self and of the problems of existence, and out of a complementary, real, non-abstractive approach to God, allied to what Newman calls real as against notional assent to religious truth.

The present study, which has taken as a point of departure what appears to be a real difficulty in St. Ignatius' thought, does not at all want to pretend that St. Ignatius' thought is everywhere dominated by mandala-type constructs, or that the elements here discussed explain everything that has to be explained, but only to suggest some of the reasons why St. Ignatius' remarks on the soul-*and-body* in exile can legitimately and understandably take the form they do. The remarks cannot be written off as defying rational explanation, for the reason that careful study shows more and more that there is no completely private way of picturing the self to the self, or even of erring in such a representation—only unfamiliarity with investigations in this field of consciousness can occasion the illusion that there is. To enter into the exile and estrangement of the human situation with the vigor and earnestness and honesty of this mature man turned saint is inevitably to engage a huge field of human experience with an economy exceedingly—even disconcertingly—rich, the study of which can be profitable, and about which a great deal is already scientifically known.

The obvious limitations of an article such as the present are due to the fact that so little has been done to relate this economy to what we know otherwise of the ascetical and mystical life. Exploration on all fronts is still the order of the day, with the intellectual humility which fruitful exploration demands. St. Ignatius himself was living in another age, and obviously he did not know—nor did he have to know—that he was making use of imagery which would have a particular interest to a twentieth-century phenomenologist or anthropologist. Indeed, for this very reason, the fidelity with which his imagery follows an economy only latterly subject to abstract formulation attests the utter authenticity of his spiritual language. The curious dimension of his own which St. Ignatius adds to the prison-cage imagery may be in certain ways without counterpart in his sources, but it is not without counterpart in the symbolic inheritance of mankind.[15]

This symbolic inheritance forms a direct connection between the depths of the Catholic spiritual heritage and a large and growing mass of contemporary thought, much of it of the first order, growing out of anthropology, phenomenology, psychological analysis, and even literary analysis. The connection deserves exploitation, not only because the mind is concerned with all truth, but especially because it offers mystical and other theology a place on the contemporary intellectual front which so far it all too little enjoys.

It might be added that this kind of exploitation, which is already to some extent under way, was once easier for Scholastic theology than it is today, for many of the frames of thought which have to be assimilated were present in the old medical and paramedical literature—astrology and alchemy—and in the old physics which was once a great part of that Scholasticism of which theology was only a small part and which is now awakening such keen interest among psychological analysts. Much of what had been discarded was worthless detritus, but many of the frames of reference were not. Concepts elaborated for use with an impossible physics are not necessarily useless for metaphysical or psychological purposes, especially since, because their connection with physics was bogus, they probably had hidden metaphysical or psychological roots to start with. At any rate, many of the phenomena on the current intellectual front indicate a profound relevance of the *Spiritual Exercises* and of Catholic spirituality as a whole to the contemporary mind, precisely as contemporary. And, on the other hand, present-day interest in the real as against the purely formalistic side of things, and the current development of techniques of talking about this real side—techniques which past ages had not very fully developed —promise certain insights into spiritual writings and reality deeper in some ways than those we have hitherto enjoyed. After all, the abiding worth of the *Spiritual Exercises* lies here: not that they provide some sort of system independent of the self, of *engagement*, of making a choice, but that they are a technique of *engagement*, of making a choice which has never been made before and can never be made again. They confront the self and the real.

NOTES

[1] The texts of the *Spiritual Exercises* here cited or referred to, Spanish and Latin, are from *Monumenta Ignatiana*, Series secunda, *Exercitia spiritualia sancti Ignatii de Loyola et eorum Directoria* (Madrid, 1919).

[2] For the occasional slight divergence of the Vulgate from St. Ignatius' thought and emphasis, see Henri Pinard de la Boullaye, S.J., "La Vulgate des Exercices de saint Ignace, ses caractères, son autorité," *Revue d'ascétique et de mystique*, XXV (1949), 389-407.

[3] G. Longhaye, S.J., *Retraite annuelle de huit jours d'après les Exercices de saint Ignace* (3rd ed.; Paris: Casterman, 1925), pp. 58-59.

[4] Maurice Meschler, S.J., *The Spiritual Exercises of Saint Ignatius*, trans. from the German (Woodstock, Maryland: Woodstock College, 1889), p. 67.

[5] Henry A. Gabriel, S.J., *An Eight Days' Retreat for Religious* (St. Louis: Herder, 1914), pp. 54-55.

[6] "Ansí mismo en el 2.° ejercicio, haciéndome pecador grande y encadenado, es a saber, que voy atado como en cadenas a parescer delante del sumo juez eterno, trayendo en ejemplo como los encarcerados y encadenados ya dignos de muerte delante su juez temporal."

[7] Cf. Arturo Codina, S.J., *Los orígenes de los Ejercicios espirituales de S.*

Ignacio de Loyola (Barcelona: Biblioteca Balmes, 1926). Besides this excellent detailed study, there is much other literature which cannot all be cited here.

[8] One of the pioneer attempts to exploit symbolic analysis theologically is Victor White's *God and the Unconscious* (London: Harvill Press, 1952), where the size of the task demanded of modern theologians, as well as its urgency, is well brought home. Closely related to such psychological and symbolic analysis is the phenomenological and/or personalist, "existentialist" analysis being used for the study of the Scriptures by R. Bultmann, Mme. Herrade Mehl-Koehnlein, etc.

[9] See Louis Beirnaert, S.J., "Symbolisme mythique de l'eau dans le baptême," *La Maison-Dieu: Revue de pastorale liturgique,* No. 22 (2° trimestre, 1950), pp. 94-120. This article had appeared earlier in *Eranos-Jahrbuch,* 1949 (Zurich: Rhein Verlag).

[10] For example, in the work of Fr. Victor White already cited, or in Kurt F. Reinhart, *The Existentialist Revolt* (Milwaukee: Bruce, 1952), etc.

[11] Ortega y Gasset, "The Self and the Other" (an address originally delivered in Buenos Aires, 1939), *Partisan Review,* July-August, 1952, 394.

[12] See Jolan Jacobi, *La psychologie de C. G. Jung,* trans. V. Baillods (Paris: Delachaux et Niestle, 1950), esp. pp. 147 ff., and the bibliography of Jung's works, pp. 179 ff.; Richard Wilhelm and C. J. Jung, *Das Geheimnis der goldenen Blüte, ein chinesisches Lebensbuch* (Zürich: Rascher, 1944); Wilfred Daim, *Umwertung der Psychoanalyse* (Vienna: Herold, 1951); Igor A. Caruso, *Psychoanalyse und Synthese der Existens* (Vienna: Herder, 1952), pp. 214 ff. These works are abundantly illustrated with mandala figures, both of the artistic and of the personal clinical type.

[13] Cf. the works just cited in the foregoing note, particularly Caruso, Daim, and Jacobi.

[14] A triangle or trinity of any sort is male; the fourth principle is concerned with the manifestation in the cosmos, is variable and female, tending toward evil. Cf. Victor White, *God and the Unconscious,* p. 249.

[15] In the *Autobiography* or *Testament* of St. Ignatius—the titles often supplied to the document headed *Acta P. Ignatii ut primum scripsit P. Ludovicus Gonzales excipiens ex ore ipsius Patris,* published in *Fontes narrativi de S. Ignatio de Loyola,* I (Monumenta historica Societatis Iesu, LXVI; Rome, 1943), 354-507—there occur several instances of symbolic visions; symbolic, that is, in the sense that they were not of Christ nor of the saints, but representational in a kind of emblem-book fashion or in the manner of present-day abstract painting. These images St. Ignatius found puzzling, sometimes above suspicion and sometimes not, so that they were one of the occasions for his interest in rules for the discernment of spirits. For example, at Manresa, he saw a thing "hanging in the air," serpentlike, but difficult to apprehend accurately, which he delighted to look at (*ibid.,* 390); at another time, a representation of the creation in which figured "something white, out of which rays shot, and from which God sent forth light" (*ibid.,* 402); or

again, something like white rays shooting down from above at the time of the elevation of the Sacred Host at Mass (*ibid.*); or, once more, a many-eyed, colored, shining object, apparently the same as the serpentlike object mentioned above, which he was now able to recognize as diabolical (*ibid.*, 406); etc. In measuring these and his other visions by their relations to the Church's teachings and to his own personal obligations in accord with her teachings, and in noting whether they brought real peace of soul or ended in agitation, St. Ignatius applied to these apparitions Christ's saying: "By their fruits you shall know them." But he had a keen sense of the way such signs could engage the reality of his own life, as his sober approach to them and careful description of them shows.

❧ FIFTEEN ❧

The Barbarian Within

OUTSIDERS INSIDE SOCIETY TODAY

I

THE outsider theme is both an old theme and a preoccupation and symbol of our time. Earlier ages are aware of individual characters as outsiders—Lear or Ulysses or Job. But our interest in the outsider penetrates through individual characters to the pure abstraction itself. Besides a movie, two earlier recent books, one by Richard Wright and one by Colin Wilson, have taken as their title the unqualified term *The Outsider*, which has also become the name of a quarterly announcing itself as "vigorous" and "new." How new it can be is questionable, in view of the many other exercises in the dialectic of the "in" and the "out" which of late have been flooding the market. From the lowbrow, middlebrow, and highbrow tastemakers of Russell Lynes (an aggressive early in-and-out sponsor) one moves through David Riesman's inner-directed and other-directed (or outer-directed) characters and Vance Packard's status seekers (outsiders pushing in), on through the "U" and "Non-U" people of Nancy Mitford's set into the utter explicitness of the Benton and Schmidt *In and Out Book*, which tells what is IN and what is OUT in capital letters.

Externalism has become established orthodoxy. At an increasing number of levels, being "way out" has replaced being "in" as the most trenchant expression of "belonging," of social acceptance. All support for such expression is not merely journalistic or faddist—the latest manifestation of popular un-think. Outsidedness has been the concern of some of our most serious and humanly meaningful contemporary thinking. In the modern world, farthest out of all (and hence really in) are the heady but truly intellectual heights of the existentialist dialectic of self-versus-other (inside-looking-out versus outside-looking-in) which dominates so much of the profoundest thinking of our time. On the other hand, this same externalism works itself out in ways which are patently democratic in the grossest sense, and even commercial: Grove

Press has certainly found the existentialist in-and-out game one of the most lucrative developments in twentieth-century philosophy.

One of the remarkable features of the outsider theme as it charms us today is its appeal to the few and the many conjointly. Outsiders make headlines not only in the *Evergreen Review* and the *Chicago Review*. They make them in the daily press as well, and with a frequency attesting the alacrity with which the average "decent" American secretly identifies with those who are "out." Teen-age outcasts especially, such as American neighborhood toughs, British teddy boys, and their equivalents the world over, are more than ever before staples of the city desk. Youth itself, of course, is an element never entirely "in," and by contrast with these unhappy youngsters, outsiders because of inexperience as well as misbehavior, the middle-aged gangsters has lost news appeal, having become in some quarters almost a symbol of security.

The accent on youth in the American heritage (no one is allowed to dress like a real grandmother any more) and the prolongation of adolescence made necessary by a technological civilization's demand for a protracted period of formal education doubtless helps further interest in the outsider question. But so do other things in the United States, such as the American's haunting remembrance of the abandoned fatherland of his ancestors, the still vicariously felt experience of the lonely frontier, and the present American (and global) preoccupation with "integration," racial and other, which represents a concerted effort, if as yet not always a successful one, to bring the outsider in.

Interest in social outcasts is of course not new and not restricted to the United States. It reaches back through Richard Hovey's and Bliss Carman's shabby-genteel *Vagabondia* literature of the 1890's on past Daniel Defoe's Moll Flanders and Robinson Crusoe (social ostracism romantically transmuted into geographical isolation), through Renaissance rogue literature, the medieval François Villon and his goliard brethren, on through Apuleius and even Homer, for whose Odysseus the prototype seems to have been a more ancient character of the clever-rogue-and-outcast type. And the story of paradise lost itself ends in exile, long a preoccupation of Hebrew and Christian thought, literature, and prayer. *To thee do we cry, poor banished children of Eve.*

Nevertheless, today's interest in the outsider is somehow special, intensified by the structure of society in a newly populous planet whose inhabitants, by contrast with their ancestors of a few millenia, or even of a few centuries, ago, are now for the first time living with an awareness of the global dimensions of human relationships. The mass media of communication, and more particularly the electronic media of instantaneous telecommunication which bring the news on the quarter hour, have made it normal for individuals to participate daily and even continuously in significant activities of the entire human race over the face of the globe. In technologically advanced societies—and all societies will soon be such—it is necessary and inevitable for individuals so to open their interior consciousnesses to outside goings-on. The interior of the individual is called on today, as it never was until recently, to live through at each moment the going exterior activities of the entire human race.

Technology—by no means so simply and purely exterior as is sometimes supposed—has established this new interior-exterior frontier. In the images which technological society projects for itself through its public communications media such as the press, radio, and television, mankind somehow finds itself divided quite naturally into the "beat" and the "square" on the basis of insideness and outsideness, participation and nonparticipation, belonging and rejection.

The beatnik is such a society's deliberate outsider, the voluntary reject, the calculatingly uninvolved. I take "beatnik" here as referring to the figure, partly real and partly a symbolic transformation, embodying the patterns of behavior, real and imaginary, which have given this concept its currency in our day. The beatnik's quick reduction of everything to classes (not only beat and square, but the whole assembly-line vocabulary of chick, cat, and the rest) even in direct address (where the other has no proper name but becomes simply "Man") and his avoidance of direct or complete statement (Man, like you can't help it) are calculated to advertise that he is keeping out—and "way out"—that he is not committed to any person, for all real commitment is personal at root. But action is impossible outside some context of commitment, and the beat's maneuvers to establish himself as solidly "out" with regard to society as a whole unavoidably establish him as solidly "in" with other "beats."

The beatnik, however, is never so "way out" with regard to "square" society as he might like to think, for he is inextricably involved in this society's highly developed communications media, and indeed could not find or sustain his own peculiar ambitions without such media. He needs phonograph records and tape, radio and television awarenesses, and the ability to roam in high-speed cars (modern transportation is largely a communication device) over great highways which could not be constructed without today's close-knit communications and could not be made to function without the electronic instruments needed to patrol them. The beatnik's intense kind of outsideness is unthinkable before human society has developed the special complementary insideness which comes from its present tight intercommunication system. A paleolithic beatnik was impossible.

Involvement with mass communications has resulted finally in the assembly-line beatnik. Despite their in some ways unquestionable externality, mass communications nevertheless give the human race today its minute-to-minute awareness of itself as a whole. Aware through its press, radio, and television that it is spawning beatniks unwittingly, society becomes reflective about the process. The beatnik is seized on as a symbol to be consciously exploited, with beatnik night clubs and beatnik parties for the kiddies (costumes are encouragingly inexpensive). At this point, inevitably, the cult of the outsider moves back inside, and big business undertakes the mass production of beatniks. A St. Louis firm advertises nationally its zip-collar sweat shirt with "beautiful official Beat Generation emblem" which gives you "your chance to join the exclusive Beat Generation" for $4.95 plus $1.95. Exclusiveness sells widely.

Life magazine a few years ago blessed the mass production of beatniks by running a special feature on the beats for its consumer-culture clientele, picturing as in a department-store advertisement the equipment necessary for a beat "pad," with all items numbered and labeled—primly and condescendingly, so that *Life* readers can be reassured that this is not themselves, but also with consumer's guide accuracy giving the same readers to know what is the real thing and what isn't, so that if they *should* just want to set up a beat "pad" of their own on a do-it-yourself basis, they could be sure to do it right and not lose status.

By eliciting this kind of hypocrisy from his would-be censors, including *Life* magazine, the beat can nurse a wry, but decisive, victory. For, wrong as he may be, the beat is invulnerable to any attack which implies that he is wrong because his critic is right. There is always in human society and in my own life something which warrants criticism and withdrawal. The outsider can only laugh when he hears others say that he is wrong in his withdrawal because the insiders are so good. He has been inside, or at least has looked in, and he knows they are not. A self-righteous insider cannot win. Only if, like Dostoevsky's Underground Man, he faces up to the full truth about himself can the insider hope to meet the threat the beatnik poses. To meet this threat the insider must abandon all complacency. The insider must acknowledge complicity with the beat. He is not so different as he likes to pretend to be. After all, the beat items so carefully inventoried by *Life* are many of them part of ordinary family living: hi-fi loudspeaker, Italian wine bottle, empty beer cans, ill-tended house plant. This is not only San Francisco's North Beach; it is America. The insider may as well avow his likeness to the beatnik—his fascination has already given him away. He must avow that he himself has faults, grave ones, and that society has, too, and he can only protest that even so, society has claims.

Of course, such a realistically harsh appraisal of society makes the insider in some sort an outsider, too. To this extent, the beatnik can claim achievement, for to this extent his achievement is positive: he has brought the squares to acknowledge their own involvement in the forces which have produced him, and to acknowledge that the established order is not entirely good and in this life never will be.

II

The outsider-insider dialectic is by no means entirely new. It is endemic to the West's understanding of its own culture and appears in many guises, most notably in the dialectic of Greek and non-Greek, or Greek and barbarian.

Barbarian and outsider, however, if closely related, are not entirely the same. Of the two, outsider is the more thinned-down, the more geometrized, and by the same token the more easily manageable. The concept of the "outsider" is both striking and poignant because of its gruesome starkness: it represents what is essentially the plight of human existence in terms of unadorned geometrical position. We are fascinated by the idea of being "in" or being "out" because we find it incongruous and mildly intolerable that one person be estranged from another simply because the two are on different sides of something represented as a mere physical border—a door, a fence, a wall, perhaps a "line" (party or color), or whatever it is that maintains an inside and an outside. Position with regard to a mere object should not define human relations. We are fascinated by the gruesome concepts which imply that it does.

Barbarian is a more complex concept to analyze, and certainly more rewarding. It developed not merely in terms of a spatial analogy but seemingly out of what is more subtle and human, a cultural relationship focused in linguistic behavior. The original barbarian was the man who could not speak Greek. *Barbaros* is seemingly an echoic word, imitating the supposed sound of strange tongues—the Latin *balbutiare*, to stammer, appears to have similar roots. Defined in terms of speech, the barbarian is defined not in extrahuman, geometrical terms, but in terms derived from human life itself, from the eminently human activity of verbal communication.

The communication system to which the barbarian finds himself referred and by which he is defined is not the one he knows. Those inside this communication system, the Greeks, who are the ones bestowing on him the name barbarian, take toward him a depreciatory attitude. They imply that he is badly off because he does not know Greek, that he is aware of this fact, and thus that he would like to know Greek and be integrated into Greek civilization if possible. From the Greek point of view the barbarian is thus in one way a projection of Greek self-confidence. But also, in another way unavoidably implied by this first, he gives evidence of the Greek lack of self-confidence manifested by the need for admiration. The Greek draws assurance from the admiring glance of the barbarian whom he professes to despise.

This Greek-barbarian situation dramatizes in its own way the human condition of interdependency. It is a special case involving the quest of security and integrity within a dialectic of inferiority and superiority. The barbarian, as the Greeks considered him, is a peripheral man, insufficient to himself, camped outside a civilization which he feels—however dimly and resentfully—promises him greater integrity than the civilization which was his own by birth. He may be more or less articulate about his position. The barbarian on the Greek perimeter may have expressed—and we can conjecture probably did express—positive scorn for the Greeks. But in so far as he was on his own barbarian terms caught up into Greek civilization, he registered his sense of dependence (subconscious though it may have been) upon the Greeks. As a raider, the barbarian is dependent upon the civilization upon which he makes inroads. To this extent, the Greeks were justified in their assumption of superiority, even when they may have been going down in defeat: their riches were being preyed on—and this was proof that they were indeed riches.

What were the riches of the Greeks? When we think of the Greeks as contrasted with barbarians, we think not merely of their material wealth but much more of their cultural self-possession, a kind of cultural self-containedness. And there is warrant for this, at least if we regard those within ancient Greek civilization who profited from it most, the 10 per cent or so who, like Sophocles, Socrates, Plato, and Aristotle were on the top, not slaves. These achieved what they achieved from the growth within their culture—and thus within themselves—of a kind of integrity or wholeness of view. Although one might add that the Sophists were barbarians in so far as they viewed law as extrinsic force, and thus that historic ancient Greek civilization in its entirety was far from "Greek" in the technical antibarbarian sense, nevertheless, in a way which is historically meaningful, for the Greeks civilization did consist in a kind of wholeness of view or integrity, such as Werner Jaeger has explored in his *Paideia*. Greek integrity was limited, of course, much more filled with holes, of which the Greeks themselves were often aware, than poorly informed rhapsodizers about Greek "rationality" allow, as Eric Robertson Dodds has shown in *The Greeks and the Irrational*. The Greeks knew that they had no really coherent answers worked out for many basic and essential questions. "I was evil from birth," says Oedipus—thereby showing that Sophocles's tragedy cannot really be fully accounted for by Aristotle's *hubris* or any known rational explanation. In his massive work, *The Odyssey: A Modern Sequel*, Kazantzakis provides a good sample of something very like the ancient Greek mind protracted into our own day—independent, zestful, vigorous, sometimes to the point of boring us with its effusions, thoroughly incomplete, but unflagging in its determination to be self-reliant, even when it does not fully know what self-reliance can mean.

How far one can push this integrity in historical detail has been and perhaps still is matter for painstaking investigation. Here the point is that, as contrasted with the barbarian, the Greek felt within his culture a germ of integrity. A germ is not adequate, of course, and the Greek, like all men, was basically insecure. Nevertheless, in so far as he was Greek and not barbarian, he was one who was willing to live with his insecurity. One can ask for no more as a starting point.

Although any culture (and every society has a culture) possesses some integrity which it seeks to maintain, when we speak of a culture as barbarian by comparison with Greek, we refer to it as turned somehow outside itself for a larger integrity which it is seeking. Integrity has to be built from within, but the process of building it is a social transaction, and a reciprocating one: the child develops his integrity as a response to that which he senses in his elders, particularly his parents, and these, in turn, develop their integrity further by living with the efforts of their children. At the very moment when the son is living up to the expectations of the father, the father is in another way most intensely living up to the expectations of his son. In either case the process is dark and obscure, for integrity is of the deep interior, but the process is also in a way exteriorizing, for the model which urges us on to establish our own integrity is "other," is in some sense "out there."

This exterior element in the process of establishing integrity is heightened by the fact that in human affairs the response of interior to interior has to be effected through external means. One of the most evident of such means is sheer imitation or annexation of something belonging to another. Such annexation is a well known phenomenon in the case of individuals: the child who apes his father or older brother, the Oxford students who, consciously or unconsciously, used to imitate Newman's mannerisms. Certainly such annexation is one of the phenomena manifest in those we think of as barbarian. As contrasted with the Greeks, the Romans were barbarians in this sense—as indeed were all the cultures outside the Greek which later took on a Hellenic cast. The cultured Roman, from Cicero on, remade his language out of Greek sources, described it with the help of a grammar derived from Greek (the Romans had no way of theorizing about their language as it really was, but only through analogy with the Greek), and indeed often used the Greek language itself when moving in sophisticated society. This is not to say that all elements in Roman life were in the present sense barbarian: there were Roman Stoics who could be regarded as in some way Greeks, if (as has been successfully maintained) rather small-souled ones, because of their insistence on inwardness and self-reliance. Yet even here two things must be noted: first, a Roman Stoic was necessarily a barbarian in the sense that the Stoa itself was originally a Greek school, not a Roman; secondly, the Stoic aim is in a sense security rather than integrity, since it seeks to avoid or assuage all personal tensions and to minimize risk—the Stoic advocated never making a wager except on a sure thing.

Medieval Western Europeans have long been called barbarians with reference to the ancient Romans (and indirectly to the ancient Greeks). Everywhere in Europe they uniformly carried on their most consciously cultural pursuits not in their own tongues but in the language of the ancient Romans, and, to give their cultures some kind of continuity with Greco-Roman culture, they "fixed" their histories (as in the legend deriving the British race from a Brutus supposed to be Aeneas' great-grandson) and even their political institutions (as in the case of the quasi-fictitious concept of the Holy Roman Empire).

As a Christian, medieval man felt a conscious superiority to the ancients, but this conscious superiority sat uneasily upon a strong subconscious inferiority. Men of the Middle Ages went to the Latin translations of the ancient Greeks to explain to themselves elements in Christian doctrine for which their own intellectual resources were all too inadequate. The ancient Roman culture had not had the integrity which the medieval Western European liked to impute to it. It was highly derivative from Greek and its lack of self-containedness evident from this fact was only made more telling by the admixtures of Arabic culture which accrued to it before it came into medieval hands. But the barbarian's type of insecurity, bred of a need for integrity and a kind of despair of finding it within himself rather than within the more sophisticated culture with which he had established contact, led him to project an integrity into something outside himself on which he fastened.

In accord with this barbarian frame of mind, medieval man habitually viewed the pursuit of knowledge as some kind of recovery effort, an exploitation of what others somehow already knew. Not only did the philosophers (a rubric which included physicists and mathematicians— in fact, all learned men except students of language, medicine, law, and theology) together with the physicians, the lawyers, and the theologians teach by commenting on texts, but even the poets looked to *auctoritas* or "authority" for source material and details as well as for the whole warrant and structure for their productions. A creative writer today may turn to Sophocles or to John Donne as a source of plot or character or tone, but he does not ordinarily in the course of his work refer the reader, as Chaucer and his contemporaries do, to what is said by "the book" or "my author," citing sources as part of his very process of telling his story.

The "others" to whom medieval man imputed the command of knowledge on which he drew were commonly his more or less distant predecessors. Their knowledge was uniformly in a peculiar condition, being accessible only in manuscript form, where it was permanently removed and insulated from dialogue and incapable in itself of the kind of development which dialogic exchange offers. Moreover, with his underdeveloped historical sense, man in the Middle Ages was unable to make the kind of correction in earlier thinking which is possible when thinking is assessed in terms of its historical context. Under these conditions the use of *auctoritas* by scholastic philosophers and theologians took a turn which involves what we today should consider calculated dishonesty. To the author one was following, one imputed a kind of inerrancy, sometimes to the extent that when the author's works said something with which one could not agree, one pretended that they said—or at least meant—quite the contrary. By the thirteenth century this practice had become a kind of convention, and seems to have disturbed no one. What was really at stake was not at all the exact sense of Aristotle's or another's words, such as the present-day scholar would want to ascertain, but the ability to maintain the conviction that one's "authority," Aristotle or another, had in his possession some sort of genuinely *integral* vision.

Under these circumstances it is not surprising that Western European man in the Middle Ages appears often unaware of the fact that he had himself made real, and often tremendous progress over his predecessors. The striking advances in logic which were effected by Peter of Spain and those medieval logicians who followed him and which carried this science far beyond where it had been left by Aristotle seem not to have struck the medieval mind generally as advances at all, and it is only today with the work of Duhem, A. C. Crombie, Anneliese Maier, and others that we are becoming aware of medieval progress in optics, physics, and related fields. By and large, the medieval mind took for granted that earlier man knew all sorts of things even when there was no record of his having expressed them.

Perhaps the most spectacular evidence of the barbarian imputation of omniscience to a preceding culture is seen in medieval interpretations of the first chapter of Genesis. Here the Hebrew concept of the world, vague and thoroughly unscientific, and left that way in the presentation of a divine revelation concerned principally with supramundane matters, pictures the earth as more or less flat, with waters somehow heaped around its sides up and over the "firmament," or solid element in the heavens, which keeps the water from coming down when it is not raining and lets it through when it does rain. Medieval theologians pretty much *en bloc* managed somehow to read into this text the cosmos as Aristotle and Ptolemy imagined it: our earth as a globe made up of the four "elements" earth (soil) water, air, and fire, and surrounded by a series of concentric, transparent spheres which consisted of a fifth, inalterable element and bore successively the moon, Mercury, Venus, the Sun, Mars, Jupiter, Saturn, and the fixed stars. This construct was entirely foreign to and in fact quite irreconcilable with the Hebrew view of the cosmos. The medieval mind reconciled the two anyhow.

As a Christian, medieval man had to acknowledge that the ancient pagan vision of creation had been incomplete. But the barbarian Christian was terribly distressed if he had to own that the vision was utterly mistaken. He needed to believe in its integrity. Somewhere, somehow, in the past there had been someone who had everything straight in every direction and dimension in which it was given him to see, at least in principle. There are of course a great many such barbarian Christian minds among us still today—perhaps nowhere more than among American Catholics.

The barbarian type of insecurity which assuages its pangs by finding outside itself an order or integrity by which it can live appears intimately connected with the development of modern science, which has its confused but unmistakable beginning in medieval European culture. Science offers us a purchase, elaborately structured, on the actuality outside us, enabling us to make external order permanently our own. One of the striking phenomena of medieval and Renaissance thought, which I have attempted to document in my *Ramus, Method, and the Decay of Dialogue,* is the preoccupation with establishing schematic relationships among the various "arts" and other areas of knowledge, even though the knowledge being ordered was in many cases so sketchy as to be virtually nonexistent. There is not and, I suspect, never will be a complete science even of physics, much less of mathematics, totally developed, with all its parts and possibilities exhausted. Yet already in the twelfth and thirteenth centuries men were treating of the structure and interrelation of the sciences as wholes, undismayed by the fact that they had not one single integral science worked out with what we today could consider even an approximation of reasonable completeness. Fascinated with the idea of an integrating structure, of which they had found circumstantial suggestions in the world around them, they could not forego the pleasure of elaborating comparable structures—however prematurely—in what was closer to them, their knowledge itself.

The scientist truly humble about his science, as most scientists are, is a Greek, willing to live with acknowledged insecurity, not a barbarian. But the populace remains, probably always, barbarian in the image of science which it projects. For the popular press, the mythical thing called science has all the answers, or soon will have. It is a kind of totality, an integral something. Such a popular image of science, generated perpetually in the minds of the less informed even as the more informed are discarding it, will persist because there is some foundation for it. Science is born of a vision of completeness. As Alfred North Whitehead has suggested, the Judaeo-Christian milieu provided the foundation for science by teaching that God made absolutely all reality outside Himself and that He was infinitely wise, so that ultimately there was available somewhere a complete explanation of everything down to the least detail, however long it might take man to find it. The integrity of all science, its completeness, is thus ultimately in the intellect of God. But in a further and very special sense science provides in a kind of exterior form minor visions of completeness in the hypotheses which the scientist "projects" outside himself and outside the ambit of his knowledge, afterwards testing to find whether the facts match the projection. The scientist here is radically barbarian in this sense: he looks for integral explanation in a truth which he does not in fact formally possess, but which he proposes as a mere "let us suppose."

The medieval complex of barbarianism comes to a marvelous maturity in St. Thomas Aquinas' view of theology. Unlike most medieval theologians, St. Thomas thought of theology itself as somehow an integral science. His science of theology not only offers in some measure a framework of integrity somehow outside one's own self and yet susceptible to personal appropriation by study, as other sciences do, but, unlike other sciences, draws its own first principles or origin from a kind of ultimate "outside" in the sense that these principles come from outside the entire created world, directly from divine revelation, from the Word of God, although from the Word as Incarnate in the created world. At this point, that from which theology borrows its integrity of course ceases to be exterior, for faith comes through the Word, Jesus Christ, to the interior of the individual soul. Yet the integrity of theology, if real, is indeed borrowed, and theology itself remains, as compared with the teaching activity of the Church, a barbarian production. Erasmus was right on this score, although wrong in using barbarian as a narrowly depreciatory term.

The barbarian question becomes a live and vivid one in the Renaissance. By contrast with the medieval man who preceded him, the Renaissance humanist was something of an antiscientist and definitely considered himself an antibarbarian. It is true that he achieved a sense of community with the ancients which medieval man had not had. Rudolph Agricola, Hegius, Erasmus, and their congeners and epigoni felt and somehow conveyed to others a sense of ancient Greek and Roman authors as still living influences, so that communing with them became for a time something very like dialogue, despite the disabling effects of preoccupation with written records of thought and expression.

This success of the humanists is often described in terms of a reaction to medieval man's failure to establish contact with the ancients. The humanists stumbled upon a mine of manuscripts which medieval man had not known. To a certain extent this is true. And yet medieval man had maintained a great deal of contact with ancient authors, as modern scholarship more and more makes evident. The relative success of the humanists was rather in great part due to the nature of the medieval contact—to the fact that it was barbarian in the sense that medieval man often imputed to the ancients the awed deference of an inferior to a superior. John of Salisbury and others can be cited as instances of medieval men who were not barbarian in this sense. And they are cited rightly, for they protest quite vocally against too great subservience to ancient writers. But the urgency of their protest attests the tendency on all sides to be too subservient.

John of Salisbury and others like him are medieval representatives of the tendency which became more marked in the Renaissance, when the ancients were viewed with less deference and more real man-to-man respect. Of course, the Renaissance, too, provides instances of too great subservience to antiquity, but its more typical spokesmen are men such as Ben Jonson, whose advice that one value the knowledge of the ancient Greeks and Romans but at the same time raid them as though one were their master sounds extraordinarily high-handed by comparison with the unquestioning deference of the typical medieval formulary rhetorics such as those of Matthew of Vendôme and Geoffrey of Vinsauf.

It is ironic but inevitable that the humanists, genuinely antibarbarian as they proposed to be, could not manage in the last analysis to be truly Greek, but assimilated themselves in the large to the Romans (barbarians from the Greek point of view). The fact is highly significant that, despite the early sixteenth-century advocacy of Greek as at least the equal of Latin, it was always Latin which dominated in the Western humanist milieu. C. S. Lewis is quite right in *The Oxford History of English Literature* when he says of the humanists that "the desire was for order and discipline, weight, and decorum; and men rightly felt that these qualities were to be learned from the Romans rather than the Greeks." Order and discipline, weight, and decorum are matters on which the barbarian, making his way up in the world, is likely to put a high premium. They are the virtues of the bourgeoisie, often taken as typifying the intelligent barbarians within an intellectual culture. Indeed, "discipline" itself refers to what is proper to the disciple or learner.

This alignment of the humanists with Romans rather than Greeks is, moreover, a product of their own history. As descendents of barbarians, they had not been able to negate their own ancestry, however much they may have thought they were doing so. They did not abandon but merely revised their fathers' ambitions. They still felt themselves outsiders in that they looked to a culture other than their own for their integrity, for although they were able for a time to identify themselves with this culture, that of ancient Greece and Rome, with an intensity which minimized their outsideness, they were in reality more widely separated from it by time and social institutions than their more patently barbarian fathers had been. Indeed, the increased distance between them and ancient Rome accounts in a large measure for their overarticulateness about ancient Roman culture. The orientation toward the ancient world which had, after all, been a dominant feature of medieval culture, was becoming less automatic. One had to shout louder to reach the ancients as they receded into the distance.

Under these circumstances it was inevitable that the old formalism would again set in. By the seventeenth and eighteenth centuries the works of the ancients with which the humanists had managed to carry on a simulated dialogue came to be regarded quite commonly as a body of writings guaranteeing almost magically to those "formed" through the educational process that integrity which even the earlier barbarian devotion to science could no longer promise so convincingly, since under the impact of the new cosmology the older scientific world found itself, as John Donne saw it, "all in pieces, all coherence gone."

Much could be said about the Catholic-Protestant situation of the sixteenth century in terms of the Greek-barbarian theme—indeed, altogether too much to admit of inclusion here. In so far as it parallels to some extent the opposition of humanist to scholastic, the opposition of Protestant to Catholic corresponds to that of Greek to barbarian—and partakes of the same ambivalence. Early Protestants aligned themselves with antiquity and against medieval barbarianism by ambitioning a return to a presumedly pure primitive Christianity, and in this sense were Greek.

But this same recourse to a culture other than that in which they were nurtured reveals not the Greek but the typical barbarian cast of mind—a "pure" primitive Christianity being an utterly typical barbarian projection. Hand in hand with the barbarian rejection of the indigenous culture goes the Protestant rejection of nature as totally corrupt. At this point the Protestant stand is barbarian, whereas the Catholic acceptance of nature and the Catholic insistence that God acts through Christ with a grace which transforms the human soul intrinsically (not merely extrinsically, or through imputation, as in classic Protestant doctrine), appears as Greek. The situation is further complicated by the fact, a commonplace today, that, whatever their disavowals, sixteenth and seventeenth century Protestants as well as Catholics were deeply imbued with "barbarian" scholastic philosophy even when they were denouncing it. Altogether, perhaps nothing would reveal the tangle of complications which make up the Reformation and later the Catholic Counter Reformation more intriguingly than the application to the situation of the Greek-barbarian theorems. But the application would be an almost endless undertaking.

In the generations since the humanistic-scholastic tiff, no larger cultural issues have raised so explicitly the barbarian question. Nevertheless, in treatments of subsequent history the theme is constantly returned to, for whatever insights it may afford. A great many disturbing movements, not a few of them successful, have been labeled as "barbarian": free enterprise, progressive education, civilization in the United States generally, and more recently Nazism, Fascism, and Communism. The entire revolutionary momentum itself, which gathered its forces several centuries ago in the depths of the Hebrew-Christian psyche and has since spread to all mankind, has been seen by some as purely barbarian in its roots and manifestations. So has almost anything which has impinged from the outside on Western culture, for better or for worse.

III

In the title of his book, *The Holy Barbarians*, Lawrence Lipton can shock the uninformed by calling barbarians "holy" because in its popular application and even in serious cultural analyses until rather recently the term barbarian has been taken as automatically depreciatory. But recent analysts have grown increasingly aware that it can be neuter in implication. Barbarians turn out rather regularly to be the custodians—often the only custodians—of the culture on which they prey. And if they transform such cultures, transformation is inevitable and can well be good, since no nonbarbarian or "Greek" culture is anything more than a quite limited human achievement, destined by its very limitations to be transmuted into something else. Of course, transformation of a culture can also be bad, but this is not necessarily due to the fact that its transformers are barbarians. It can be due to certain positive defects which the culture may have. We must continually remind ourselves that every culture is probably in some way barbarian with regard to every other, although in varying ways and degrees, and that every culture which cannot survive contacts with other cultures is by that very fact certainly limited, for mankind is obviously destined to possess itself as a whole. Two adjoining cultures cannot be kept out of contact with each other, and if one or the other feels the need to keep out of contact this fact itself manifests a defect, a lack of self-possession.

To say that a culture is barbarian, therefore, as this term is taken here, is to say neither that it is good nor that it is bad. It is to say that it feels that the integrity it seeks is in some way possessed by, or enshrined in, or symbolized by a culture outside itself to which it must adapt.

To the Greek, barbarian is a derogatory term because the barbarian is an outsider. But the term is far more derogatory by implication in the mouth of what we may call a "practicing barbarian," one who regards Greek culture as a paramount good, something to be emulated at all costs. Since for such a man all that he is not is good, by inference he himself is bad. The inference, of course, is not true. For no culture is worth uncritical and unselective emulation.

For the advance of civilization barbarians may be necessary. They supply vigor, for a properly administered inferiority complex can compel high achievement. And they force discrimination. No culture is worth preserving just exactly as it is. All cultures need improvement, and need it rather badly, and the operations of barbarians on a culture, whatever the immediate effects, can result in a sorting out of what is valuable from what is not.

The very concepts of Greek and barbarian are aids to discrimination. For the Greek-barbarian disjunction cannot be applied to any cultures simply or en bloc. There are no complete Greeks or complete barbarians, only partial ones. There are no total outsiders of any kind. These dialectically related concepts, Greek and barbarian, like other similarly related concepts such as classic and romantic, are useful precisely because they do not fit the whole of a given situation but fit the situation only in part—that is, they are useful largely because of the ways they do not fit. In saying that a culture is Greek, one is forced to say how it is so by contrast with some certain barbarianism, and vice versa, since every culture (like every person) is both Greek and barbarian, so that one is saying nothing until one has worked out a specific ground for a statement involving these terms. If every culture is both Greek and barbarian, nevertheless no two cultures are Greek or barbarian in exactly the same way.

This is rather strikingly evident in the case of contrasting cultural groups today, and notably in the case of the United States and the Union of Soviet Socialist Republics. Khrushchev's pronouncements which have taken the United States as the measure of technological achievements—"*We* are going to outdistance *you*"—are typical examples of the barbarian outsider's defense mechanism in the face of a culture which he envies. On the other hand the American reaction to the

Russian educational performance also shows signs of the barbarian's defense mechanisms. This composite of reactions suggests that with regard to technologically contrived well-being Americans are not barbarians at all, but the ultimate Greeks. Such well-being is felt as interior to American culture, so that in realizing a reign of material sufficiency, Americans feel that they are drawing on nothing at all beyond their own interior resources. To be surpassed in the production of material well-being really distresses Americans seriously, not so much because it gives them to feel that they are being deprived of material comforts as because of something deeper: they are losing something of their own interior orientation. But the material well-being native to the American psyche is an import in Russia, the object of calculated striving supported by a self-consciously materialistic system of thought which the Russians have annexed and which strikes an American, rightly or wrongly, as a bit naïve, however effective it may prove.

At the same time, however, with regard to intellectual achievement, Americans tend to be barbarians, viewing—not ungrudgingly—such achievements as existing at their optimum in cultures other than their own: in Europe or in the past or in the future, or even—the abiding "other" in American life—in nature. It does Americans no harm at all to be told or to tell themselves that other cultures have better ways of training the mind than they do. They want to believe this. The smart of such a conviction distresses Americans not at all, but simply drives them, as nothing else could, to better their own educational procedures.

In activity connected with education, American life presents several facets of a curiously obvious barbarian cut. Most spectacular perhaps is the rash of Greek-letter associations distinctive of American universities and colleges. Membership in these associations certainly ensures no very effective contact with ancient Greek civilization—most members can recognize few letters of the Greek alphabet beyond those naming their own organization, and the latter only if they are capital letters. But membership does confer the "Greek" status of being "in." The associations are commonly styled fraternities (brotherhoods) or sororities (sisterhoods) to make this fact plain. The Hellenic façade is deliberately maintained. Interfraternity or intersorority or inter-fraternity-sorority groups are commonly referred to as "Panhellenic" groups of one sort or another, and students who do not belong to the fraternities or sororities are referred to as barbarians or "barbs." Greeks are in and barbs are out. Membership in the Greek-letter associations is achieved by passage though initiation rites closely (if unconsciously) paralleling the *rites de passage* of primitive societies which anthropologists have described as marking entrance into a new state of being.

It is, of course, tempting to write off all this self-conscious Hellenism as a mere "accident." College age is sure to be an age of initiations. It is so everywhere. Someone started Phi Beta Kappa in America, and the Greek letter ideas "somehow" caught on. But there are no such "accidents." The "somehow" cries for explanation of one sort or another. There must be a reason why this idea, and not others, swept all before it. And one does not have to cast out all other explanations to observe that one reason could well be the deep drive within the American to move from the barbarian status in which he feels he is born (for no one is born into a fraternity or sorority, but always adopted) into that of a true Greek, however confused or even unconvincing this imputed Hellenism might be. In college or university the drive manifests itself with full academic explicitness. Early American education was like other Western education in being centered around the study of Latin and Greek, skill in the latter being rarer and an indication of greater prestige—or of being further "in." But only in America did the implications of the early classical educational system (a barbarian system, of course, in America as elsewhere) hit home with this peculiarly obvious force.

Another phenomenon in the American academic world of interest on a similar score is the high concentration of scholastic philosophy in the United States, where a scholasticism or neoscholasticism more or less connected with its medieval counterpart is far more widespread than in any other country of the world. In so far as scholasticism, as explained above, called forth from the humanists the charge of barbarianism, the vigor of its modern counterpart in the United States is worth noting. The vigor is due to no one cause but rather to a combination of various circumstances—but that does not mean that it is fortuitous. The culture of the United States favors this particular "barbarian" mode of thinking in ways often intriguing even though indirect or coincidental.

One of the chief circumstances favoring such thinking has turned out to be the American devotion to a liberal education in the sense of a protracted general education, a devotion which itself evinces a desire to strengthen assurance that an individual really "belongs." For the most part, in other countries, the teaching of philosophy as a part of a liberal or general education is restricted to the secondary schools, where alone general education is purveyed, it being assumed that the student can be inducted into the full range of essential knowledge early, so that the university remains exclusively a specializing organ. But in the educational system of the United States, where general education persists even at the university level, scholastic philosophy is made part of the Catholic program of *higher* education and in Catholic institutions is taught to all students who aspire to undergraduate degrees.

The effect of neoscholasticism in the United States, moreover, is not restricted to Catholic circles. The University of Chicago, for example has known strong, if somewhat ambiguous, neoscholastic influences under Robert M. Hutchins, Mortimer Adler, Richard McKeon, and others, and has developed a school of literary criticism manifesting strong neoscholastic traits. The typically American "Great Books" programs often show high interest in scholastic and neoscholastic works. Professors Jacques Maritain and Etienne Gilson, distinguished deans of European scholastic philosophers, have been annexed by North America, the former being long established at Princeton and the latter teaching regularly at Toronto, where American students flock to his classes. The recent intensive study of the influence of scholastic logic and formal rhetoric on English literature has been done largely in American universities such as Harvard, Yale, Columbia, North Carolina, St. Louis University, the Catholic University of America, the University of Chicago, the University of Illinois, and the University of Wisconsin. More than other groups, Americans like to write and to read books such as *The Thirteenth, Greatest of Centuries*. But the historical roots of scholasticism in the United States do not lie only in Catholic ground. American Puritanism itself was in great part scholasticism, as Perry Miller and others have shown. And the American mind, although a many-faceted thing, reflects in not a few of its facets a formal, apersonal, and schematic pattern which attests connections with much in the scholastic heritage.

Looking also beyond educational circles, one might say that although certain aspects of life in the United States are of course not barbarian, doubtless American life is best described as barbarian rather than Greek in its over-all cast. The special position in history of the American north of the Rio Grande makes him an established outsider: he is the one who more than any other set himself up outside Old World society. He has long looked to this society—perhaps too long—as his measure of achievement. It is interesting in this connection that visitors in Europe from the United States are so often drawn to Germany as to the culture closest to that of the United States. Germany is a focus of barbarian culture in Europe. Tangent to the classical world from antiquity and always drawn to Mediterranean culture by a powerful inferiority complex (*los von Rom!* has stirred the German spirit in its intimate depths) the German-speaking world remains psychologically outside—further outside than the British Isles, which had been an integral part of the ancient Roman culture. The tension between modern Germany and ancient Greece is documented in books such as E. M. Butler's *The Tyranny of Greece over Germany*. And yet the same German-speaking world has performed the typical barbarian role of preserving the exterior civilization it seizes on: German scholarship, rather more than Italian scholarship and far more than Mussolini's grandiose imperial scheming, has kept alive ancient Rome and Greece.

The Latin American, less likely to be impressed by Germany when he visits Europe, is in certain discernible ways less barbarian than his neighbors north of the Rio Grande. For in Latin America European culture encountered a country far more populous than that which constituted the present United States and Canada. The relationship of the emigrants to the Europe which they had left was complicated in the extreme by a new relationship with masses of people around them who were not European at all. The immigrants were outsiders to two cultures, that which they had left and that to which they had come, but because they were more inclined to view the indigenous American culture as barbarian, they felt themselves less barbarian with regard to Europe, where, moreover, as South Europeans they preserved close historical continuity with classical Mediterranean culture. The South Europeans in Latin America were emissaries of the Greeks at the outposts of civilization. The Latin-American psyche, at one level, has thus retained a continuity with the European experience which Americans north of the Rio Grande do not know.

The strong commitment to the future which has always been part of the United States psyche identifies it in a still further way as barbarian. For the barbarian can be seen quite readily as the man of the future. He is the man who is viewed as not having anything to offer out of his own past or present, and whose achievement thus lies necessarily in the future if it lies anywhere at all. To the barbarian, all the glories of the *past* and *present* empire *will* fall.

This raises the question as to the relationship of barbarianism and what might be called Nietzschean man in the sense of the man who insists on living at the edge of things somewhat disdainful of past and present, peering prophetically into the future. Is such a man a barbarian? Is he one who must prey on something not himself? Such a Nietzschean is a barbarian certainly in so far as his effectiveness depends on his ability not simply to find truth but also to astound the bourgeois—but a kind of inverse barbarian, since he desires not to learn from the "others" (the bourgeois), but to make them unlearn what they think they know. But the bourgeois himself is even more consummately barbarian if he believes that by maintaining his "way of life" he is preserving a well established and permanent security or "well established order" (and much more if he believes that he is *re*-establishing it) rather than that he is working toward such security. For the conviction that order is here—which contrasts markedly with the Greek willingness to live with a certain order in a context of disorder—shows only that one has smugly identified oneself with a merely hypothetical or projected order of an imagined Greek instead of living the more strenuous and upsetting life which consists in working toward an order never to be obtained in this life. For total security is never the possession of any living man, who must work out his salvation in fear and trembling to the very end of his life, and much less is it the possession of any human culture organized by these perilously organized individuals. Anyone who thinks of integrity as being in reality an actually achieved possession must be thinking of it by implication as someone else's, for he should know that it is patently not his or his culture's. Thus in this sense his is the barbarian's view, measuring things by an integrity which someone else is supposed to have.

In so far as Nietzchean man is willing to live with the fact that the reality of human life, the node which we actually hold in our possession, is never fully ordered, that the possibility of chaos is built in, he is willing to live with a limited integrity, and to that extent is Greek. But in so far as he situates a hoped-for integrity in the dream of a future *Uebermensch*, a Superman, he is a barbarian of the most hopeless sort. And in so far as he denies God, he is not being barbarian where he should be. Because if we must have integrity from another—

as we must—the other is not the mere future but God, Who is here now.

IV

As the newer nations and hitherto "backward" groups of men take their place more and more in the sun, the barbarian issue comes more alive than ever. Are the Indians of South America barbarians? In a basic sense, it appears not. In Latin America they preserve their own pre-Columbian civilization, at least to a great extent. American Indians in the United States and Canada, on the other hand, perhaps because of their small numbers from the beginning, have been more barbarian, but not so much as another group, American Negroes, who, in so far as they are one of the subcultures making up the United States, have been true, vigorous, aggressive, progressive barbarians, making the culture which was once largely that of white Europeans alone more and more their own (while contributing to it massively themselves) until, as has been said more than once, they become the most American of all Americans.

In other countries, however, as less advanced peoples come into contact with modern technological civilization, they are less barbarian today than they would have been in an earlier age. For the age of barbarianism in the strict sense has passed, in that mankind has matured to the point where each culture and subculture is highly reflective about itself and about all cultures and their relationships to one another. The barbarian's adulation of another culture is now tempered with global consciousness. The "other" culture is no longer so much "other" as it used to be, and hence is approached more critically.

Moreover, to the Greek the barbarian as such is no longer so entirely "other." The outsider can now claim the interest of the insider precisely because of his otherness. Society reaches out to the outcast not too generously yet, but more generously than ever before, at least in those countries where social betterment has become a major concern. Race relations work is a special instance of what happens when man becomes sufficiently reflective about the question of otherness. The development of a personalist philosophy in our day provides the most clear-cut instance of improved interest in the other, for at this point the quest for the universal—that which is not other, but the same—in being yields to attempts to deal with what is utterly "other" and induplicable, the person, the person's commitments, and the particularities of history.

At this point the fate of the beatnik becomes most tortuously ironic. A professional outsider, he becomes of paramount interest to philosophers themselves precisely because of his declared intransigence. He is a kind of barbarian in reverse, for he insists that he, the outsider as outsider, is the real Greek who has the integrity which the insiders or squares have sacrificed to a cheap security. The beatnik's reversal of role here is not due merely to perversity or intransigence. It is in a way inevitable, for it corresponds to a profound reversal within thought itself. In classic philosophic thought grown out of the Greek world into the present, the focus of interest has been the universal, the nonunique, the duplicable, which has by and large been taken to be the sole subject of true science and philosophy. But this approach to reality has been under siege as recent philosophical developments of a phenomenological and personalist or "existentialist" cast have pressed the cause of the individual and unique with a vigor never evident before. Hitherto, the unique was the outsider, philosophically inconsequential. Today the philosophical spotlight covers him inexorably as he struts and frets his hour upon the stage. Indeed, the philosopher's interest would be even greater if the beatnik were only as unique, as far out, as he would like to be.

What is more, the beatnik knows all this. He knows that the squares have an interest in him, which is even an academic interest. *A Casebook on the Beat* has recently been published by the University of California Press to implement study of the outsider in society today. The beatnik cannot avoid knowing that his outsideness guarantees that he is really in. But this makes him less an outsider, and hence less interesting. At this point his real motives become garbled to the point of total unmanageability. Does he really want to be out only in order to be in? Or does the fact that, being out, he is really in only annoy him and make him push harder than ever to be out? No one knows. The difficulty in assessing his motives is, in fact, built into the motives themselves, because his very revolt is an assertion of the state he revolts against. The beatnik is caught in *the toils which ensnare every man who sets up a program which at its heart is negative*. Such a man is derivative in his very assertion of independence, and his program is an elaborate self-delusion at heart.

And yet the beatnik is highly significant for our age. His revolt in its very futility and his consequent plight illustrates what is evident on many other scores: the barbarian's case is weakening, for man's global consciousness is growing so that other civilizations themselves are all in a sense our own, no matter what or where they are. For the same reason, of course, the Greek's case is weakening, too, since all civilizations must look outside themselves more than ever now to other cultures. The historical awareness which marks all the serious thinking of modern man is an awareness of otherness, and this means that it includes an awareness of the limitations of our own achievements. The beatnik's trouble is that it is no longer possible to be a barbarian without being a reflective one.

Furthermore, as man's relationship to time has changed with the accumulation of knowledge which enables him to write history, he has increased his sense of the richness of his immediate milieu and in doing so has found much of his otherness at his finger tips. In earlier ages, university lecturers were expected to spend their time commenting on the work of others who had to be far removed from themselves in time. Medieval and Renaissance professors of medicine commented on Galen, who flourished in the second century of the Christian era. St. Thomas Aquinas commented on Peter Lombard, who had died about 1160, and, although St. Thomas Aquinas himself died in 1274, his works did not displace Peter Lombard's in many places until several hundred years later. This academic system of speaking into the more or less distant past continued well into the age of Kant. And when the English language was introduced as a subject for university study during the nineteenth century, Old English came in first. But today, while we do not neglect the past (much more available to us than it ever was to earlier man), we focus more and more on the present, which, because we know so much more fully than earlier man its connections with the past, presents itself to us as a rich and varied manifold. We find otherness around us, and are Greeks and barbarians with regard to our own times.

And thus if in some ways the barbarian-Greek tensions are lessening in society, in another way they remain. There is barbarian and Greek permanently in us all. Each of us is divided between his drive inward and his drive outward, between self and other. The ultimate other is God—and yet this is no relief, for *this* Other is to be found chiefly within. When we achieve our integrity in Him, it is interior but still does not come from ourselves. He is ours when we are His.

Here there is special hope for the Christian. If his relationship to God is in a sense that of barbarian to Greek, this relationship has been tempered by Christ, for it has been brought to fruition in His Person. It is no accident that the Christian climate was the one which initially made assimilation of barbarian by Greek and of Greek by barbarian feasible on a large enough scale to fix the term "barbarian age" classically in the early Christian era for good. The Christian climate is a climate in which tensions do not die but come to fruition, a climate not of indifference but of active conciliation. The Christian is in the world but not of it. He is an outsider living from within.

Index

IMPRIMI POTEST: Linus J. Thro, S.J., Provincial, Missouri Province, St. Louis, Missouri, August 2, 1961

NIHIL OBSTAT: William M. Drumm, *Censor Librorum*, St. Louis, Missouri, August 17, 1961

IMPRIMATUR: ✠ Joseph Cardinal Ritter, Archbishop of St. Louis, St. Louis, Missouri, August 17, 1961